TRUE CANADIAN

UNSOLVED MYSTERIES

Ed

Butts

PROSPERO B·O·O·K·S

Library and Archives Canada Cataloguing in Publication

Butts, Edward, 1951–
True Canadian unsolved mysteries / Ed Butts.

Includes bibliographical references.
ISBN 1-55267-508-4

1. Crime—Canada. 2. Cold cases (Criminal investigation)—Canada. I. Title.

HV6807.B88 2006   364.10971   C2006-906309-5

This collection produced for Prospero Books.

Key Porter Books Limited
Six Adelaide Street East, Tenth Floor
Toronto, Ontario
Canada M5C 1H6

www.keyporter.com

Electronic formatting: Jean Lightfoot Peters

Printed and bound in Canada

06 07 08 09 10 5 4 3 2 1

To the memory of my friend
Harold Horwood

Acknowledgements

The author would like to thank The Archives of Ontario, the Public Archives of Canada, the Metropolitan Toronto Research Library, the editors of Key Porter Books, and as always the staff at the Guelph, Ontario, Public Library.

Contents

Introduction

The mystery story has been the bread and butter of fiction writers since Edgar Allan Poe first startled readers with "Murders in the Rue Morgue" in 1841. Since then writers of short fiction, novels, plays and TV, radio and film scripts have intrigued audiences with "whodunits." The best of them weave tangled plots that can be unravelled only by the likes of Sherlock Holmes, Philip Marlowe or Miss Marple. Because these stories are fiction, the audience has one basic expectation: to have the identity of the villain revealed at the end of the story. This is something over which the author of fictional mystery has total control.

With true-life mysteries the situation is different. The non-fiction mystery writer must stick to the known facts. He or she cannot invent. Speculate? Yes, as long as the reader is told that the writer is speculating. An author writing about the mystery man known as the Mad Trapper of Rat River can certainly offer an informed guess as to who that killer *might* have been. But the author cannot state, "This is who he was" without conclusive proof. At that point, of course, the story ceases to be a mystery.

Historical mysteries are simply old (and sometimes not-so-old) puzzles that have not been solved, and in some cases never will be. Nonetheless, they fascinate us because their intricacies can be just as bewildering as those created by fiction writers, and because they are *true.* The solution to an unsolved historical crime might seem tantalizingly obvious, but it cannot be taken for granted. Until the solution is *proven* it is theory, not fact.

Many countries have unsolved mysteries that have become legend. Historians still speculate over the identity of England's Jack the Ripper. Lizzie Borden of the United States remains an enigma, and the claim that Lee Harvey Oswald acted alone in the assassination of John F. Kennedy is hotly contested to this day.

Canadian history, too, is laced with mysteries. It is well-spiced with stories of unsolved murders, unexplained deaths, missing persons and individuals whose activities were so strange, they themselves have come to be known as "mystery men." Those stories, rather than tales of lost gold mines, UFOs and the supernatural (fascinating though they may be) make up the narratives of this book.

Some of the people in these chapters were famous in their own time. Sir Harry Oakes discovered a fabulous gold mine in Ontario and rubbed shoulders with royalty. Charles Hall was a renowned Arctic explorer. Both men died under mysterious circumstances. The Manchur family of Wakaw, Saskatchewan and the Westwood family of Toronto were ordinary people whose names became famous because murder came to their doorsteps, leaving no trace of the guilty.

Typically, these stories have been ignored or understated in Canada. Some have been chronicled by other Canadian writers, but Canadians in general remain unaware of them. To my knowledge there has not been a TV miniseries about Simon-gun-an-noot's incredible thirteen-year run from the law for a murder he did not commit, or a documentary film study of the mysterious Kinrade murder, which in some ways so resembled the more widely known Lizzie Borden case. But some might say that is just the Canadian way. As with so many other things, we keep our mysteries close to the vest.

THE MYSTERY OF THOMAS WALKER'S EAR

A Dangerous Affair

Unlike the severed ear of Robert Jenkins, which touched off a war between Britain and Spain in 1748, the mutilation of Thomas Walker's ear did not lead to armed conflict. But the incident did throw Britain's new colony of Canada into a political and legal scrap that lasted years and cost Governor James Murray his position. According to some accounts, the trouble began with the billeting of soldiers in private residences. Actually, trouble had been brewing for some time before the billeting crisis arose. Merchants who had arrived in Canada from Britain and the American colonies resented Murray's refusal to grant them any real political power. In the governor's opinion, the traders were "the most cruel, Ignorant, rapacious Fanatics, who ever existed." The merchants also objected to Murray's obvious admiration for the French Canadians, whom he called "perhaps, the best and bravest Race on the Globe." The traders certainly did not agree with the governor's resistance to the policy to completely anglicize the colony. The billeting issue did serve to bring matters to a head.

Under the military government that was imposed following Quebec's surrender, British soldiers were billeted in privately owned housing where their hosts were required to provide them with bedding, firewood, candles and the use of kitchens and cooking utensils. With the establishment of civil government in 1764, magistrates were officially exempt from billeting, though it seems that at first nobody made an issue of the situation one way or the other. The man who did take the matter from being a trivial point of law to an affair of dangerous, if overblown, proportions was Thomas Walker.

English-born Walker had been established as a merchant in Boston for ten years before moving to Montreal in 1763. He became involved in the fur trade and settled into a fine house in town. Walker was an ambitious but argumentative man who took a quick dislike to the military authorities in the colony. He had influence among the mercantile class, and Murray thought he could be useful if handled properly. He made Walker a magistrate, and soon regretted it.

Walker became a leader among the Montreal merchants and frequently quarrelled with military authorities. In September 1763, he lost a lawsuit filed against him by an employee. Walker defied the military court whose ruling had gone against him. Only when threatened with arrest did he pay the paltry sum of seven pounds.

The billeting of soldiers in communities was a common practice, especially in the winter when comfortable quarters for officers were scarce. Technically, magistrates did not have to take in soldiers, but prior to Thomas Walker's arrival there had not been any difficulties. Then, in the fall of 1764, Captain

Benjamin Payne of the 28th Regiment was billeted in quarters that had just been vacated by another officer. The following day the landlord, a man who was a merchant and magistrate, ordered Payne out, saying that he had rented to rooms to another party. Payne refused to leave. The landlord had the captain arrested and thrown in jail, an extremely embarrassing experience for a British officer and gentleman. Thomas Walker's signature was on the warrant.

Weeks later another officer from the 28th moved into his billet, and found that he had no bed, fireplace or any other conveniences. His landlady told him she was acting on advice from Mr. Walker. On December 4, a corporal in the 28th was evicted from his billet, again on orders from Walker.

Obviously, Walker was using the billeting issue as a means of striking at the military, and in so doing was earning the hatred of soldiers, particularly the men of the 28th Regiment. So many letters of complaint concerning billeting arrived at James Murray's office in Quebec City that he sent two justices of the peace to Montreal to look into the matter. But before those men could begin their inquiries the seething anger of the soldiers erupted into violence.

At about nine o'clock on the night of December 6, Thomas Walker was sitting down to supper in his home. With him were his wife Martha, his clerk John Lilly, and a friend identified only as Miss Hurd. Waiting on the diners were a servant, William Fontaine, and two unnamed black maids.

Suddenly the door burst open and six or seven men rushed into the room. The intruders were well-disguised with masks, blackened faces and nondescript clothing. All were armed.

Screaming "This is murder!" Martha Walker fled through the kitchen into the yard, where she hid in a cow shed. Miss Hurd and the two maids were right behind her. Fontaine ran upstairs with one of the invaders in pursuit. The terrified servant jumped out a window just as a slash from the man's sword cut off his coattail. John Lilly put up a fight, but after he'd received a few blows to the head he ran from the house. That left Walker alone with the attackers.

By his own account, Walker felled two of his assailants with his fists as he tried to reach a bedchamber where he had guns. But the gang overwhelmed him. As he grabbed one by the throat, he said, the others threw him to the floor and beat him mercilessly. One gave him a blow to the head, which Walker later said he feared would be his death wound. Then Walker felt an agonizing stab under his right ear, which he was also afraid would prove fatal.

Certain that he was dying, Walker groaned and stretched out his arms. Surely that would show the assassins that their foul mission of murder had been accomplished. He would report one intruder as saying, "The villain is dead. Damn him, we've done for him!" (Quotes from the 18th and 19th century records often have a suspiciously melodramatic quality to them). Scarcely three minutes after they had barged into the house, the attackers fled.

Thomas Walker was not dead, though he would insist ever after that the intruders had been determined to kill him, and only his vigorous resistance had saved his life. Quite likely, if the intruders had wanted to murder him, that night would have been his last. But they did give him a savage beating. His body was "as black as a hat, and so swelled up that you can barely know the remains of his face or the colour of his skin." Surgeons found fifty-two separate contusions on his body—which he would later inflate to two hundred. Though painful, the injuries were mostly superficial. There was one, however, that would mark him for life. One of the villains had sliced off half of Walker's right ear!

That same night, as Lieutenant Synge Tottenham, adjutant of the 28th Regiment, sat down to his evening meal, the door to his quarters was flung open. Two disguised men bounded in. One of them tossed Walker's ear on the table, telling the lieutenant it was "for his supper." The men left, and Tottenham made no attempt to pursue them. He would deny having any knowledge of who they were or what they'd done.

Nobody in the Walker household could identify any of the attackers, but Walker had no doubt that they were soldiers from the 28th. Quite likely, he thought, the whole regiment had been in on it. Moreover, he was certain they would return to finish him off. He did not feel safe on the street. At home he kept himself "locked up in my room with a bar at my outer door... a sword by my side, a brace of pistols in my bosom, one of my large ones with ball and buckshot lying on my table."

In Montreal there was a general outrage over the assault on Walker's home. The French Canadians detested the man as thoroughly as the soldiers did, but the merchants were on his side. The town was rife with gossip that soldiers were responsible for the deed. While few people would have felt personal sympathy for the insufferable Walker, many would have found it disturbing that soldiers, who were supposed to maintain order, should commit so lawless an act. Visitors to Montreal reported that the town was divided into two hostile camps; one supporting Walker and the other siding with the 28th Regiment. As a precautionary measure, Governor Murray transferred the 28th to Quebec City and sent another regiment to Montreal. He went to Montreal to personally conduct an inquiry.

A few days after the assault a letter signed "Matthew Gospel" was left in a place where authorities would be sure to find it. The anonymous author accused sergeants James Rogers and John Mee, and privates James Coleman and John McLaughlan, along with several others, of the Walker incident. All the accused were with the 28th Regiment. The letter said the men had gathered at Mee's house to change their clothes. The writer identified Rogers as the one who had cut off Walker's ear.

Investigators soon found bedding and a jacket, both bloodstained, that belonged respectively to Rogers and Mee. They learned that two or three hours before the attack, Rogers had borrowed a sword from another soldier. Sergeant Mee admitted that Rogers had been to his house the night of the sixth, but he denied having had anything to do with the assault.

Rogers, Mee, Coleman and McLaughlin were arrested and locked in jail. Rogers, in fact, was thrown into a dungeon. News of this brought the 28th Regiment to the brink of mutiny. It was all the officers could do to maintain order. Some soldiers actually managed to spring Mee, Coleman and McLaughlin from jail, but the three were soon recaptured.

Thomas Walker recovered remarkably well for a man who had received two "mortal" wounds. He had been antagonistic toward the military before the attack. Now he was on the verge of paranoia. He demanded that a trial be held in Montreal before an all-Protestant jury. Murray initially agreed to this. Then he found that it would not be possible because the few Protestant residents of Montreal were already prejudiced in favour of one side or the other. He changed the venue to Quebec City, further enraging Mr. Walker. Events now took a bizarre turn.

The 28th Regiment had retained for the defense of the accused men a lawyer named William Conyngham. This man had the reputation of an absolute scoundrel. He had served as clerk of the peace and as coroner, and had been dismissed from both offices due to malpractice. Murray described him as, "the most thorough paced villain who ever existed."

It is probably not remarkable that a cad like Conyngham should be a good friend of Thomas Walker. It was baffling though, that Walker allowed Conyngham to advise him on the case. Quite possibly he thought that the attorney would betray his clients in the interests of a friend.

Conyngham himself told Walker that the trial had been moved to Quebec City. Predictably, Walker flew into a rage and swore that he would not go to Quebec. Conyngham encouraged him in his anger and indignation. The shifty lawyer even drew up a letter of protest for Walker to send to Murray, outlining the merchant's objections. Among other things, the trip to Quebec would be too costly for Walker and his witnesses, and the presence of the 28th Regiment there made Quebec a dangerous place for him.

Governor Murray attempted a compromise by moving the trial to Trois Rivieres. This was still unacceptable to Walker. He and his wife hid to avoid being officially summoned. John Lilly was subpoenaed, but refused to appear.

Meanwhile, Murray had offered a reward of three hundred pounds for information leading to a conviction. If the informant were a soldier, there would be an additional two hundred pounds, a free discharge from the army and transportation to any British colony, since remaining in Canada might not be healthy for the man who talked. The governor was making every effort to bring the guilty parties to justice. He hoped that one of the accused would be tempted by the reward and turn King's evidence. No one stepped forward.

Sergeant Rogers was brought before the Summer Assizes at Trois Rivieres in 1765. Without Walker and his witnesses there was little chance of a conviction. Rogers was acquitted. There seemed no point in putting his companions on trial, so all four were released.

Now Walker complained bitterly that the military was shielding the guilty. He was so obsessed with his hatred of the army, he could not see that he had been manipulated by Conyngham and that his own obstinacy had handcuffed the Crown. To add to his indignation, Murray dismissed him from the office of magistrate.

Walker, who had refused to go to Quebec City to help in the prosecution of the men accused of attacking him, now travelled all the way to England to lay his case before James Murray's superiors. He carried with him not only his own litany of complaints, but also the exaggerated charges other Montreal merchants had against the governor. When Walker returned to Canada in 1766, he brought a letter from the Secretary of State instructing Murray to reinstate him as magistrate. A month later Murray was recalled to England to give an account of his administration. He was eventually vindicated on every count, but did not return to Canada. Sir Guy Carlton was appointed his successor.

With Murray gone, Walker was sure that the mystery of who had cut off his ear would now be solved. That reward for information leading to a conviction was still in effect. In November 1766, someone stepped forward to claim it.

The would-be informer was an ex-soldier named George McGovock, formerly of the 28th Regiment. He had been living in Walker's home for about four months. McGovock was a man of vile reputation, having been convicted at various times of robbery, rape and desertion. Nonetheless, on his disposition six perfectly respectable men were arrested and, at Walker's insistence, held without bail. They were Captain John Fraser, Major Daniel Disney, Captain John Campbell, Lieutenant Simon Evans, a merchant named Joseph Howard, and Luc de la Corne, formerly an officer under Montcalm. McGovock also named sergeants Rogers and Mee, but by that time those men had been transferred out of Canada.

Montrealers were shocked that these men should be arrested at bayonet point in the dead of night and then incarcerated without bail, all on the word of a rogue like McGovock. A petition on their behalf was signed by both English and French residents of Montreal and presented to Sir Guy Carlton. The new governor did not believe it to be his place to interfere with the judicial system, so the men remained in jail until the March 1767 Assizes in Montreal.

Lieutenant Evans was the first to be brought before Chief Justice Hey. In addition to McGovock, the prosecution had two witnesses who implicated Evans in the attack on Walker. A soldier named James Case stated that he had seen Evans come out of Walker's house on the night in question. Another soldier,

Henry Mirtz, testified that he had been employed by Evans to write letters in French to the lieutenant's fiancée. When the young woman reproached Evans for involvement in the attack, Mirtz said, the lieutenant dismissed the affair as a "*coup de jeunesse.*" In the jury's opinion these men were lying. They threw out the indictment and Evans was discharged, much to Walker's disgust. He told the jurymen that when he'd seen their names on the panel, he'd known he could expect nothing better. All Montreal now believed that Thomas Walker didn't care *who* was punished for cropping his ear, as long as that person wore a uniform.

Of the six accused men, only Major Disney had a true bill brought against him by a jury. At the subsequent trial, Thomas and Martha Walker, both of whom had earlier stated that they could not identify any of the disguised intruders, now claimed they recognized Major Disney. But the major had an alibi, sworn to by four people, that he was at a dinner party at the time of the assault. Under cross-examination McGovock contradicted himself so often that the chief justice instructed the jury to dismiss his evidence. The jury took less than half an hour to find Disney not guilty.

Now Disney and several others of the accused tried to sue Walker for malicious prosecution. The foreman of the grand jury brought a lawsuit against him for defamation of character. These actions came to nothing, as did an indictment against McGovock for perjury.

Thomas Walker remained in Canada, ever a troublemaker and malcontent, until the American Revolutionary War. He took the side of the rebels, and when the American commissioners went to Montreal in 1776 they stayed at his house. When they returned home, he went with them. Walker died in Boston in 1788. He went to his grave without ever having learned who had mutilated his ear. Whoever that man was, he and his companions took to their own graves the answer to early Canada's most troublesome mystery.

MYSTERY MAN

Henry More Smith

Every country has had its rogues and scoundrels, but few can lay claim to a felon as mysterious as Canada's Henry More Smith. His crimes were not extraordinary. Smith was a petty thief, a con man and a liar. But his eccentric behaviour while in jail made him a local celebrity, and his uncanny ability to escape fetters remains unexplained to this day.

When Smith (or whatever his real name was) first appeared in Windsor, Nova Scotia, in July of 1812, he was about twenty years old and dressed like a gentleman. He called himself Frederick Henry More and said he was from Brighton, England. He did not say much about his past, except that he was a tailor. He accepted a job as a farmhand with a pious Baptist Loyalist named John Bond who lived at Bawden, between Windsor and Truro.

Bond was happy to learn that his hired man was a God-fearing teetotaller who read his bible and joined the family for evening prayers. He was not pleased, however, when his daughter Elizabeth took a shine to the lad and wanted to marry him. As charming as young "Frederick" was, he was penniless and therefore not a suitable match for the daughter of a prosperous farmer. The young lovers defied Mr. Bond, and eloped in March of 1813.

The couple were married and settled in Windsor, where Smith went to work as a tailor and peddler. He made frequent trips to Halifax for material and supplies. His pack was always full of watches, silverware and small household items. No one connected him with the sudden rash of burglaries in Halifax. Nor did anyone suspect that the young tailor who could turn out a coat in record time was stealing garments and bolts of cloth from the best homes and shops in the city.

Then a young Windsor man was accosted on a Halifax street by an angry Haligonian who accused him of stealing a coat; the very coat, in fact, that the young man was wearing. The Halifax man had the Windsor man arrested. The astonished youth insisted that he had bought the coat from his tailor in Windsor, Frederick Henry More. A judge issued a warrant for the tailor's arrest, and constables went to his house. The only people there were Elizabeth and the couple's baby. Smith had been warned that the law was after him. He'd packed his bag with as much swag as he could carry, and fled on a stolen horse. Elizabeth and the child probably never saw him again.

In July of 1814 Henry More Smith, now using the name by which he is best known, arrived in Saint John, New Brunswick. He was soon in trouble there for stealing a horse from a man named Knox and selling it to an army officer. Smith made a run for it. Knox, sworn in as a special constable, went after him. Three days and 170 miles (273.5 km) later, Knox caught up with his man in Nova Scotia and hauled him to Kingston, New Brunswick where there was a good, solid jail.

The sheriff of King's County was Walter Bates, a Loyalist from Connecticut. Little did he know as he locked Smith up in the criminal room (as opposed to the debtor's room) of his jail that the young outlaw would have more than a passing impact on his life. Smith would, in fact, be the most difficult prisoner Bates ever tried to hold in his jail.

Smith had a hearing at the Circuit Court to determine if he could be tried at the next assize for horse theft. He pleaded that he was a penniless, friendless immigrant from England and a "victim of ill circumstances." He said he'd bought the horse he stood accused of stealing, never dreaming that the cad who'd sold it to him was a horse thief. He even had a receipt with a (forged) signature on it. When the magistrate asked Smith how he made his living, he replied, "By my honesty, sir."

Then he told the magistrate that Knox had beaten him, kicked him, and struck him with a pistol. Knox, of course, denied all this. In spite of Smith's tales of woe, he was committed for trial, and returned to his cell.

Smith began to complain of a pain in his side. He said it was the result of the beating Knox had given him. He claimed he was sick, too, because Knox had forced him to ride during a rainstorm. People in the town felt sorry for the unfortunate young Englishman. Smith still had his peddler's portmanteau, so Sheriff Bates allowed visitors to come to the jail to buy articles of clothing and other items. The prisoner was accused of horse theft, but nobody seemed to suspect that every item in his bag was stolen.

Smith used the money from his sales to retain the services of a lawyer, Charles J. Peters of Saint John. But that was just for show. He had his own ideas on how to get out of jail.

Since Sheriff Bates could not be at the jail all the time, he employed a man named Walter Dibble and his nineteen-year-old son John as part-time jailers. Smith went to work on all three of them. He knew they were pious men, so he made a great show of reading aloud from his bible. Then, in the midst of a passage, he would suddenly be seized with a violent coughing fit.

Smith's act went well beyond a fake cough. He showed Sheriff Bates a large, swollen bruise on his side. He said it had been there ever since that roughneck Knox had beaten him up. He complained of the cold and of being sick to his stomach, so Bates tried to keep his cell warm. He provided the prisoner with food that was "adapted to the delicacy of his constitution."

Smith's health deteriorated. He complained of loss of appetite, chills, headaches and dizziness. Then he began to cough up blood. Alarmed, Bates brought in a doctor. The medicine the physician gave the sick man did no good. By September 15, Smith was running a high fever and could not walk.

The Reverend Elias Scovil began making regular visits to the jail. He listened as the ailing Smith spoke with tears in his eyes of his approaching death, and of his poor old parents in far-off England. Reverend Scovil prayed for him. There was not much else to be done.

On September 23, Bates found Smith unconscious and naked on the floor of his cell. He had the sick man put back into his bed and revived with smelling salts. Smith feebly said that all in his family were subject to such fits. He didn't think he would survive another one.

Bates sent for the doctor again. After another examination, the doctor quietly told the sheriff that the prisoner probably would not last the night. Bates wrote to Charles J. Peters, informing him that his client was not long for this world.

Smith willed his clothing to John Dibble, and all the money he had left, three pounds, to Walter Dibble. Then the deathwatch began. The Dibbles and Scovil kept a solemn vigil. Mrs. Scovil sent her servant, Amy, to the jail with a comfortable feather mattress for the poor man to die on. But when Amy arrived at the jail, the place was in an uproar.

Minutes earlier John Dibble had gone into the cell to check on Smith and found the dying man writhing in pain. In a voice that was barely a whisper, Smith asked for a warm brick for his feet. Young Dibble hurried down the hall to put a brick in the stove. He did not lock the cell door. When he returned, Smith was gone!

John ran down a corridor to a room where his father was sitting with Reverend Scovil—a room Smith had to have passed on his way out. When he told them Smith was gone, they thought the poor fellow had died. They couldn't believe it when John explained that the man had escaped. How could a man who was at death's door get up and walk out of the jail?

Just then Amy arrived with the mattress. "Take it away, Amy," the Reverend snapped. "Smith is gone!" Amy went back to the house and told Mrs. Scovil that poor Smith was "...dead and gone."

When Sheriff Bates was told that Smith was gone, he, too, thought the poor soul had passed away. When he realized the prisoner had escaped, he immediately sent search parties off in all directions. The men found nothing except one man on the road who reported seeing Smith's ghost, "...scudding past me as fast as quicksilver...his feet not touching the ground."

Smith's escape caused a sensation. Many people thought that Bates and the elder Dibble had arranged it. The two men were Freemasons. The rumour went around that Smith, too, was a Mason, and his fellow members had let him go. On the day Smith was to have been tried for horse theft, Bates and Dibble were indicted for negligence. The angry sheriff posted a twenty-pound reward for Smith's recapture.

Smith, meanwhile, was sleeping in barns and looting farmhouses of food, money and anything else he could carry off easily. He was apprehended by one man who suspected him of being an American spy (the War of 1812 was on), but the fast-talking Smith convinced a magistrate in Fredericton that it was all a mistake. Then he added insult to injury by stealing another horse from Mr. Knox.

A warrant for the arrest of Henry More Smith was issued to every sheriff and magistrate in New Brunswick. The reward was raised to eighty pounds, a substantial amount of money at that time. Everytime a farmer or a townsman reported a theft, Smith was naturally assumed to be the culprit. The searchers who patrolled the country roads in search of the felon were at one time joined by a young man who called himself Bond. What better place to hide, Smith thought, than among the men who were looking for him!

Sheriff Bates had no solid leads on Smith's whereabouts until the second week of October, when he learned that a tavern owner near Woodstock had been robbed of some expensive clothing and several other valuable items. The sheriff sent out a posse that traced Smith to an Indian camp on the St. John River. They learned that Smith had hired a Native guide to take him through the woods and across the American border. The constables cursed their luck at missing their quarry, but they were also glad that New Brunswick was rid of the villain. Now he was the Americans' problem.

Things were not going well for Smith, however. Before he could reach the border, his guide deserted him. The man either doubted Smith's willingness to pay him, or he was unnerved by the pistol Smith now carried in his belt. Without a guide to take him through the bush, Smith was forced to use the roads. On October 10, two men named Putnam and Watson collared the fugitive and took him to Fredericton. He admitted to the magistrate there that he was Smith, the escapee from the Kingston jail. When asked how he had escaped, Smith answered, "The gaoler opened the door and the priest prayed me out."

Putnam and Watson put Smith in a canoe for the trip back to Kingston. He was handcuffed, pinioned, and tied to the centre bar, so he'd be sure to drown if he tried capsizing the boat. After two days on the St. John River they stopped at the farm of Robert Bailes, one of the people whose house had been burglarized. Bailes was so pleased to see the thief in irons, he invited Putnam and Watson to stay the night. In the morning he would take them to Kingston in his wagon.

After supper Putnam and Watson went to bed, leaving Bailes to watch the prisoner. Smith told the farmer he had to use the privy. Bailes didn't trust Smith, so he woke Watson. He, too, was suspicious, and didn't want to let Smith out of the house.

The obliging Smith offered a solution. He couldn't escape, he said, if Watson had a rope on him. Watson thought that made sense. He tied one end of a rope around Smith's arm and wound the other end around his hand. Then they stepped outside. They were barely out the door when Smith spun around and smashed

Watson over the head with his handcuffs. As Watson slumped to the ground, Smith slipped off the rope and vanished into the darkness. By the time Watson regained his senses and alerted the others, Smith was long gone.

Putnam and Watson shamefacedly reported the escape to Sheriff Bates. The sheriff didn't blame them. He, too, had been a victim of Smith's wiles. But he did look forward to the day when he had the scoundrel back in his jail.

Smith went right back to stealing. His hideout was an isolated shack on a farm owned by Jack Paterson, about two miles from Fredericton. He slept in the daytime, and at night he went to work, robbing farmhouses as well as homes and shops in town. He stole a pony to help him carry off the swag. One of his victims was the Attorney General of New Brunswick. While that gentleman hosted a dinner party in his mansion, Smith crept into the front hall and cleared it of the guests' coats.

Smith was probably building up a supply of goods to set himself up as a tailor and peddler in the United States. Soon his little robber's lair was full of stolen goods. But staying too long in one place proved to be Smith's undoing.

One morning Jack Paterson took a stroll around his property and found a stranger sleeping in the shack. The young man awoke and said he'd been on the road late and just wanted a place to sleep for the night. He hoped the farmer didn't mind. Paterson said he didn't mind at all. In those days it was common for travellers in rural areas to take shelter for the night in barns and other farm outbuildings. Paterson left the shack and continued on his rounds. But when he looked back, he saw the stranger heading the other way at a dead run. He thought the man must be either a thief or an army deserter. Paterson rounded up some help and the search was on. Before nightfall Smith was locked in the Fredericton jail. When Paterson searched the shack, he found a treasure trove of clothing, silverware, clocks and other stolen items.

Smith was sent back to Kingston on a sloop. He was bound with a padlocked iron collar and ten feet of chain, and a pair of handcuffs. The little ship docked at Kingston on October 30, just before midnight. In the morning when he was taken off the boat for delivery back to jail, Smith was greeted on the dock by a crowd of townspeople. In Kingston, Henry More Smith was a celebrity.

Sheriff Walter Bates searched Smith carefully before putting him in his old cell. The cell was twenty-two feet (6.7 m) long, sixteen feet (4.8 m) wide, with three-foot (.9 m) thick walls of limestone and mortar on three sides. The fourth wall was a partition from the next cell. It was made of timber a foot (.3 m) thick and covered with plaster. The cell door was made of two-inch (5 cm) plank lined with sheet iron. It was held in place by three strong iron hinges, and secured by three heavy padlocks. The door had a small, iron wicket window, also fastened with a padlock. The cell's only small window to the outside was double-grated with iron bars inside the pane of glass. A person leaving the cell would have to pass through two more padlocked doors to reach the outside. The keys to all locks were kept by Walter Dibble.

Now that Bates knew what a slippery customer Smith was, he took extra precautions. He had Smith chained to an iron bolt in the floor. The prisoner could reach the "necessary" and the wicket in the door, but he could not reach the window. Bates did grant Smith one small mercy. The young man's hands and wrists were badly swollen, so he removed the handcuffs. It didn't seem likely that Smith would be going anywhere. Nonetheless, Bates inspected Smith's irons regularly.

For twelve days Smith seemed to be well-behaved. Then on November 12, an inspection of Smith's cell revealed that one of the bars in the window had been cut through, and could be removed and replaced. Another bar had been partially cut. A few more nights' work, and Smith would have been gone.

Sheriff Bates demanded to know how Smith had done it. Smith obligingly handed over a case knife and a small file. He claimed he'd left them behind when he'd made his first escape. He said he'd used them to cut his chain before going to work on the window. It hadn't been difficult to hide the cut end of the chain from the sheriff's inspections.

Bates thought Smith might still have hidden tools, so he searched the cell again. He found a small saw in the crack between two stone blocks in the wall. Smith refused to say where he'd gotten it. Bates searched Smith's clothing and bedding again, and found nothing. He fastened the prisoner with a new chain, and locked handcuffs on him. Then he went home to bed.

He was soon awakened by an urgent message from Walter Dibble. Smith had been caught sawing away at the bars on the window again. When the prisoner realized he'd been seen, he dropped something into the privy.

"Smith, you keep at work yet," the sheriff said as he entered the cell. Unbelievably, Smith was sitting on his bunk, free of chains and handcuffs.

Bates and Dibble searched Smith's clothing again. They looked in the privy. They took the bunk apart. Nothing! The next day the exasperated sheriff brought the doctor in and made Smith strip naked in his presence. This time they found a ten-inch (25.4 cm) saw blade concealed in his undershirt. Bates was certain that Smith had no more escape tools. Nonetheless, he had the window bricked in, leaving only a tiny opening at one corner.

Now began the most bizarre chapter in Smith's story. Up to that point he had been relatively docile, if somewhat tricky. Henceforth the mischievous imp was replaced by a madman given to outbursts of violence. Moreover, he would perform feats that still defy explanation.

On November 16 Bates found Smith's cell nearly demolished. Smith had broken a padlock, and used his chains to smash the plaster off the walls. He threatened to burn the jailhouse to the ground.

At that time horse theft was a hanging offence. Bates might well have been looking forward to having Smith tried and then out of his hair, one way or the other. He was dismayed when he received a letter from a magistrate advising him that due to heavy snow that made travel difficult for witnesses, the trial would have to be postponed. Meanwhile, Bates was to use "any severity necessary" to ensure Smith did not escape again.

In compliance with those instructions, Bates loaded Smith down with forty-six pounds (20.8 kg) of steel fetters and iron chains. Smith's arms and legs were so restricted in movement that he could shuffle but a few feet in any direction. He could not reach his mouth to eat unless he sat on the floor.

For the next few weeks Smith howled and screamed like a madman day and night. He mixed senseless ravings and bloody threats with prayers and quotations from the bible. He ranted about his wife and his aged parents. Bates wrote some of it down for use later in court. When the weather turned colder Bates provided Smith with straw and blankets. Then he took the blankets away when Smith tried to hang himself with one.

When the prisoner became silent again for a while, the sheriff became suspicious. He inspected the cell, and found that Smith had worked loose the iron staple fastening the chain to the floor. He had also broken his iron collar. The sheriff brought in new fetters. Smith resumed howling and ranting.

As the temperature dropped further, Bates worried that Smith would freeze to death in his unheated cell. But for some reason the cold never seemed to bother him. In fact, Smith's chains were actually warm to the touch, as though heated by some supernatural energy. People began to whisper that Smith was in league with the devil.

In mid-February of 1815, two men arrived from Nova Scotia with a letter from Elizabeth, who had heard of her husband's trouble. She wanted to sell a colt she owned and send the money to Henry. Smith refused to even see the messengers.

Smith was a slender young man, yet he broke chains and iron collars as fast as Bates could have them replaced. No one could explain how he did it. One might be inclined to think that Bates, who wrote an account of the events, was exaggerating. But other people witnessed these things, and an iron collar that Smith twisted like a piece of leather was kept as an exhibit in the jail for many years.

On March 5, Smith was allowed his first bath in four months. He tried to eat the soap. On March 11, Dibble resigned as jailer and was replaced by James Reid. The new jailer soon found his patience being tried to the limit. He caught Smith working away at a stovepipe hole, trying to break through the partition to the debtor's room, which was vacant and unlocked.

Reid sent for Bates. When the sheriff arrived, he found Smith shadow-fencing with a wooden sword. Bits of chains and handcuffs hung from nails like trophies. Once again Bates brought in new chains, and once again Smith broke them.

But in spite of all this wizardry, Smith couldn't get out of the Kingston jail. At last, on May 4, he went on trial before Judge John Saunders. The weird behaviour continued.

On the first day of his trial, Smith took off his shoes and socks. He tore his shirt, snapped his fingers and clapped his hands. When asked how he pleaded to the charge of horse theft, Smith remained silent. Judge Saunders warned him against faking madness, but to no avail. The jury finally decided that the prisoner "stood mute by the visitation of God." Court was adjourned for the day.

On the second day Smith was so violent, he had to be bound hand and foot in the dock. His lawyer argued that the evidence against him was circumstantial. The jury disagreed, and found Smith guilty. Judge Saunders sentenced him to be hanged.

Smith was locked in his cell to await execution. He was placed on a diet of bread and water. But he continued to break every chain and manacle placed on him.

Now his behaviour took yet another strange turn. Using straw from his bedding and bits of his own clothing, Smith constructed several puppets, which Bates described as life-sized and very lifelike. Then he scratched the forms of men and women on the walls of his cell. He incorporated the puppets and the scratchings into a show that he performed between bouts of screaming. Bates gave him a fiddle so he could play a jig while he used his feet to make the puppets dance. The sheriff wrote to the attorney general of New Brunswick that the performance was "better worth the attention of the public than all the waxwork ever exhibited in this province."

The letter was published in New Brunswick's *Royal Gazette,* and caught the attention of the public. People flocked to the jail and paid admission to see the condemned man's amazing puppet show. Smith used the money for the purchase of material so he could make more puppets. He eventually had a "family" of twenty-four puppets, and by August he was one of the most famous men in New Brunswick.

Smith's death sentence was commuted by the colony's supreme court. With the noose no longer dangling over his head, Smith ceased his ranting and became more talkative. He told Bates that his real name was Henry Moon. He came from a well-to-do family, he said, and had been educated at Cambridge. He also claimed he could tell fortunes. He told Bates and some other visitors things about themselves that, supposedly, he could not possibly have known except by some mystic means.

Smith might have spent a long time in the Kingston jail, but authorities decided they'd sooner be rid of him. The court released Smith on the single condition that he get out of New Brunswick and stay out. If he ever returned, more charges could be brought against him. Upon hearing this news, Smith danced around the courtroom like a raving lunatic, and asked the judge for a shoelace. At the urging of the magistrate, Bates put Smith on a boat for Nova Scotia.

Walter Bates eventually wrote a book about his troublesome former prisoner, *The Mysterious Stranger, or, Memoirs of Henry More Smith.* In order to finish his account, he wanted to find out what had become of Smith after his banishment from New

Brunswick. Tracing Smith's movements wasn't difficult, because he left a trail of robberies everywhere he went. He had been jailed in Connecticut, New York and Maryland, and chased out of Ohio. In the American jails Smith had repeated some of the tricks he'd pulled in New Brunswick: near-fatal illness and the breaking of chains and fetters.

Bates was able to follow Smith's wanderings to Upper Canada, where in 1835 he was jailed in Toronto for burglary. Beyond that, no record exists of the mystery man who called himself Henry More Smith. He vanished from history, leaving people to wonder: who was he, and how did he do the things he did?

THE MYSTERIOUS DEATH OF CHARLES FRANCIS HALL

Was the Captain Poisoned?

For three and a half centuries after the first European explorers probed its eastern approaches, the region of land and sea now known as the Canadian Arctic was one of the greatest of all geographic mysteries. In wooden ships powered first by sail, and later aided by steam engines, daring men gradually charted the islands and waters of the world's largest archipelago. Their initial goal was a route that would take them through that massive puzzle to the Pacific Ocean—a Northwest Passage. The discovery of such a passage would bring glory to the man who found it, and would open to Europeans a new door to the riches of the Orient.

That quest would cost many of the explorers their lives. It would also add new mysteries to the lore of the Arctic. What was the ultimate fate of Henry Hudson and his companions after a mutinous crew cast them adrift in 1611 on the bay that now bears his name? What became of the men of the James Knight expedition of 1719 after they were stranded on Marble Island in Hudson's Bay? Why did the well-planned and well-provisioned Franklin Expedition of 1845 meet with utter disaster?

While some explorers were still trying to solve the riddle of the Northwest Passage, others set their sights on a new goal: the North Pole. Unlike the discovery of a Northwest Passage, which all hoped would be of commercial value, the quest for the Pole was strictly a hunt for glory. There would be fame, to be sure, for the first man to reach it. But this was a time of flag-waving nationalism, when adventurers from many countries strove for "firsts": first to climb an unconquered mountain, first to reach the remote source of a great river, first to plant his country's flag on the North or South Pole!

Charles Francis Hall was born in Vermont in 1821. As a young man he published two small newspapers in Cincinnati, Ohio, but his passionate interest was the Arctic. He read every book he could find on it, and regarded as heroes the captains who had sailed into the frozen north. By the late 1850s he was fascinated with stories of the search for the Franklin Expedition.

Over a decade earlier the Royal Navy commander Sir John Franklin had sailed from England with two ships to find the Northwest Passage, and then vanished. Subsequent expeditions, some of them financed by the commander's wife, Lady Jane Franklin, had failed to find any survivors, though in 1859 explorer Francis McClintock found relics and some bodies on King William Island. Hall suddenly decided he had a God-given duty to go to the Arctic and find any of Franklin's men who might still be alive. He sold his businesses, left his wife and children in Ohio, and went to New York. There he met Henry Grinnell, founder of the American Geographical Society, patron of American Arctic exploration and Lady Franklin's representative in the United States.

Hall intended to spend a season living with the Inuit—still called Eskimos at that time—and learn their language and their ways. Most people who heard this considered Hall somewhat mad. No white man had ever gone to live alone among the Inuit. To most of the whites who had encountered them, the Inuit were filthy, lazy, degenerate savages.

Charles Francis Hall, however, was quite unlike most of the other explorers—mostly British with a few American exceptions—who had ventured into the Arctic. He was eccentric, obsessive, and often tactless. He was quick to take offence, and would hold a grudge. He was a difficult man to get along with. But he thrived on solitude, and that aspect of his nature would serve him well in the vast loneliness of the Arctic.

Hall didn't have much money, but with some help from Grinnell he secured passage on a whaling ship, the *George Henry,* commanded by Captain Sidney O. Budington. In May 1860, the whaler sailed from New London, Connecticut, bound for the Arctic. In August the ship anchored at the mouth of what was then called Frobisher Strait, discovered by Sir Martin Frobisher in 1576.

Hall hoped to sail through the strait in his own small boat to King William Island, where he would begin his search for Franklin's men. However, Hall learned what the local Inuit already knew; that the strait was actually a bay. Hall also discovered artifacts left behind by Frobisher's men. He collected hundreds of relics that were eventually sent to Britain.

Hall had the good fortune to meet Ebierbing and Tookolito, an Inuit couple the whites called Joe and Hannah. This remarkable pair had been taken to England by whalers and spent two years there. They had learned English—Hannah was fluent—and had been presented to Queen Victoria and Prince Albert. Hannah and Joe became Hall's lifelong friends, and were invaluable in teaching him their language and customs.

Nonetheless, Hall, typical of "civilized" men of his time, had a condescending view of the Inuit in general. He called them "untamed children of the icy north," and felt they would benefit from exposure to Christian missionaries and the white man's influence. He wrote:

"One has to make up his mind, if he would live among that people, to submit to their customs, and be entirely one of them. When a white man for the first time enters one of their tupics (tents) or igloos, he is nauseated by everything he sees and smells—even disgusted with the looks of the innocent natives, who extend to him the best hospitality their means afford."

Writing of the interior of an Inuit dwelling, Hall described "a dirty set of human beings mixed up among masses of nasty, uneatable flesh, skins, blood and bones scattered all about... hanging over a long, low flame, the *oo-koo-sin* (stone cooking kettle) black with soot and oil of great age, and filled to its utmost capacity with black meat, swimming in a thick, dark, smoking fluid, as if made by boiling down the dirty scrapings of a butcher's stall."

Hall added that the dishes the family used to eat this "soup" were also filthy. But *before* the meal was put into them, the bowls were given to the dogs to be licked clean. The American survived because he learned to adapt to such conditions.

Hall explored the country around Frobisher Bay. He discovered and named the hundred-mile (160.9 km) long, 3,500-foot

(1,067 m) high Grinnell Glacier. But his own small sailboat was wrecked in a storm, preventing him from setting off to look for Franklin's men.

On September 27, 1861, Hall found the *George Henry* waiting for him at Rescue Bay on Cumberland Sound. Captain Budington was astounded to see Hall still alive after so many months with the "Eskimos." Hall had hoped to return to the United States to fit out a new expedition, but ice in Davis Strait made it impossible for the *George Henry* to get out.

The whalers spent a long, miserable Arctic winter. They resented Hall sharing their food. He responded by going on a hunger strike, which Budington finally convinced him to end. Quarrels and fights were common. Hall left the ship to go on lengthy journeys of exploration, during which he lived off the land as the natives had taught him.

The *George Henry* finally sailed again in August 1862. When she reached St. John's, Newfoundland, all aboard were shocked to learn that the United States was now in the grip of a bloody civil war. When Hall reached New York, he wrote to the federal government offering his services, but received no reply. That was just as well. He was not interested in the war. He wanted to return to the Arctic.

Because of the war, however, sources for funding had dried up. Hall had brought Joe and Hannah with him. He went on the lecture circuit. The Inuit couple dressed in their native costumes were a surefire draw. He also "rented" them for a short time to P.T. Barnum's museum in New York. Sadly, Joe and Hannah's infant son died while they were in the city. When Captain Budington was about to sail north again, he offered to take Joe and Hannah with him. Hall was furious with him for that, even though the Inuit stayed with him in New York.

Hall still had to raise more money. He wrote a book titled *Arctic Researches and Life Among the Esquimaux,* which was published in London in 1864, and New York in 1865. By July 1, 1864, Hall was ready to sail again. Once more he had managed to arrange free passage on a whaler, the *Monticello.*

Hall was still convinced that some of Franklin's men could yet be alive, living somewhere with Inuit. He wanted the *Monticello* to drop him at Repulse Bay, near the Melville Peninsula. But the ship's skipper made a mistake and set him ashore far to the south at Depot Island in Roes Welcome Sound. It was too late in the year for Hall to have any chance of reaching Repulse Bay.

Hall spent the winter in an Inuit village, listening to their stories of strange white men and their ships from many years before. Some of the tales were indeed from actual encounters the people had had with whites. But other stories were exaggerations of tales they'd heard from other Inuit. Hall believed every word. Hall once visited a ship in the whaling fleet and had a meal with the crew, but otherwise he lived like an Inuit.

Hall spent the next four years among the Inuit. His journal, much of it written by the light of an oil lamp that he also used to thaw his ink, reveals the highs and lows of his spirits. Sometimes he wrote of going all the way to the North Pole, as though it were a mere matter of walking until he got there. At other times he was thrown into despair by what he considered the backward and superstitious ways of the Inuit.

"How terrible is my situation here, the only white man among a savage people...never again will I put myself in the power of an uncivilized race...a whisper, a tip of the finger is enough to throw all seeming order here into an earthly hell."

Once an *angeko* (medicine man) tried to persuade Joe to trade wives. Hannah would have nothing to do with such an arrangement, and Hall supported her, even though it was risky for him to do so, because an *angeko* was held in awe. Hannah prevailed. Then tragedy struck again when her second child died.

All the time that Hall wandered with the Inuit, he tried to convince them to take him to King William Island where he might find survivors from Franklin's crew. But the Inuit went where they wanted, guided only by their quest for food and the traditional taboos that Hall found exasperating.

In August 1866 Hall met whalers who had a letter for him from Henry Grinnell. It included a message from Lady Franklin, encouraging him to continue his search for the missing men, even though she knew that "my own dear husband has long been beyond the reach of all rescue." Hall had come to the end of his patience with the Inuit. He tried to recruit whalers to join him in an excursion to King William's Island. He failed. But a little over a year later, in the fall of 1867, he persuaded five whalers to go with him.

For several months Hall and his party, which included Joe and Hannah, chased down one rumour after another and found nothing. The whalers began to grumble, quite likely because Hall was a critical and demanding leader. By the end of July 1868 they were on the verge of mutiny. Hall argued with a man named Patrick Coleman, whom he accused of inciting the other men. When Coleman threatened him—or so Hall claimed later—Hall pulled a gun and shot him.

Hall immediately regretted his rash action. He tried to nurse Coleman back to health, but two weeks later the man died. The only account of the shooting that ever reached the outside world was Hall's. He was never officially charged with any crime. As soon as they could, the other whalers deserted him and rejoined the whaling fleet.

Not until the spring of 1869 did Hall finally make it to King William Island, accompanied by Joe and Hannah and a few other Inuit. He did indeed find relics from the Franklin disaster, including a silver spoon with Franklin's crest on it and some skeletal remains. Local Inuit told him that many years earlier they had given some seal meat to about thirty starving white men, but then had gone away and left them to fend for themselves.

Hall was angered by what struck him as cold-heartedness on the part of these Inuit. Considering the time he had been with them, Hall should have realized that the Inuit quite likely would have had little food to spare for so many strangers. In their own daily lives they often looked starvation in the face, and sometimes had to abandon old or sick family members so the rest could survive.

Hall was bitterly disappointed—if unjustly—in the Inuit, but he had lost none of his love for the Arctic. He could have no doubts now that Franklin and all of his men had perished. He turned his gaze to the North Pole. All his years in the frigid land had not been for nothing, he decided. They had been preparation for what would be his greatest adventure yet. On August 13, Hall, Joe and Hannah boarded a whaler for the voyage to New York.

When Lady Franklin learned of the artifacts Hall had brought back from King William Island, she wanted him to go back to search for her husband's journal, which she was sure must be cached somewhere on the island. Hall said he'd be honoured to lead such an expedition, *after* he had been to the North Pole. No amount of argument could shake him from that, not even when Lady Franklin traveled to the United States to meet Hall personally.

Hall briefly visited his family. Then he was off to raise funds for his expedition. Hall was famous now, so his lectures drew large audiences—though he actually hated public speaking. He had an interview with President Ulysses S. Grant, and was awarded $50,000 for the expedition. Hall was absolutely confident that he would plant the American flag at the North Pole.

Hall would not have to hitch a ride on a whaler for this epic journey. He would sail to glory on the 387-ton steamer USS *Periwinkle,* which was completely refitted and renamed *Polaris,* the official name of the expedition. As commander of the expedition Hall would have the rank of captain.

But Hall had absolutely no qualifications to command a ship. Therefore Sidney Budington, who had first taken Hall into the Canadian Arctic, was made master of the *Polaris.* Another captain, George Tyson, whom Hall had known at Frobisher Bay, was taken on as assistant navigator. First mate was Hubbard Chester, formerly of the *Monticello.* William Morton, another man with Arctic experience, was second mate. Joe and Hannah, with their twelve-year-old adopted daughter Punny, would also be aboard.

Engineer Emil Schumann was German, as were seven of the crew. Of the three scientists selected for the voyage, two were also German. That meant the ship's company was half German and half American. That fact alone might have intimated coming trouble. The potential for disharmony escalated with the addition of Dr. Emil Bessels, another German, as ship's physician and a member of the scientific team.

Dr. Bessels was not Hall's first choice, and the commander had to be persuaded to take him along. The two men took an instant dislike to each other. Hall was known for his bluntness. Bessels was said to be very sensitive. He also had a tendency to be insubordinate.

Nonetheless, when Hall was ready to sail, he told the American Geographic Society, "I have chosen my own men; men who will stand by me through thick and thin. Though we may be surrounded by innumerable icebergs, and though our vessel may be crushed like an eggshell, I believe they will stand by me to the last."

The *Polaris* sailed on June 29, 1871. For part of the voyage she was accompanied by the U.S. Navy tender *Congress* so that when Hall reached the Arctic Ocean he'd be able to continue with a full load of supplies. Like most of his fellow explorers he believed that beyond the maze of islands lay a wide-open polar sea. But he didn't know how long it would take the *Polaris* to thread her way through.

Within a week of embarkation Hall also had a full load of trouble. Dr. Bessels and the other German scientist, Frederick Meyers, would not obey his orders. As well-educated men, they considered themselves superior to him. Meyers was downright insolent. Captain Budington certainly knew more about running a ship than Hall did, but he also professed to know more about the Arctic. Of course, that rankled Hall. Budington also quarrelled with George Tyson, a captain in his own right who was not accustomed to being subordinate to another ship's officer. Matters became worse when Budington was caught pilfering food from the supplies and Hall admonished him. Budington threatened to quit. The German and American crewmen did not get along.

When the *Polaris* and the *Congress* reached Disco Island off the coast of Greenland, Hall asked the other ship's skipper, Captain Davenport, for help. Davenport called the men of the *Polaris* together and gave them a tough talk on the need for discipline. He reminded them that Hall was in command. He threatened to put Meyers in irons and take him back to the United States. At that, every German in the *Polaris* crew threatened to quit.

Davenport did not arrest Meyers. He had a chaplain go before the assembly and say a prayer asking God's blessing on the endeavour. The reverend added his own plea for charity, co-operation and good fellowship among shipmates. He might as well have whistled into the Arctic wind.

Soon after the *Congress* turned back, Tyson found that Budington was pilfering again, this time from the liquor supply. He told Hall, but Hall decided to overlook the infraction. Nothing mattered to him now except pushing north. Then Hall did a strange thing.

He had brought along his journal and other documents connected with his second expedition. Hall had intended to work on them to prepare them for publication. When the *Polaris* reached Godhaven, Greenland, Hall left them with an official there for safekeeping. Did this man who had always been brimming with confidence suddenly have a foreboding of disaster? Had it occurred to him that he, like Franklin, might end up in an icy tomb?

Further up the Greenland coast Hall stopped at Upernavik to pick up an Inuit named Hans Christian Hendrik. Hans had assisted Arctic explorer Elisha Kane, and his knowledge of the land and waters could be valuable. But when Hans came on board he brought his wife and three children, as well as a load of tents, cooking gear, weapons and other baggage. He would not leave any of it behind, so Hall had to find places to stow it all.

Hall's original plan was to sail west through James Sound. Now he changed his mind and set a course north, into the narrow waters that separate Greenland and Ellesmere Island, Canada's northernmost territory. Hall was sure that channel led to the open polar sea. In his attempt to navigate its previously uncharted northern extremity, Hall would sail farther north than any other man up to that time. But he wouldn't find his polar sea.

By the end of August Captain Budington was anxious to find a safe harbour where the *Polaris* could lay up for the long Arctic winter. He quarrelled with Hall and Tyson, and called Hall an amateur behind his back. Tyson, for his part, thought Budington was a coward who had little interest in reaching the North Pole.

The crew was also getting nervous. In his journal Tyson wrote contemptuously, "I believe some of them think we are going over the edge of the world." Tyson himself seemed willing to sail into the jaws of hell if that's where Hall wanted to go. Then at 82 degrees 11 'N the *Polaris* reached impassable ice. The current was pushing her back down the channel. In what is now called Hall Basin the crew moored her to an ice floe while the ship's officers had a meeting.

Tyson and first mate Chester urged Hall to press on, but Budington wouldn't even discuss that option. For once Hall agreed with him, though grudgingly. Winter was setting in, and it would be foolish to risk the whole expedition—not to mention their lives—on a reckless gamble.

Hall attempted to take the *Polaris* to the northern tip of Ellesmere Island (which he called Grant's Land). But pack ice drove the ship back, almost wrecking her in the process. The *Polaris* found refuge in a small cove on the Greenland coast. Hall named it Thank God Harbour. There he raised the American flag. It wasn't the North Pole, but it was the most northerly spot on the globe over which any flag waved. The date was September 10, 1871.

Hall wasn't about to sit and wait out the long winter. He had tramped across more miles of Arctic ice than any non-Inuit alive. He believed he could reach the Pole by sledge. First he would make a scouting expedition to plot out a route. Then he would make his run for the Pole itself in the spring.

To accompany him on the first trip, Hall chose Joe, Hans Henrik and Hubbard Chester. He wanted to take Tyson, but (according to Tyson) had to leave him with the ship because he needed a man he trusted to watch Budington. The captain resented the implication.

The four men left on October 10. Two weeks later they were back. Hall was tired, but he said he'd had a good trip and was sure he could reach the Pole in the spring. By now the *Polaris* was more a big cabin than a ship.There was ice under her keel and her sides were banked with snow as insulation against the extreme cold. Outside, a man's spit crackled and froze before it hit the ground. Inside, the coal stoves kept the cramped quarters at near tropical temperatures.

The sudden exposure to the heat might have had a dizzying effect on Hall when he first entered. He asked for a cup of coffee, and a pot was brewed for him. When Hall took a drink from the steaming cup, he immediately became nauseous and vomited. He said his stomach burned. He told Hannah there'd been a strange, sweet taste to the coffee.

Hall took to his sickbed, but apparently no one thought he was seriously ill. He had complained of stomach ailments before this. The coffee had not made anyone else sick. Dr. Bessels advised against giving Hall an emetic, which would have purged his digestive system. By morning the commander's condition was worse. Then he became delirious.

For a week Hall raved. He had an insatiable thirst. He said he had been poisoned. He accused everyone, especially Dr. Bessels, of trying to murder him. He thought he saw poisonous vapours coming from Bessels' mouth. He refused to take any food or medicine, especially from the hand of the doctor. Still, Bessels tried to fight Hall's high fever with quinine injections.

After a week Hall began to show improvement. He was rational, and was soon well enough to go outside. "I am as well as I ever was," he said. But Hall would trust only Hannah to prepare his meals, and even then had a crew member taste his food and drink before he would touch them.

Then the explorer was stricken again. Shortly after midnight on November 8, Hubbard Chester awoke Budington and told him, "Captain Hall is dying." Budington hurried to Hall's cabin. He found the commander sitting on the edge of his bunk, glassy-eyed and twitching. He was trying to spell the word "murder"!

Charles Francis Hall died in the gloom of an Arctic night. While far to the south his countrymen awakened to the morning sun, Hall was buried on the bleak Greenland shore. Hannah wept.

According to testimony given at an inquest much later, when Hall died Captain Budington said, "There's a stone off my heart."

The captain denied making the statement, but admitted telling a sailor, "we are all right now...you shan't be starved to death now, I can tell you." Dr. Bessels allegedly said Hall's death was the best thing that could have happened aboard the *Polaris*...and then laughed. Frederick Meyer expressed relief that Hall was dead, so command would now fall to the ship's officers.

If Meyer thought things aboard the *Polaris* would improve with Hall gone, he was wrong. In fact, the opposite was true. Technically Budington was in command, but he was now little more than a quarrelsome drunk. None of the other officers seemed able to take charge. As Joe put it later, "No cap'n; nobody cap'n. Cap'n Budington, he cap'n. Cap'n Tyson, he cap'n. Doctor, he cap'n too. Mr. Chester, cap'n. Mr. Meyer, cap'n; me cap'n; everybody cap'n—no good."

Budington had no intention of continuing on to the Pole. "Whoever wants to go north, let them go," he said, "but I won't." Tyson and Chester made one attempt to complete Hall's mission, but one of their whaleboats was crushed in the ice and they had to give up.

On August 12, 1872, the ice broke up enough for the *Polaris* to begin the journey home. Bad luck was not finished with the ill-starred expedition. For the men, women and children on board, the ordeal was just beginning.

In mid-October a series of mishaps resulted in nineteen people being separated from the ship and stranded on a huge ice floe, eight kilometres (five miles) in circumference. They included Tyson, Meyer, Joe, Hannah and Punny, and Hans Hendrik and his whole family. They drifted on this ice island for *five months.* Their incredible journey is a tale in itself. Had it not been for Joe and

Hans, who were able to hunt seals and polar bears, the entire party would have died. They were finally rescued by a Newfoundland sealer off the coast of Labrador and taken to St. John's.

Meanwhile, the rest of the *Polaris* crew had been forced to abandon ship off the coast of Greenland. They spent a hard winter ashore and then headed south in their whaleboats. A Scottish whaler picked them up. Miraculously, the only member of the *Polaris* Expedition to die was Hall. But what was the cause of his death?

During his illness Hall ranted that he'd been poisoned. But who would murder him, and why? Budington, Bessels and Meyer clearly detested him. Budington was strongly against continuing with the expedition. But only Dr. Bessels had access to poison—the arsenic in his medical supplies. At that time, many medicines contained small amounts of the substance. Bessels could have been putting it in the quinine he administered to Hall. What, however, would have been his motive? In spite of his contempt for Hall—and the rest of the ship's officers for that matter—Bessels had been in favour of continuing north. Could the doctor have murdered his patient simply because he didn't like the man? Could someone else have stolen arsenic from Bessels' medical supplies and used it to kill Hall?

It is worth noting that when a search party found the remains of the *Polaris* men's camp on the Greenland coast, they retrieved several journals that had been left behind. Pages for the dates covering the time of Hall's illness and death had been torn out. Hall's own journal and other papers were missing, supposedly lost but possibly destroyed. Lacking solid evidence, and going by Dr. Bessels' diagnosis, the American court of enquiry concluded that the fifty-year-old explorer had died of a stroke.

However, in 1968 Chauncey Loomis, Hall's biographer, received permission to go to Greenland and exhume Hall's body. Due to the dry Arctic cold the corpse was quite well preserved. Loomis took hair and fingernail samples and sent them to the Centre for Forensic Medicine in Toronto for testing. The results were startling. In the last two weeks of his life, Hall had received a lethal quantity of arsenic. He had, in fact, been poisoned!

Arsenic could have been the reason for the unusual sweet taste of Hall's coffee. It could have caused the vomiting, the raging thirst and the mania. But even Loomis' hard evidence does not necessarily mean that Hall was murdered.

Hall was a rugged individualist. With few exceptions, he placed little trust in other human beings. In keeping with his policy of self-reliance, he kept his own medicine chest. Quite likely it was stocked with the arsenic-based remedies that were so common then. Given Hall's mistrust of Dr. Bessels, he might well have tried to doctor himself back to health, and taken a fatal dose of his own medicine. Of course, by 1968 Dr. Bessels was long past questioning. Did he poison Captain Hall? The truth will never be known.

THE MARY CELESTE MYSTERY

Gone Without a Trace

Many people believe the story of the *Mary Celeste* to be mere legend, like that of the dreaded *Flying Dutchman*. The *Mary Celeste* was in fact a real ship, sailed by real men. The question as to the fate of her people has become one of the most enduring mysteries of the sea.

Ghost ship! The image is common in the lore of the sea. It might be a phantom vessel passing in the fog, seen only by superstitious sailors. Or it could be a derelict, bobbing ruined and empty on the swells like a floating, haunted mansion. The *Mary Celeste* defied both definitions. She was no phantom, though at times she has been dismissed as a myth. She was a real ship, registered in New York. Real men walked her decks, worked her sails and guided her wheel. Nor was she a wreck, waiting only for the sea to pull her down. When found on the open ocean she was in good shape and her cargo was intact. The problem was, not a soul was on board. For well over a century she has posed a riddle, and perhaps even held a clue to an unsolved crime.

The *Mary Celeste* was a 282-ton two-masted brigantine, schooner rigged. She was about a hundred feet (30.4 m) long, twenty-five feet (7.6 m) in the beam and eleven feet (3.3 m) in depth. Originally christened the *Amazon,* the vessel was built in 1860 at Spencer's Island, Nova Scotia. At that time, Bluenose shipbuilders were reputed to rank among the best in the world.

However, when the *Amazon's* skipper died suddenly on her maiden voyage, the vessel was quickly cursed with the reputation of being a bad luck ship. Six years later the *Amazon* was caught in a storm and ran aground at Cow Bay, Cape Breton. More mishaps followed. Like an unwanted waif of the sea, she was bought and sold several times before she finally became the property of an American firm based in New York in 1869. The new owners renovated the ship and renamed her *Mary Celeste*, even though many sailors considered it bad luck to change a ship's name.

In 1872, the owners hired a new skipper, Captain Benjamin Briggs of Massachusetts. Briggs, thirty-seven, was from an old seafaring family and had a solid reputation. He was a staunch Christian, a teetotaller, and a bit of a disciplinarian. Days before setting out on the voyage that would carry his name into legend, Briggs wrote to his mother:

"Our vessel is in beautiful trim. I hope we shall have a fine passage, but as I have never been in her before I can't say how she'll sail."

Making up the rest of the *Mary Celeste's* crew were two other Americans, first mate Albert C. Richardson, twenty-eight, and steward and cook Edward W. Head, twenty-three; the Danish second mate, Andrew Gilling; three Dutch sailors, Volkert Lorenson, Arian Martens and Boy Lorenson; and one German sailor named

Gotleib Gondeschall. Two passengers would be aboard: the captain's wife Sarah, thirty, and their two-year-old daughter Sophia. It was not uncommon for a captain to take family members on a trip. Sarah commented in a letter to her mother-in-law that the ship's crew seemed to be a decent lot.

The *Mary Celeste* sailed from New York on November 7. She was bound for Genoa with a cargo of 1,700 barrels of raw alcohol. As far as is known, the ten people on board were never seen again.

At about 3:00 p.m. on December 4 or 5 (the date is disputed because standard time zones had not yet been established) the Nova Scotian brig *Dei Gratia,* Captain David Morehouse commanding, bound from New York to Genoa with a cargo of petroleum, sighted the *Mary Celeste* about 380 miles (611 km) off the coast of Portugal, midway between the Azores and Cape Roca. One other ship, a German steamer, would also report seeing the *Mary Celeste* in that area. Captain Morehouse thought the brig seemed to be in trouble.

As he drew his vessel near, Morehouse could see that the ship's lower topsail jib and foretop staysails were set, responding to the whim of the wind. All other canvas was either furled or in tatters. Rigging swung like gallows rope, and the main staysails lay wet and heavy over the galley chimney.

The *Dei Gratia* came within calling distance of the strange vessel. Morehouse could read the name, *Mary Celeste.* He recalled that the brig had left New York a few days ahead of the *Dei Gratia.* By now she should be in the Mediterranean. He hailed the ship, and got no answer. One of his men suggested that the crew were below, drunk. Morehouse thought that unlikely with Captain Briggs in command. He summoned his first mate,

Oliver Deveau, and sent him in the ship's boat with two other men to investigate the ghost ship.

Deveau and one man explored the *Mary Celeste* while the third waited nervously in the ship's boat. All was eerily quiet, in spite of the sounds one normally hears on a sailing vessel at sea. Canvas flapped in the wind. Water sloshed in the hold. Wind whistled through the rigging. The wheel spun back and forth, as though in the hands of an invisible helmsman.

Looking around, Deveau saw that the main peak halliard was broken. To add to Deveau's bad feelings, a hatch cover lay upside down on the deck, and the ship's boat was missing. It had evidently been launched, but why? Puzzled and maybe a little spooked, Deveau sent his man back to fetch Captain Morehouse. When the captain came on board, the two men examined the *Mary Celeste* together.

The brig was generally in good order. She had shipped some water but her pumps were working. The galley was well-stocked with food, and the water casks were as full as could be expected. In the forecastle the sailors' chests lay as though they had just been stowed, with the owners' valuables untouched. Washing hung on a clothesline. Only a few razors carelessly left lying about gave any hint of a sudden and hasty departure. In the galley all was neatly in place, just as it should have been after the cook cleaned up.

In the captain's cabin they found toys, money, a sewing machine with cloth still in it, and some of Mrs. Briggs' clothing. A pillow on the bed had the impression of a child's head. The cover of Mrs. Briggs' harmonium was raised, and there was sheet music nearby.

Captain Briggs' watch hung from a lamp, and on the table was an unfinished letter from first mate Richardson to his wife. The captain's chronometer and some of the ship's papers were gone. Notes were logged on a slate, the last date of entry being November 25. That reported the ship reaching the island of St. Mary in the Azores. It indicated that the *Mary Celeste* had been drifting for up to ten days and had covered, unmanned, some five hundred miles (804 km). It wasn't unheard of for an abandoned ship to travel so far, but it was not common, either.

There was no solid evidence of violence, but the Canadian sailors found two puzzling clues, besides the displaced hatch cover. A cutlass under the captain's bunk had traces of what appeared to be blood on it. There were deep gashes in the railing that ran around the ship's deck. The brig was trailing a long stretch of rope that was frayed at the end. Baffled, Captain Morehouse decided to take the *Mary Celeste* to Gibraltar and claim salvage. He put half of his crew aboard the ghost ship (most went aboard reluctantly), and set sail for the British stronghold.

The *Mary Celeste*, with cargo, was valued at $42,000. According to maritime law, the captain and crew of the *Dei Gratia* were entitled to half of that. The salvage claim should have been a mere matter of paperwork. The American consul on Gibraltar, Horatio J. Sprague, did not expect any problems. But Frederick Solly Flood, the British Attorney General of Gibraltar, did not buy the story Morehouse and Deveau submitted in their signed report.

Flood was a man who felt he had to live up to his grandiose full title, "Advocate and Procter For The Queen In Her Officer of Admiralty." He believed that skullduggery was afoot; that the *Mary Celeste* was a victim of piracy or mutiny. He turned the affair from a routine salvage claim into what amounted to a trial for Captain Morehouse and his crew.

An inspection of the ship's hold showed that some of the barrels of alcohol had been "tampered with." Then there was that "bloodstained" sword, and the unusual cut marks on the railing. Flood theorized that the crew of the *Mary Celeste* had drunk themselves into a frenzy, murdered the captain and his family, then escaped in the ship's boat. He refused to release the *Mary Celeste* from the court's authority, pending further investigation. He was certain the missing seamen would turn up in some port or would eventually visit their homes.

While the *Mary Celeste* sat in Gibraltar's harbour, the Canadians of the *Dei Gratia* grumbled over if and when they would get their salvage money. They found themselves the subject of rumours and innuendo. Stories of murder, fraud and conspiracy spread from official offices to waterfront taverns. Captain Morehouse, impatient with the delays, ordered Deveau to take the *Dei Gratia* on to Genoa and deliver her cargo. This infuriated Solly Flood, who felt that Morehouse was interfering with the investigation by sending away an important witness.

Investigators did not think there was much to support Flood's theory of drunken mutiny and murder. A doctor said the "bloodstains" on the sword were rust. The displaced hatch cover could have been blown out of place by a build-up of alcoholic gas in the hold. The "tampered-with" barrels could easily have leaked. Moreover, the alcohol they contained was a crude type unfit for human consumption. Even if it had been potable stuff, Captain Briggs was known to run a tight ship, and would not have allowed his men to imbibe. The men themselves were all known to be reliable mariners.

With no mutineers to prosecute, and the American consul pressing him, Flood had to release the *Mary Celeste* to her owners. But the Attorney General still insisted there was a conspiracy of some sort, and that Morehouse and Deveau were part of it. He would allow the Canadians only a fifth of the salvage value, instead of the traditional half. This was "punishment" for a crime he could not prove they had committed. Flood publicly aired his opinion that Morehouse and Briggs had plotted the whole thing so they could share in the salvage. After all, it was rumoured the two captains were close friends and had even dined together in a New York restaurant the night before the *Mary Celeste* set sail. There was no logic to Flood's charges, but he clung to them to his dying day.

The story of the abandoned ship spread from port to port and caught the imagination of people everywhere. As the tale became more widely known, new "facts" were added. Perhaps one of the most oft-told of these was the discovery in the galley of plates still bearing partially eaten meals. Everybody had a suggestion as to just what had happened. Mutineers, pirates and sea monsters were all blamed for the disappearance of the ten people. Still, the incident might have eventually been forgotten had one of the most popular fiction writers of the day not seized upon it as the inspiration for a short story.

Arthur Conan Doyle, creator of Sherlock Holmes, wrote a tale called "J. Habakuk Jephson's Statement" in 1884. In this story, the Briggs family and the crewmen of the *Mary Celeste* are murdered by a gang of Africans led by the villainous Septimus Goring, a former slave bent on revenge. The story was widely read, and many people thought that Doyle had written a factual, historical account. Still others came to believe that the *Mary*

Celeste herself was straight out of Doyle's imagination. Thus began a wave of speculation and conjecture about the mystery of the *Mary Celeste.*

Here and there men came forward who claimed to know the *real* story of what happened. They were either charlatans who passed themselves off as surviving members of the missing crew, or they said they'd heard the story from an old salt in some exotic port. More amazing than their far-fetched yarns was the fact that contemporary journalists took them seriously.

In one such tale, Briggs is a half-mad skipper who bullies his wife and crew, yet has a special playdeck built on the bowsprit for his little daughter. One day during that fateful voyage, the baby's quarterdeck is dislodged with little Sophia in it, and is about to fall into the sea. All nine adults rush to the bowsprit to rescue the child. The makeshift playpen collapses, dropping everyone into the sea.

In another wildly imaginative version, the *Mary Celeste* comes upon an old, deserted steamer that just happened to have a safe loaded with gold. Overcome by greed, and afraid that authorities might take away the windfall, Briggs scuttles the steamer and rows away in his lifeboat with his family, crew and the money. He leaves the empty brig to puzzle investigators.

There was even a "true account" that echoed Solly Flood's idea of a conspiracy. In this story, Briggs and Morehouse are a pair of drunken brawlers better suited to the bridge of a tramp steamer than the command of a brigantine. They plot a salvage scam. On board the *Mary Celeste* is a cook named John Pemberton, better known as "Young Poison." Pemberton witnesses a bizarre drama in which Briggs (double-crossed by Morehouse) and his family and crew are murdered by the men of the *Dei Gratia* and dumped into the sea. Pemberton escapes death by promising Morehouse he will keep his mouth shut. Now, years later, he is telling the whole story in a book titled *The Great Mary Celeste Hoax,* published in 1929. The book, written by Laurence J. Keating, was itself a hoax.

As the years passed and the mystery remained unsolved, the stories became more and more fantastic. Added to pirates and giant squids were such culprits as UFOs and the Bermuda Triangle. Twentieth-century novelists and scriptwriters would draw upon the mystery for books, movies and TV shows. There was even a 1935 film called *The Mystery of the Mary Celeste,* (also called *Phantom Ship*) starring horror film icon Bela Lugosi.

No one will ever know just what happened on the *Mary Celeste* between the time she cleared the port of New York and the day the Canadian ship found her. But experienced seamen who looked into the mystery independently agreed on a very probable theory. It had nothing to do with mutiny, monsters or UFOs.

Gas escaping from the alcohol in the hold might have built up enough pressure to blow off the hatch cover. Captain Briggs, fearful that the whole ship might explode, overreacted. He ordered all on board into the ship's boat, then rowed away to a safe distance. A long rope attached the lifeboat to the brig's main peak halliard. When he was certain the danger had passed, Briggs would take his family and crew back to the ship.

But in the rough water the rope broke, and the hapless souls in the small boat could not get back to their ship. Either the lifeboat capsized, drowning them, or they died on the open sea of hunger, thirst and exposure. With sails still set, the *Mary Celeste* blew across the water, a wood and canvas ghost, until she was spotted by the *Dei Gratia.* The scenario cannot be proven, but it is credible and it sensibly ignores any conspiracy plot.

The *Mary Celeste* sailed for another twelve years, on the Atlantic and on the Great Lakes. Cursed with a bad reputation, she changed ownership many times. Superstitious sailors refused to work on her. Finally, in 1885 she ran aground on the Rochelois Reef off the coast of Haiti. Ironically, this time the tragedy really was the result of attempted fraud. Her owners and captain had loaded her with junk, which they listed as valuable cargo. Then they deliberately wrecked her so they could collect insurance.

Those involved with the scam could not have met with more misfortune if they had desecrated a pharaoh's tomb. The captain and the first mate died suddenly before they could be brought to trial. One of the ship's owners committed suicide. All of the companies connected with the fraud went bankrupt. Shortly after the *Mary Celeste* was wrecked the steamer *Saxon* and the schooner *Mary E. Douglas* both came to grief. By coincidence—or fate—both vessels had been used as transport by Kingman Putnam, the insurance agent investigating the case of the *Mary Celeste.*

In 2001 American novelist Clive Cussler and Canadian film producer John Davis discovered the remains of the *Mary Celeste* off the coast of Haiti. Not much was left of the infamous brig. Some ballast stones, timbers and artifacts were retrieved and sent to Nova Scotia for study.

Today the *Mary Celeste* remains an enigma, and Captain Briggs and his family and crew are phantoms of legend. We have a plausible explanation of the mystery, but no definite solution because no one who was there ever turned up to verify it. The only witness was the sea, and she is the mistress of secrets.

MYSTERY MAN

Doctor Thomas Neill Cream

In 1888 London, England, was in the grip of terror as a mysterious killer prowled the streets at night, murdering and mutilating prostitutes. The fiend was never caught, his identity was never discovered. But the name by which he became known is as chilling today as it was when he was engaged in his orgy of murder: Jack the Ripper!

Almost 120 years have passed since the Ripper stalked the poverty-ridden Whitechapel district of London. Over those decades many professional and amateur sleuths have tried to solve the riddle of the killer's identity. Numerous suspects have been investigated. One was a Canadian, Dr. Thomas Neill Cream, a sadistic misogynist who, whether or not he had anything to do with the Ripper murders, was in his own right a monster.

Thomas Neill Cream was born in Glasgow, Scotland, on May 27, 1850, the eldest of eight children. In 1854, his family immigrated to Quebec City where his father became involved in the lumber and shipbuilding business. The younger brothers in the Cream family followed their father's example, but young Thomas had no interest in business. He was a scholarly type who preferred books and was even said to teach Sunday school classes. In 1872, he persuaded his father to send him to Montreal's highly esteemed medical college at McGill University. Cream applied himself to his studies, showing a particular interest in the anesthetics of the time. He allegedly wrote an impressive thesis on the subject of chloroform.

Cream liked to dress in expensive clothes, and was sometimes seen travelling around town in a "carriage and pair," most likely rented. His fellow students considered him a fop. His lifestyle might well have been beyond the range of the allowance his father provided, because in 1874, Cream pulled what may have been his first crime, an insurance fraud.

The young medical student took out a $1,000 policy on the personal belongings he kept in his rooms at a Montreal boarding house. Within three weeks a fire mysteriously destroyed some old clothing in the rooms, but did little other damage. Cream tried to collect the whole $1,000. The suspicious insurance company would pay only $350.

Cream graduated in 1876, but was soon in trouble over something more serious than a few burned rags. He had seduced a young woman named Flora Brooks, daughter of a hotel owner in Waterloo, Quebec, a village southeast of Montreal. When Flora became ill, the family physician examined her and told her parents she'd had an abortion (quite illegal at that time). Flora confessed that the man who had both caused and terminated the pregnancy was Thomas Neill Cream.

Flora's father and brothers sought out Cream in Montreal and hustled him off to Waterloo (some stories say at gunpoint) to marry the girl. The marriage didn't last.

The morning after the wedding Flora awoke to find a note on the pillow where her new husband's head should have been. The letter said that Thomas had left for England to further his medical studies so he could better provide for their future. He would be sure to write to her. A little over a year later, Flora died of a mysterious illness. Investigations carried out after Cream had become notorious would reveal that he had been sending his wife "medicine." Flora Brooks, who had so briefly been Mrs. Cream, was quite likely the doctor's first victim.

London was a whole new world to a young man from the fledgling Dominion of Canada. It was the capital city of an empire that encircled the globe. It was one of the wealthiest cities in the world; nonetheless, a huge proportion of its population lived in desperate poverty. London was a place where a bright, ambitious young doctor could make his mark. Thomas Cream would ultimately do that, though not as a healer.

Cream had been well-trained at McGill, but he wanted to further his studies and become a surgeon. In order to qualify for surgical college he registered as a student doctor at St. Thomas Hospital in Lambeth, South London, one of the seamier parts of the city. He attended classes while working as an obstetrics clerk.

But young Cream was distracted by the diversions of London, particularly wealthy young women. In his youth Cream was fairly handsome, in spite of having crossed eyes. He dressed well and could be very outgoing and charming. The colossal ego that would eventually dominate his personality might, in those early years, simply have been taken by people who met him as self-confidence. Young society women were apparently quite taken with the promising Canadian doctor. And if a young "topper" like

Cream found himself alone of an evening, there were other women from whom a gentleman could get whatever he wanted for just a few shillings.

Cream failed his first entrance exam for the Royal College of Surgeons. He might very well have blamed this setback on the women who had kept him from his studies. He knuckled down to work, and passed the second exam with flying colours. He was accepted into the Royal College of Surgeons in Edinburgh. There he excelled in, among other skills, midwifery.

Cream graduated in 1878. He was now qualified to hang out his shingle in London or any other British city. But for reasons unknown he left Britain for Canada, and set up practice in another London—in Ontario.

The Canadian London, with a population of 20,000, had certainly grown since its days as a small pioneer community. It was a major town by provincial standards, and a good place for an honest young doctor to put down roots. But Cream, by the standards of the time, was not an honest doctor. He was willing to break the law—for a fee.

In the Victorian Age becoming pregnant out of wedlock was one of the worst things that could happen to a young woman, especially if she came from a respectable family. The shame attached to the situation might compel a father to throw his daughter out of the house and tell her, "Never darken my door again!" Or a family might move to another town where the parents could pass the baby off as their own while the mother assumed the role of a big sister. Some young women were driven to suicide. Others sought out the services of an abortionist. In all but a very few instances abortion was illegal in Canada, the

United States and Britain. Doctor Cream saw the operation as a means of making extra money.

In May 1879, the body of an unmarried young woman named Kate Gardener, a chambermaid in a local hotel, was found in an outhouse behind the building in which Cream had his office. The corpse reeked of chloroform. An autopsy showed that the girl had been pregnant.

Cream was questioned, and he admitted the girl had come to him for an abortion. Naturally, he had refused. Drugs like chloroform were easily obtainable at that time. Dr. Cream suggested that the girl had taken her own life. That wasn't likely. There was no chloroform bottle near the body, and marks on the deceased's face indicated that someone had forced the chloroform on her. The police suspected murder, and would have bet their badges Dr. Cream was responsible. But they didn't have any hard evidence. The doctor's second victim went into the ground. But the rumours that flew around London ensured that the good doctor had no more patients. He made tracks for Chicago.

Chicago was the fastest-growing, most rip-roaring boomtown between San Francisco and New York City. It was a rail centre, a major Great Lakes port, a growing industrial centre, and in the words of one chronicler, "the wickedest city in the world." Crime and corruption were rampant in the Windy City. Prostitution was a major source of income for organized criminal gangs, and often the only source of income for destitute women. Whatever her background, a prostitute often found herself in need of an abortionist.

Thomas Cream, as far as his training was concerned, was not a hack doctor. Had he been incompetent, he would not have made it through the medical schools in Montreal and Edinburgh. But he had evidently developed a pathological hatred of women. He wanted them sexually, but on every other level he despised them. Though he was said to have a liking for pornography, he would speak of prostitutes and lower-class women in the most degrading terms. There would later be speculation that Dr. Cream had difficulty performing sexually, and used a variety of aphrodisiacs. When the concoctions didn't work, he sought release through other means.

In Chicago, Dr. Cream did not repeat the mistake he had made in London. Instead of having women seeking abortions come directly to him, he employed a network of midwives who referred clients. The operations were not done in Cream's own surgery, but in other locations, behind locked doors and drawn curtains.

But even these precautions did not keep police from his door. Early in 1880, a botched abortion caused the death of a Canadian-born prostitute named Mary Anne Faulkner. Cream was arrested, but his well-connected lawyer convinced the jury that a clumsy midwife had performed the operation, and Dr. Cream had been summoned to try to save the poor girl's life.

Then another of Dr. Cream's patients died mysteriously. Ellen Stack had been taking an "anti-pregnancy" medication Dr. Cream had cooked up himself. The main ingredient was strychnine! Once again, police could not tie the Canadian doctor directly to the crime.

Cream had now allegedly killed two women in Canada and two in the United States.Whether the killings were deliberate or accidental, he had gotten away with it. His fortunes took a decidedly bad turn with the death of his only known male victim.

Like many unscrupulous doctors of the time, Cream whipped up his own "cures" for illnesses that baffled medical science. He claimed to have an elixir that worked wonders for epilepsy. An epileptic named Daniel Stott sent his pretty wife Julia to Dr. Cream for the wonder drug. Cream seduced Julia, and then decided that Daniel Stott had to go. The patient died suddenly on June 14, 1881. His medicine was laced with strychnine.

Dr. Cream might well have gotten away with this murder, because the unfortunate Mr. Stott appeared to have died during an epileptic seizure. But Cream tried to blackmail the pharmacist who had made up the prescription (to which Cream had added the poison). The District Attorney of Chicago became suspicious and had Stott's body exhumed. Strychnine was found in the stomach, and a warrant was issued for Cream's arrest. The doctor fled to Ontario, but was caught and sent back to Illinois. Rather than be tried as an accomplice in her husband's murder, Julia turned state's evidence. In November 1881, Dr. Thomas Neill Cream was sentenced to life imprisonment in the Illinois State Penitentiary in Joliet. When the news reached Montreal, McGill University permanently revoked Cream's license to practise medicine. Meanwhile, Cream had plenty of time to ponder the fact that a woman was responsible for all his troubles, and to think about the kind of revenge he would like to inflict upon all females.

Six years after Cream went to prison, his father died in Quebec, leaving a substantial inheritance to his children. It was no secret that the state government in Illinois was corrupt, and that money could buy anything, including a pardon. Thomas Cream's brother, Daniel, bribed the right people. On July 21,

1891, the ex-doctor walked out of prison a free man. Cream went first to Quebec City to pick up the $16,000 that was his share of the inheritance. In September he took ship for England, and set foot on British soil again on October 1.

Cream looked much older than his forty years. His hair had thinned, he'd grown paunchy, and his once neat moustache looked unkempt. There was a sallow look to his skin, and he suffered from frequent headaches. Whenever he spoke of women, it was with the utmost contempt.

With a small fortune at his disposal, Cream could have stayed at a fine hotel or rented lodgings befitting a gentleman. Instead, he took a cheap apartment in his old neighbourhood of Lambeth, not far from St. Thomas Hospital. He had good reason for choosing to live in a slum.

The residents of Lambeth were among London's poorest. Those who had jobs worked hard for very little pay. The unemployed survived by whatever means they could. For destitute women, prostitution was often the only recourse. It was not only degrading, but also extremely dangerous. Women alone on the streets at night were easy prey for footpads (a 19th-century term for muggers), rapists, and even murderers. The memory of Jack the Ripper, whose brutal slaying of five prostitutes was just three years earlier, still haunted the city. But other women had been killed besides those five. Their deaths, for various reasons, were not thought to be the work of the Ripper.

Victorian morality, with all its hypocrisies, was largely responsible for placing these women in danger. The police were obliged to close down brothels, forcing the women onto the streets. Bobbies arrested any woman who looked like she might be soliciting, so the women avoided police officers. They were therefore completely vulnerable.

Cream passed himself off as Dr. Neill from St. Thomas Hospital. He disguised himself with false whiskers and thick spectacles. He looked like a lonely old gentleman who just wanted some female companionship for an evening, a harmless man whom a girl could trust.

His first victim was nineteen-year-old Ellen "Nellie" Donworth. Nellie had a soldier boyfriend who lived with her, but she earned her living on the streets of Lambeth. At six o'clock on the evening of October 13, she told her friend Annie Clements that she had a date with a "gentleman."

A short while later another friend, Constance Linfield, saw Nellie come out of a pub arm-in-arm with a "topper." Constance thought Nellie had picked up a paying customer, and paid them little notice. Within half an hour yet another friend, James Styles, found Nellie leaning on a gate, barely able to stand. He thought she was drunk and took her home.

By the time they reached Nellie's flat and Styles laid the girl on her bed, she was writing in agony and clutching at her chest and stomach. She told Styles the gentleman had given her two drinks out of a bottle with some "white stuff" in it. Styles sent for help. Nellie, meanwhile, began convulsing so violently that Styles and the soldier boyfriend could barely hold her on the bed. Police arrived and ordered her removed to St. Thomas Hospital. Nellie died on the way. The autopsy showed that her stomach was full of strychnine.

Soon after Nellie's murder, the coroner received a letter written in what was later proven to be Cream's handwriting. The letter offered to bring the murderer of Ellen Donworth to justice, if the British government would pay him three hundred thousand pounds. It was signed, "A. O'Brien, Detective." When this outrageous offer drew no response, Cream wrote anonymous blackmailing letters to a member of parliament and a police magistrate, threatening to "expose" them as the killers unless they paid him substantial sums of money. These letters were turned over to the police. Within a week of the Donworth killing, Cream struck again.

Matilda Clover, twenty-seven, had been forced into prostitution when deserted by her baby son's father. She was struggling with alcoholism, and was taking a sedative prescribed by a doctor to help her fight the condition. Matilda shared rooms in a house on Lambeth Road with her landlords, Mr. and Mrs. Vowles, and their maid, Lucy Rose. On October 20, while cleaning Matilda's room, Lucy saw a note on the bureau. Later in court, she recalled to the best of her ability that it said:

"Meet me at the Canterbury at 7:30 if you can come clean and sober. Do you remember the night I bought you your boots? You were so drunk that you could not speak to me. Please bring this paper and envelope with you. Yours, Fred."

That night at about nine o'clock, Matilda came home with a man whom she took into her room. Lucy saw that he was tall, whiskered, and wore a top hat and frock coat with a cape; obviously a gentlemen. Lucy did not get a good look at his face because the light in the hall was dim. She assumed he was "Fred."

Matilda left the man in her room while she went out to get some ale. Lucy didn't see Matilda return. Sometime later, she saw the man leave alone.

At about 3:00 a.m. the whole house was awakened by Matilda's shrieks of pain. Lucy and the Vowles ran to Matilda's room. They found her naked on the bed, "all of a twitch" and vomiting. She doubled over and had a white-knuckle grip on the bedposts. Between retching and screaming she said that Fred had given her some pills to prevent pregnancy. She was sure she'd been poisoned. (Cream had actually given Matilda not pills, but gelatin capsules—something quite new—packed with strychnine.)

Matilda's doctor was summoned. He could do nothing for her. She died screaming. The doctor believed her death had been caused by a mixture of alcohol and the sedative he had prescribed. Lucy told the police about the mysterious Fred and his "pills," but the information seemed hardly worth looking into. The doctor had already told them the likely cause of death. Matilda Clover was an alcoholic prostitute. Her kind died in the mean streets and back alleys of London slums all the time.

Cream evidently did not know that Matilda's death was not yet being treated as a homicide. Once again he tried blackmail. He wrote a letter to a well-respected London physician threatening to go to the police with evidence that that good doctor had poisoned Matilda Clover. The price of his silence was 2,500 pounds.

"Answer by personal on the first page of the *Daily Chronicle* any time next week. I am not humbugging you. I have evidence strong enough to ruin you forever."

The doctor ignored the threat.

Meanwhile, Matilda had not even been laid in her pauper's grave when Cream picked up his next potential victim at the Alhambra Theatre. Her real name was Louisa Harris, but because she lived with a man named Charlie Harvey she called herself Lou Harvey. She was a streetwalker, but she was not as trusting a soul as Ellen Donworth or Matilda Clover.

Cream and Lou spent the night in a hotel in Soho. Before they parted company the next morning, "Dr. Neill" arranged to meet Lou that evening so he could give her some pills. He said they would take away some spots she had on her forehead.

Lou Harvey might have been forced by necessity to sell her body on the streets, but she was nobody's fool. She did keep the appointment with the man who called himself Dr. Neill, because she couldn't afford to miss a date with a paying customer. She was not about to swallow pills that came from the hand of a stranger. Lou was especially suspicious when Dr. Neill wanted her to swallow the capsules on the spot.

Lou pretended to put the capsules in her mouth, but actually palmed them. Then she threw them away. Cream, believing she had taken his poison, suddenly bade her good evening, claiming to have an important engagement at St. Thomas Hospital. He told Lou he would meet her at a music hall at eleven o'clock. Lou kept that appointment, but Cream did not. He thought Lou Harvey was dead.

When Cream wasn't stalking streetwalkers, he was solidifying a relationship with a fine society lady named Laura Sabbitini. Introducing himself as Dr. Neill, he'd met her while on an outing to Berkhamstead, where she lived. Laura was pretty, charming and respectable; just the kind of woman a gentleman with social ambitions would want for a wife. Laura needed money for a dress-designing business she had her heart set on, and Dr. Neill gallantly provided the funds. He also took Laura and her widowed mother to the theatre and the finest restaurants in London's West End.

Cream's courtship of Miss Sabbitini was interrupted when he received a telegram calling him back to Canada on family business. He sailed on January 7, 1892. He intended not only to settle domestic affairs, but also to secure the British franchise of an American drug company. While in Quebec he met a Toronto businessman named John McCulloch, who represented a company dealing in coffee, spices and extracts. By this stage of his criminal career, Cream had been getting away with crimes for so long (if one discounted that unfortunate episode in Chicago) that he felt—perhaps after a drink or two—he could do a little bragging about his activities as an abortionist.

He showed McCulloch some "whitish crystals" that he said he gave to women in capsules "to get them out of trouble." He also showed McCulloch the false whiskers he used "to prevent identification when operating." McCulloch would eventually reveal all of this in court.

Having tied up his family affairs in Canada, Cream went to the United States to look after business interests there. He paid a brief visit to New Jersey. It may have been entirely coincidental, but before Cream sailed for England, New Jersey authorities had two mysterious murders on their hands. Also worth noting is that while Cream was in Quebec, he had five hundred copies printed up of a leaflet that said:

ELLEN DONWORTH'S DEATH
To the guests of the Metropole Hotel
LADIES AND GENTLEMEN,

I hereby notify you that the person who poisoned Ellen Donworth on the 13th last October is today in the employ of the Metropole Hotel and that your lives are in danger as long as you remain in this hotel.

Yours Respectfully
W.H. Murray

The circulars were sent to Cream in London, but he never used them. "W.H. Murray" was the name he signed to some of the blackmail letters. The purpose of the circulars remains a mystery.

Cream was back in London by April. He popped the question to Laura Sabbatini and she accepted. Cream decided to celebrate by killing two prostitutes in one night.

Late in the evening of April 11 he met Alice Marsh, twenty-one, and Emma Shrivell, eighteen, in St. George's Circus. He accompanied them back to Alice's flat on Stamford Street. Cream told the young women he was an American doctor, just arrived in London to work at St. Thomas Hospital. He promised to give them some pills that would prevent venereal disease, if they provided him with a pleasant evening.

Alice and Emma did provide the kindly doctor with a pleasant evening. When his sexual appetite was spent, they even shared a late night repast of canned salmon and beer with him. Then the doctor opened his black bag and gave each of the young women "three long, thin pills." He said they were to take them before they went to sleep. He would give them more the next time they met.

Cream left the flat at 2 a.m. As he stepped onto the street he nodded a good evening to a constable named Comley who was doing his rounds. The policeman returned the greeting and continued his patrol, making a mental note of the other man's description.

Half an hour later, Charlotte Vogt, landlady of the house, was awakened by loud groans, cries and screams coming from Alice's rooms. She woke her husband and the two of them rushed upstairs. They found Alice Marsh on the floor at the top of the stairway. She was writhing in agony, fighting for breath and spitting up bile. Mr. Vogt swung the door open and saw Emma Shrivell in the same frightening condition. The Vogts sent for a policeman, who in turn put in a call for an emergency wagon. Alice died on the way to the hospital, but Emma lived until eight o'clock in the morning. She was able to tell the police everything she possibly could about "Dr. Fred." The description was the same as that given by Constance Linfield and Constable Comley.

At first doctors suspected the young women had suffered food poisoning from the canned salmon. But the traces of fish still in the cans was tested and proved harmless. Once again, autopsies revealed strychnine in their stomachs. Only now did the police begin to realize that a poisoner was walking the streets of London.

Now more blackmail letters began to arrive at the offices of various doctors, government officials, and even a peer of the realm. All demanded money, or the author would expose the recipients as the murderers of Ellen Donworth, Matilda Clover, Lou Harvey, Alice Marsh and Emma Shrivell. The letters were given to the police, who were perplexed. Matilda Clover hadn't been murdered, had she? And who was Lou Harvey? Scotland Yard joined the London police on the investigation.

Cream was unaware that the avarice that had compelled him to write the blackmail letters—which gained him not a penny—was slowly but surely putting the police on his trail. By this time he quite likely thought he could murder with impunity. He was always far from the scene when the victims met their horrible deaths. How could he possibly be caught?

On May 17, Cream picked up a streetwalker named Violet Beverly. He offered her "an American drink." Violet, like Lou Harvey, had more sense than her customer gave her credit for. She turned down the drink, and saved her own life.

All of London was talking about the mysterious Lambeth poisoner. It was like the Ripper case all over again. While Scotland Yard puzzled over the clues, everyone had a theory. Dr. Thomas Neill was no exception. Why shouldn't he indulge in his own notoriety?

Cream had befriended a neighbour, an American named John Haynes who was an ex-detective. Haynes had rooms above a photographic studio, and Cream (whom Haynes knew as Dr. Neill) had his picture taken there in April.

As a former investigator, Haynes had taken an interest in the Poisoner murders, and discussed the case with Cream. Still the egotistical braggart, Cream had to display an even greater knowledge of the murders. In telling how *he* thought the villain had done the foul deeds, Cream mentioned things he should not have known because they hadn't been reported in the papers. Moreover, he included the names of Matilda Clover and Lou Harvey.

Haynes was too experienced a detective not to take note of these points. He was also a friend of Inspector Patrick McIntyre of Scotland Yard. Haynes told McIntyre everything Dr. Neill had said.

Police put Dr. Neill under twenty-four-hour surveillance. They quickly learned that he was Thomas Neill Cream, from Canada. A top Scotland Yard detective, Frederick Jarvis, boarded a ship for North America to do a thorough investigation of the suspect's background and interview potential witnesses. The police had Matilda Clover's body exhumed; strychnine was found in the stomach. The police quietly began to search for a woman named Lou Harvey.

The plainclothes officers trailing Cream reported that he spent many an evening at the Canterbury Music Hall. He was less interested in the shows than he was in the women in the audience, whom he watched "very narrowly indeed." Prostitutes especially seemed to draw his attention.

Police spoke to Lucy Rose, whose report on "Fred" they had earlier dismissed. Her description of him fit Thomas Cream. Streetwalkers who ordinarily avoided police now volunteered any information the coppers asked of them. Two prostitutes, Eliza Masters and Lizzie May, were acquainted with Dr. Neill and had seen him in the company of Matilda Clover hours before she died.

As the police collected evidence in London, telegrams arrive from Inspector Jarvis in Canada. There was information about the mysterious deaths of two women in Canada, one of them Cream's own wife. Then there were the suspicious deaths of prostitutes in Chicago, and Cream's imprisonment for the murder of a man whose wife he had seduced. One can imagine what the Londoners might have said about the Illinois authorities who had released Cream after he'd served less than ten years of a "life" sentence.

The police obtained samples of Cream's handwriting. It matched that of the blackmail letters. They still didn't have any hard evidence connecting him to the murders in London, but on June 3 they arrested him on suspicion of blackmail.

"You have the wrong man!" he protested. "Fire away!"

Scotland Yard knew its case so far was slim. The evidence was largely circumstantial. The police were sure something solid would turn up, and in the meantime they had to take Cream into custody before he killed again. From jail Cream wrote to Laura Sabbitini. It was all a mistake, he said. He was a victim of rumours.

Detectives found a chemist (pharmacist) from whom Cream had purchased strychnine. His signature was on the bill of sale. They had the statements of many witnesses who had seen the murder victims with a man answering Cream's description. They had the account of John Haynes, to whom Cream had said things an innocent man could not have known. All this came out in an inquest into the death of Matilda Clover. But none of it proved Cream had given the women poison.

Cream was confident he would once again put one over on the law—until Lou Harvey walked into the courtroom! Cream was dumbfounded. He might as well have seen a ghost. From the moment Lou told of the "pills" Dr. Neill had given her—pills she had wisely thrown away—Cream's fate was sealed.

In October, Cream was tried for murder, attempted murder and blackmail. The jury took only ten minutes to find him guilty. Justice Henry Hawkins sentenced him to be hanged on November 15, 1892.

Many notorious criminals had died on the gallows in forbidding Newgate prison. The name of Thomas Neill Cream might have faded, like the others, into obscurity had it not been for the last words he uttered. Just before the trap door dropped, Cream shouted, "I am Jack…" Then the noose broke his neck. Outside the prison walls, a crowd cheered at the news that the poisoner had received his just desserts.

What did Cream try to say in his last moment of life? That he was Jack the Ripper? Cream was in an American prison when the Ripper murders happened, so how could that be?

With a mystery as large as that of Jack the Ripper, no stone, however fantastic, can be left unturned. The Ripper's identity was never discovered, and the suspects ranged from a Polish barber to a member of the royal family. There has been speculation that more than one killer was involved. It has also been said that the Ripper was guilty of more than the five "official" murders credited to him.

Jack the Ripper killed prostitutes. So did Dr. Cream. But Jack liked his murders up close and bloody. Cream preferred to slip his victims poison, then slither off to a safe place to fantasize over their agonies. But that does not mean a killer couldn't change his *modus operandi.*

Still, Cream was in prison in 1888. Or was he? The record shows that he got his ticket of leave in 1891. There is a story that says he actually slipped out of Joliet at a much earlier date, after someone was paid to take his place behind bars. That doesn't seem very likely, but it isn't impossible either.

Cream had a hood over his head when he took the fatal plunge. Were his words muffled, so that those who were in attendance didn't actually hear what they thought they'd heard? Or, with only seconds of life left to him, did Cream try to buy himself a little more time by means of a sensational lie? Those questions, concerning the man who was undoubtedly the most sinister doctor Canada ever produced, will remain forever a mystery.

THE SHEDIAC MYSTERY

A Servant Girl's Story

Timothy McCarthy and his wife Ellen were not getting along. The tavern McCarthy operated in Moncton, New Brunswick, was a successful business, taking in an average of $600 a month. But the difficulties between Ellen and Timothy were such that on October 12, 1877, McCarthy stuffed his savings of $1,000—a considerable sum at that time—in his pocket and walked out on his wife and four children. He boarded a train for Point du Chene, evidently intending to take the ferry to Prince Edward Island. Once the train was under way, however, he found that Ellen was also aboard. She got off at Point du Chene, but McCarthy took the train right back to Moncton. There he hitched up his horse and carriage and drove to the village of Shediac.

Because he was also a liquor wholesaler, McCarthy knew all of the tavern keepers in the area. He went to an establishment called the Weldon House where he put up his horse and spent some time drinking with a man named Smith. Shortly before 10 p.m. McCarthy and Smith left the tavern and a few minutes later parted company. What happened after that would become known across Canada as the Shediac Mystery.

After spending a few days in Point du Chene, Ellen McCarthy went back to Moncton. Timothy had not returned home, so she contacted his brother Edward. After searching for almost two weeks, they traced McCarthy to Shediac, where Ellen found the horse and carriage still at the Weldon House. Of Timothy there was not a sign. Ellen reported him missing to the police.

Investigating constables found numerous people who had seen McCarthy in Shediac on the night of October 12, but no one could say they had seen him leave town. He had definitely not taken the ferry to Prince Edward Island. For almost three months McCarthy's disappearance was the subject of gossip throughout New Brunswick. Had the man deliberately vanished to escape his wife, or had some other fate befallen him? Then in January 1879 a young servant woman named Annie Parker came forward with an incredible story. She told Edward McCarthy that his brother had been robbed and murdered, and that she had witnessed the crime. Edward listened to her tale, and then took Annie to a magistrate to repeat it. She made her first official statement on January 19.

Her age was not recorded, but Annie Parker was described as an uneducated young woman with a somewhat tarnished reputation. In October 1877 she was employed as a servant in the Waverly House, a Shediac hotel run by John Osborne, his wife Martha, daughter Eliza, twenty-five, and son Harry, seventeen. Parker had been employed there but a few weeks when Timothy McCarthy made his fateful visit to Shediac.

According to Parker, McCarthy was well in his cups when he arrived at the Waverly at about 10:00 that night. John Osborne was sick in bed, but Martha, Eliza and Harry were still up. McCarthy sat down with Martha and Eliza in the ladies' sitting room. Parker was scrubbing the floor in the room next door, and said she overheard much of their conversation.

McCarthy was talking about his wife and about a pretty girl in Moncton to whom he had given a new dress. An argument arose between him and Eliza over the colour of the buttons. McCarthy said they were black, but Eliza said, "I'll bet they were white."

The two allegedly had heated words. McCarthy was drunk, and was known to have a temper, so it was not unusual for him to become angry over something so petty. He pulled out a thick roll of bills and told Eliza he would take her up on her bet. Eliza replied that she didn't care what colour the buttons were and she wouldn't bet. McCarthy had a drink in the bar, then left the Waverly, saying he would be back later.

Parker said she then overheard Martha Osborne tell Eliza and Harry of her plan to rob McCarthy of that fat roll of bills. When he returned, he would undoubtedly want another drink. She would slip some white powder into it to "mortifize him," to use Parker's words.

After she had finished the scrubbing, Parker went upstairs to bed. At midnight she heard someone entering the hotel. She thought it might be her "fellow" so she got dressed and went downstairs. There she found McCarthy in the barroom with Martha, Eliza and Harry. John Osborne was still upstairs in bed.

Parker said McCarthy treated everyone to drinks, but she didn't take one herself. After McCarthy had three or four drinks, Martha slipped him the Mickey Finn; a glass of brandy with some sugar and some type of knockout powder in it. McCarthy downed it in a gulp. Then, according to Parker:

"She also put some powder in a drink and offered it to me, but I did not take it. I told her I did not drink. This was after she gave the drink to McCarthy. After that McCarthy became stupid."

Within ten minutes of swallowing the spiked drink, McCarthy became incoherent. He lay across the bar with his head in his hands. He called out his wife's name six or seven times. If he was not completely unconscious, he was quite likely no longer aware of his surroundings. Annie Parker continued:

"…the old woman came out from behind the counter and took the money out of his pocket. She took the money out of the right-hand pocket and gave it to Harry. Harry and the old woman together parted the money in two and offered me part of it, but I would not take it. Mrs. Osborne then went behind the counter. She said, 'If we put him anywhere, when he comes to he will know where his money is, and we will all be taken up.' Harry said, 'Mother, if you think he will come to, let us finish him.' There was a puncheon standing in a corner of the room, and a hatchet on it. Mrs. Osborne handed the hatchet to Harry and said, 'Strike him only once, and kill right once.' Harry took the hatchet and struck him behind the right ear, and he fell down. When he fell, the blood rushed out of his mouth and nose. He did not kill him quite dead; he drew a long breath, and Mrs. Osborne said, 'he is not dead yet,' and Harry struck him another blow where he struck him before."

Parker said that Harry took McCarthy's pocket watch. Then he made the servant girl swear on a Bible that she would never tell anyone about the murder. With the assistance of his mother and sister, Harry used a piece of bedcord to tie a large, heavy stone to the body. They carried the corpse outside and placed it in a wagon. Harry climbed into the driver's seat and told Annie to get up there with him, but she refused. Young Osborne drove off, and the women went back into the hotel. When Harry returned, Parker asked what he had done with the body. He said he had disposed of it in the Sadouc River a mile above the railway bridge.

There were bloodstains on the floor, Parker said, and she cleaned them up. She claimed that the Osbornes used McCarthy's money to pay off some debts, including a bill they owed on a piano. McCarthy's overcoat and raincoat were still hanging in the hall. Parker said she did not know what became of the raincoat, but that Eliza shortened the sleeves of the overcoat so it would fit her father. Martha warned her husband not to wear the coat to Moncton, where someone might recognize it.

Parker said that John Osborne was concerned that she knew about the murder. He was afraid she would tell because she didn't get a share of the money. Martha assured John that Annie would not talk, because she had taken an oath on the Bible. "No, she will always stay with us," Parker quoted Martha as saying.

A week after the murder, Parker said, she went to the place where Harry said he had dumped the body, and saw wagon tracks still in the sand. However, because she had sworn on the Bible to keep quiet, it was not until January that she could finally bring herself to talk. Once Annie had related her shocking story, Edward McCarthy demanded that the Osborne family be charged with his brother's murder.

A police investigation turned up information that seemed to corroborate Parker's story. The wagon she said Harry had used to take the body away did not belong to the Osbornes, but to an express driver who had left it in their barn. The man said that when he went to pick it up on the 13th, it was outside the barn and looked as if someone had used it. A night watchman said he had seen a wagon come from behind the Waverly very late on the night in question, but he could not identify the driver. The farmer who owned the property Harry would have had to cross to get to the river said that he had seen wagon tracks in his field and had found his gate unbarred. Yet another man had found a hat on the riverbank, and it was soon identified as McCarthy's.

The Osborne family was arrested, but with no body there could be no charge of murder. Spring came, and the ice went out of the river. On May 11, 1878, Timothy McCarthy's body was found at almost the exact place Annie Parker had said it would be. There was a wound behind the right ear. Now the Crown could prosecute for murder. From all appearances it seemed to be an open and shut case. It wasn't!

There was Annie Parker's story to begin with. By her own admission, Parker's character was far from exemplary. On one hand, her incredible tale seemed too complex and detailed for her to have invented. On the other hand, parts of it didn't make sense. Would the entire Osborne family have suddenly turned evil? Would they have committed such a crime in front of a girl they'd known for only a few weeks, and then trust her oath on a Bible as protection? Would a seventeen-year-old boy have been able to take the body of a big man like McCarthy, complete with heavy rock, far enough into the river to hide it from sight, all by himself? Why would Harry tell anybody at all the exact location of the body? Was Annie Parker more deeply involved than her story indicated? Why had she suddenly decided to speak up?

Other things didn't add up. The overcoat, which Parker said had been hanging in the hall, was on the body. McCarthy's watch, which Harry was supposed to have pilfered, was in the dead man's pocket. It was stopped at 1:35. The pockets also contained $250 in cash! Would the robbers have missed that? Investigators speculated that either the body had been taken out of the water and these items replaced in order to confused police, or Annie Parker was lying.

The doctor who did the post-mortem on the corpse said that the wound behind the ear could not have been fatal. But McCarthy had not drowned, either. The doctor suggested shock as a possible cause of death.

The case went to trial at Dorchester on July 18, 1878. The Osborne's lawyer, A.L. Palmer, suggested that it was quite possible McCarthy, while drunk, had fallen off the bridge and struck his head on a piling before sinking to the bottom. However, that didn't explain the large rock tied to the body. The lawyer was much more successful in casting doubts on the truth of Parker's story. Palmer suggested that the argument over the colour of the buttons was quite possibly true, but the rest of the tale was absolutely false.

Naturally, the Osbornes called Annie Parker a liar. Eliza admitted that McCarthy had been at the Waverly that night. She said he had complained about his wife following him. "He said that when he got on the island with his horse and a pretty girl, he guessed he would give his wife a damned hard chase to catch him."

Martha denied ever seeing a fat roll of bills, let alone stealing it. She testified that about thirteen days after McCarthy had been at the Waverly, Ellen McCarthy showed up at the hotel, insinuating that the Osbornes had something to do with Timothy's disappearance. Martha told the court, "She said, 'Do you think he will ever come back?' I said, 'Yes.' She commenced calling Tim names and said if he never came back she would be married in six months." The Osbornes all swore that McCarthy left the hotel sometime after 10:00 and did not return.

Under Palmer's cross-examination, Annie Parker contradicted herself on several points. Then Palmer produced three witnesses—a dentist named Campbell and two travelling salesmen—who said they had been staying at the Waverly that night and had heard nothing out of the ordinary. A fourth witness swore that Annie Parker (who had already said she didn't drink) got drunk one night and told her, "Mrs. McCarthy would keep her like a lady if she would only stick to her story that the Osbornes killed McCarthy." Now the grist for the gossip mills was the speculation that Ellen McCarthy was behind the murder and was paying Annie Parker to frame the Osbornes. That might well account for a story that Annie was not clever enough to have made up on her own. But there was no hard evidence to support this theory.

The trial lasted five weeks and ended with a hung jury. A new trial was ordered for the following November. In the meantime, John Osborne was released on bail, but the rest of the family remained in jail. Annie Parker, too, was kept behind bars as an essential witness.

The new trial began on November 13 and lasted more than a month. Once again the jury could not come to a unanimous decision. Seven were for conviction but the other five could not bring themselves to send the Osbornes to the gallows on the testimony of Annie Parker. The family was released.

The following February Annie Parker herself was in the box at a hearing to determine whether she should be tried for perjury. Dr. Campbell, the dentist who had sworn he'd heard nothing unusual the night of October 12, now gave startling new testimony. He said that when Annie Parker stated at the trial that he had not been in the Waverly the night of the murder, she had been telling the truth. Moreover, he said that if Parker said she had seen the Osbornes kill McCarthy, he could not contradict her.

Dr. Campbell said that one morning—he could not remember the exact date—he had gone into the barroom and found it freshly scrubbed. He remarked to Harry that they were "putting on considerable style." Harry told him there had been a row the night before, and he'd had to drive a drunken customer home. He showed Campbell a place on the floor where there had been bloodstains.

Campbell said that sometime later he had witnessed an altercation between Annie and Harry, over an ornamental shell Harry had.

"Annie Parker said, 'I want that shell,' and offered him some money. Harry said, 'I won't give you the shell.' Annie appeared to get angry, and said, 'I know enough to send you to Dorchester [a prison in New Brunswick].' Harry followed her into the kitchen and said, 'I know enough to send you to hell if you tell on me.'"

Dr. Campbell was clearly nervous on the stand. At times he flatly refused to answer questions. Asked why he had not given this information at the trial, he said he was afraid of the Osbornes and Annie Parker. He would give no explanation as to why he had changed his mind about talking. "My private opinion is that the Osbornes are dangerous. My reason for so believing is locked in my breast. On certain points I am prepared to tell all I know; on others I won't tell all I know, and the law can't compel me."

Annie Parker was committed to stand trial for perjury. The judge offered her bail, but she refused it, preferring to spend the months before the next assize in jail. However, she never had to take the stand again. The Crown decided not to prosecute her, and the charges were dropped. Annie Parker was released and vanished from historical record. Whatever else she, the Osbornes, Ellen McCarthy or even Dr. Campbell might have known of the murder remained a secret. The Shediac Mystery was never solved.

A MYSTERY OF THE NORTH WEST MOUNTED POLICE

Who Killed Constable Graburn?

The period of American history known as the Old West lasted roughly from the end of the Civil War until the turn of the 20th century. During that time hundreds of American soldiers were killed by Native warriors, who were themselves soldiers fighting to defend their homelands. The troopers died in twos and threes when small patrols ran into war parties, and they died in heaps in pitched battles like the one at the Little Bighorn.

In contrast, during Canada's "Wild West" period, only six North West Mounted Police constables were slain by Natives. (This number does not include the handful of Mounties killed by Metis fighters in the Riel Rebellion of 1885.) The motto of the Mounted Police has never been "We always get our man." The official motto is actually "Maintain The Right." But in the case of the first Mountie to die in the line of duty, the red-coated riders did, in fact, fail to get their man.

The North West Mounted Police was formed in 1873 to bring law and order to what had formerly been Rupert's Land, the vast western domain of the Hudson's Bay Company. Illegal American traders operating out of "whiskey posts" like Fort Stand-Off, Robber's Roost and the notorious Fort Whoop-Up had been debauching the Natives with some of the worst concoctions that ever passed for alcoholic beverages. Their various recipes included raw alcohol, hot peppers, Jamaican ginger, red ink, gunpowder and laudanum (a drug made from opium). The booze the Yankees traded to the Natives for their buffalo robes, horses and women was accurately dubbed "firewater."

The effect of the liquor trade on the Native population was devastating. The legacy of the whiskey posts was drunkenness, violence and poverty. After the Cypress Hills Massacre in May of 1873, in which thirty-one Assiniboine people were gunned down by whites following a drunken confrontation, the Canadian government passed legislation to send an armed force to the newly acquired West. This force was initially called the North West Mounted Rifles. However, Prime Minister John A. Macdonald was concerned that the Americans would be suspicious of a Canadian military force in the West, so he changed the last word to *Police.*

The Mounties quickly sent most of the whiskey traders packing. This earned them the respect of many Native leaders who had been complaining for years about the nefarious trade. It impressed them, too, that the NWMP would send a single red-coated officer to deal with a problem, while south of the border the Americans responded to similar situations with regiments of gun-toting, sabre-slashing cavalry.

This is not to say that all was harmonious in the Canadian West. White settlers were moving in. Native people were being pushed onto reservations. The buffalo, the mainstay of the tribes' survival, were disappearing. Cultures clashed, and the notion of "white supremacy" was as strong in Canada as it was in the United States.

By 1879 the Mounties had been policing the Canadian prairies for five years. They had dealt with angry Natives and white lawbreakers and had not lost a single constable to violence. This was a far cry from the situation in the American West where, in addition to soldiers killed in "Indian wars," sheriffs, marshals and deputies died with their boots on in shootouts with the likes of Jesse James and Billy the Kid. It was only a matter of time before the NWMP suffered a fatality, and the constables who manned the lonely police posts knew it.

In November 1879, Constable Marmaduke Graburn was one of the policemen staying at an outpost called the Horse Camp about sixteen km (ten miles) northwest of Fort Walsh in what is now Saskatchewan. The Horse Camp would have been just over the present day border with Alberta. It was a place where the Mounties' horses were corralled if they needed rest after a gruelling patrol or to recuperate from illness or injury. Local Blood warriors objected to the redcoats' presence at this particular location. One possible reason was that it could have been near a trail the Bloods used on horse-stealing raids. Once the Mounties had effectively chased out the whiskey peddlers, horse theft was one of the most common crimes they had to deal with. Young Native men still looked upon horse stealing as a sort of honourable sport. They resented the Mounties' efforts to put a stop to it.

Constable Graburn, from Ontario, was new to the force. He was only nineteen, and had enlisted only six months earlier.

Perhaps that was why he had the chore of looking after horses. On cattle ranches and trail drives the wrangler—the man who tended the horse herd—was lowest in cowboy hierarchy. The young constable probably looked forward to the day when he could go off in pursuit of outlaws or "renegade Indians."

On November 17, Constable Graburn and Jules Quesnelle, a scout with the NWMP, rode out to see to the horses, which were corralled some distance from the camp. Constable George Johnston, Graburn's friend who had signed up with him, stayed behind to do the cooking. That evening, after a long day with the horses, Graburn and Quesnelle rode back toward the Horse Camp. En route they stopped at a vegetable garden the men had planted, where there were probably a few potatoes or turnips in the ground. Later, as they rode into the Horse Camp, Graburn realized he had left his lariat and axe at the garden. He turned his horse around and went back alone to get them. There was no reason for Quesnelle to go with him. There hadn't been any serious trouble in the area, and Graburn was, after all, a NWMP constable.

But anybody could run into trouble on a cold night out there in the wild. Darkness fell, snow started to come down, and Graburn did not return. Quesnelle and Johnston were concerned. They went out to look for the constable, but in the dark of night it was useless. When Graburn was still not back by morning his comrades sent word to Fort Walsh.

Superintendent N.L.F. Crozier immediately dispatched a search party. Guiding the men was scout *extraordinaire* Jerry Potts. Potts was a half-Scot, half-Metis frontiersman who was one of the best trackers and scouts of his day. It was he who had guided the first column of NWMP constables across the seemingly endless, rolling prairie to wicked Fort Whoop-Up. It was said that he personally had tracked down and killed the Native responsible for the murder of his mother and half-brother.

Potts found the tracks of Graburn's horse though they were somewhat obscured by snow. Then, reading the trail the way someone else would read a book, he showed the others where the tracks of an unshod Native horse joined those of the police horse. The two sets of tracks went side-by-side for a short distance.

Then another set of unshod tracks lay over the first prints. With his years of experience, Potts could mentally recreate what had probably happened the night before. Someone had fallen in behind Graburn and the Native riding alongside him. The scout was familiar with the old trick. One man joins the prospective victim to distract him, while the killer comes up from behind. Potts had a pretty good idea what they would find.

Before long he saw marks in the snow that told him Graburn's horse had suddenly lunged forward, as though something had startled it. There was blood in the snow; snow that was now quickly melting because a warm Chinook wind had blown in. A little farther down the trail the searchers found more blood. Then they found Graburn's hat with a bullet hole in it. Potts also picked up a spent cartridge of the type used in trade with the Natives.

By now the wind was wiping out the trail in the snow the way an eraser cleans a school blackboard. The men spread out to search. One of them, Constable R. McCutcheon, found Constable Marmaduke Graburn's body where it had been dragged off the trail and dumped at the bottom of a coulee. The first Mountie to be murdered had been shot in the back and in the back of the head.

The trail had so deteriorated by this time that not even a hawk-eye like Potts could follow it. He found Graburn's horse a short distance away. It, too, had been shot in the head. This was probably done so the animal would not return riderless to the Horse Camp and thereby give the alarm to the men there. The searchers took the slain Mountie back to Fort Walsh.

The following day Jerry Potts scouted for a posse that went in search of the killers. The chinook had wiped the ground clean of snow, so there was no sign to follow. The quarry had quite likely fled over the border to the United States. Commissioner James Macleod wrote in his official report:

"There is no doubt the foul deed was perpetrated by two Indians, but we have not been able to fix the guilt upon the murderers. I feel sure they will be discovered, as when they are across the line and think themselves safe, they will be certain to say something about it which will lead to their detection, and other Indians will be sure to let us know. I am confident there was nothing in the act itself to lead to the belief that the Indians had changed in their feelings toward us, and that when the facts come out they will show that the atrocious crime was committed in revenge for some real or fancied injury done to the murderer or one of his family, not necessarily by a policeman but by some white man. All his comrades mourned the sad fate of poor young Graburn deeply, as he was a great favourite among us all."

It was of vital importance that Graburn's killers be apprehended. This was due not only to the enormity of the crime, but also because if the guilty went unpunished, the Mounties stood to lose the Natives' respect. For six months the police could find nothing that would lead to a suspect. Then they got the break they'd been waiting for—or so it seemed.

A Blood named Weasel Moccasin and an unnamed companion were arrested for stealing horses, and were taken to the Fort Walsh guardhouse. They attempted to escape, with the assistance of their wives who passed rifles to them as they made a run for it. Guards opened fire on them, several bullets actually passing through the blankets the escapees were wearing. Superintendent Crozier and Inspector John Cotton, who were playing tennis when the prisoners made their break, ran after them. They kept the two in sight until mounted constables could recapture them. Weasel Moccasin said they had tried to run because they were afraid. If he and his friend could meet Crozier after dark in his quarters, with the windows covered with blankets so no one could see inside, they would explain why.

That night, with Weasel Moccasin doing most of the talking, the Bloods said they were afraid they would be blamed for the murder of Constable Graburn, because their band had been camped very near the place where Graburn was killed. The culprit, said Weasel Moccasin, was a Blood named Kukatosi-Poka, known to the whites as Star Child.

Star Child, who was about twenty years old, was one of the Bloods who had been angry over the police presence at the Horse Camp. He had even harassed the constables there, including Graburn. He was also known for making a nuisance of himself by hanging around Fort Walsh, begging for food and other things.

Weasel Moccasin said that on the day Graburn was killed, Star Child went out to hunt prairie chickens. The rest of the band was moving the camp to a new location, and Star Child did not return to help. When he finally rejoined them that evening, Star Child was sullen. Weasel Moccasin suspected he had been up to something.

The next day when the Mounted Police rode by, searching for Graburn, Star Child seemed frightened. He left the camp and hid in the bush for four days. He was nearly frozen to death when he came back.

By now everyone knew of Constable Graburn's murder. Weasel Moccasin accused Star Child of the deed. The young warrior denied it.

Shortly after, the Bloods went to winter in the Bear Paw Mountains on the American side of the line. There, said Weasel Moccasin, Star Child boasted to him that he had in fact killed the redcoat. He had done it to avenge an insult, though he might have killed the wrong white man.

According to the story Weasel Moccasin said he heard from Star Child himself, Star Child came upon Graburn on the trail and rode with him a short way. Then they came to a large muddy area that Star Child's horse balked at crossing. Star Child indicated that Graburn should go first. As Graburn passed him, Star Child struck the Mountie's horse. Graburn became angry and pulled his rifle from its scabbard. But before he could turn, Star Child levelled his own rifle and shot Graburn in the back. The constable fell to the ground. Star Child dismounted and shot him again. He dragged the body into the coulee and covered it with snow. Then he went back and shot Graburn's horse.

Weasel Moccasin said Star Child swore the redcoats would never capture him alive. He would stay in the Bear Paw Mountains where the Mounted Police could not touch him. Weasel Moccasin also said he was risking his own life telling

Crozier all this. If his people learned of it, they might kill him. Indeed, threats were made against Weasel Moccasin later, and he was driven from his band.

Weasel Moccasin's story did not fit the Mounties' theory that two Natives were involved, but perhaps Potts had been wrong about the second Native horseman following Graburn. The second man might have ridden that trail sometime after the murder had been committed. At any rate, Weasel Moccasin's story was the only lead the police had.

At the time Weasel Moccasin told Crozier his story, NWMP Commissioner James Macleod was in Fort Benton, Montana, on business. Crozier sent him a message informing him that the man they wanted was a Blood named Star Child who was hiding out in the Bear Paw Mountains. Macleod asked the Fort Benton sheriff to bring Star Child in and hold him for extradition. The sheriff said he'd be glad to, for a fee of $5,000. Macleod did not have the authority to promise that kind of money, so for the time being Star Child remained at large. But the Mounties were sure that sooner or later he would return to Canada.

In May 1881, the police at Fort Macleod learned that Star Child was in the Blood Camp about forty kilometres (twenty-five miles) south of the post. Corporal Robert Patterson and two constables saddled up and went after him. Once again their guide was Jerry Potts.

The posse arrived at the camp at dawn. They knew the Bloods would be hostile, and hoped to take Star Child by surprise before the rest of the people could be aroused. Such tactics had worked for the police in the past. However, the fugitive heard them ride up and came out of his lodge with a rifle in his hands.

Star Child threatened to shoot Patterson if he made a single move. Patterson said something as though speaking to someone behind Star Child. When the wanted man glanced over his shoulder, Patterson tackled him. Star Child's gun went off, awakening the whole camp. While the Mountie and the warrior struggled, Potts and the other two men kept the crowd of angry Bloods back with leveled rifles.

Patterson managed to disarm Star Child, handcuff him, and lift him onto a horse. Then he shouted to his men, "Ride, boys!" The posse galloped out of the camp. A chase worthy of a Hollywood western movie ensued, with the police party riding hell-for-leather toward Fort Macleod and the enraged Bloods hot on their heels. Twenty-five hard miles later, Patterson's men came within sight of Fort Macleod. The Bloods had to turn back.

Star Child was formally charged with the murder of Constable Graburn. Then he was locked in the guardhouse. Among the whites no one doubted his guilt.

Star Child did not stand trial until October 18. He was not represented by legal counsel. He had the option of participating in the selection of his jury of six white men. He agreed on only five. He simply thought that should be enough for the job. Nonetheless, his case was heard by a jury of six. Officiating at this trial of a man charged with the murder of a NWMP constable were two NWMP officers. Superintendent Crozier was Justice of the Peace and Commissioner Macleod was Stipendiary Magistrate. The situation did not look promising for the accused.

Natives had taken a strong interest in the case. They wanted to see if an accused Native could actually receive fair treatment in a white court of law. They believed, with justification, that Natives brought before a white judge usually came off the worst for it. Before Star Child's turn in the dock came up, three Natives were tried on a charge of horse theft. The men of the jury did not even have to leave their seats to reach a "guilty" verdict. How else could it possibly go for a Native accused of killing a Mountie?

Weasel Moccasin took the stand and repeated the story he had told Crozier. Star Child offered no defense except to say Weasel Moccasin was a liar. No doubt everyone present thought the jury's decision would be an easy one to reach. It wasn't!

The jury retired, and had not reached a decision by the end of the day. When they finally announced their verdict the following day after many hours of deliberation, the court was stunned: *not guilty!*

The jurymen said there simply was not enough evidence to convict Star Child of murder. The Crown's case was based solely on Weasel Moccasin's claim that Star Child had boasted to him of killing the Mountie. The Crown had not brought forth any other witness who had heard this boast. Moreover, among young Native men, boasting of great deeds was a fact of life, even if they had not actually done them. It was a way of gaining respect and prestige. In those days, when the former masters of the prairies were being herded onto reservations and the buffalo hunt was becoming a thing of the past, respect and prestige were hard to come by. Also, the men who had found Graburn's body had said from the start they thought the moccasin prints they saw at the crime scene were too large for Star Child to have made them.

The white community believed the jury had run scared out of fear the Bloods would seek revenge if Star Child were convicted and hanged. Rumours spread that the jurymen feared for their livestock and even their own lives. But several of the men on the jury were former NWMP constables. Far from being men who would "run scared," they showed considerable courage in not making a scapegoat of a Native based on flimsy evidence.

Star Child was acquitted. But in 1883 he was caught stealing horses and sentenced to four years in Manitoba's Stony Mountain Prison. He was released on good behaviour in 1886.

Remarkably, in 1888 Star Child became a scout for the NWMP. He was instrumental in the capture of some whiskey traders and so impressed the police that his commanding officer, Richard Burton Deane, said of him: "Out of several Indian scouts that I have tried none have proved to be worth their salt but Star Child."

Only a year later, in 1889, Star Child was dismissed as a scout because he had become involved with the Native wife of a white settler. In December of that year Star Child died from tuberculosis. No one else was ever prosecuted for the murder of Constable Graburn. The official report on his death said, "Murdered by person or persons unknown, thought to be Indians." It remains so today. The killer of the first Mountie to be murdered was one man the famed police force did not get.

THE HYAMS MYSTERY

Double Jeopardy

When William Chinook Wells put his name on an insurance policy in 1892, he might well have been signing his own death warrant. The beneficiary of the $30,000 policy was Willie's older sister Martha. She would soon become the wife of Harry Place Hyams, twin brother of Dallas Theodore Hyams. Two years after Willie signed that policy, Harry and Dallas would be on trial for their lives. If proven guilty, they would be unique in the annals of Canadian crime: murdering twins whose deadly plot centred on a 250-pound (113.3 kg) elevator weight.

The Hyams twins, small, dapper men with outsized moustaches, hailed from a well-to-do New Orleans family. Their father was a doctor. Why they left the sunny South for Canada is uncertain. It was rumoured the twins were black sheep whom their more genteel relatives preferred to keep at a distance. By Harry's own account they arrived in Canada in 1886 and ran a glove factory in Kingston, Ontario. In 1888 they moved to Toronto, with their aged mother in tow (she received an allowance from the

South), and set up business in a warehouse at 11 King Street West. Later they rented another warehouse on Colbourne Street. They called themselves commissioned merchants, but their warehouses actually did very little business. Their secretary, Mabel Latimer, later testified that rarely were there more than a few sticks of furniture and some small grocery consignments on the premises. Whatever money the Hyams twins had brought with them from Kingston was soon gone, and they were running into debt with moneylenders.

In the winter of 1891–92 Harry and Dallas lived at an Oshawa rooming house where they met fellow boarders Willie Wells, eighteen, and his sister Martha. Originally from Pickering, Willie, Martha and a married sister named Annie had come into a modest inheritance of a few thousand dollars. Harry and Dallas learned of the legacy and quickly became friendly with Willie and his sisters, and Annie's husband Ebeneezer Aylesworth.

They made themselves out to be men of business, and offered Willie and Aylesworth jobs. In return, Willie and Aylesworth would each lend the twins $1,000. The money was not an investment, but a loan to be paid back on January 14, 1893. In the meantime the Ontario lads would work for the Southerners for wages—a sort of interest on the loans.

Initially Willie and Aylesworth were to run a hotel in Fort Erie the Hyams planned to buy, but the deal fell through. Harry and Dallas called the two into their office, where some stacks of money lay on a desk. They told the pair they could take their loans back, but if they did they did could forget about any jobs. The alternative was to go to work in the Colbourne St. warehouse. The loans would then be repaid at the time agreed upon.

Willie and his brother-in-law took the jobs. Mabel Latimer could not tell them that the stacks of money they had seen were mostly small bills topped with large ones.

Willie and Aylesworth spent most of the workday making handwritten copies of old business statements. The Hyams said that was cheaper than having them printed. But some of the documents were so out of date, they were useless. Other people in the warehousing business laughed when they heard of it. Mabel Latimer worked from nine to five (for six dollars a week) addressing envelopes to businesses listed in the city directory. The envelopes were then filed away. She would testify later that she saw Harry and Dallas toss bundles of the copies Willie and Aylesworth had made into the fire.

There was so little to do in the warehouse that Willie had time for horseplay. He would ride up and down in the "hoist," as the freight elevator was called, for fun. The elevator was a rickety device that had as part of its mechanism a 250-pound weight attached to a cable. That weight could be replaced with a lighter one if required. Willie was apparently fascinated with the elevator, because he often "monkeyed" with it. He also liked to ride his bicycle in the warehouse. The Hyams cautioned him about that, because of the danger of falling down the open elevator shaft.

Meanwhile, Harry was courting Martha Wells. Annie Aylesworth didn't particularly like the Hyams brothers and tried to discourage Martha from becoming too familiar with Harry. Her warnings were in vain, however, because Martha accepted Harry's proposal of marriage. But even as Martha agreed to become his wife, Harry said they could not be wed as long as his mother was alive.

By the summer of 1892, the Hyams, the Wells and the Aylesworths were all living in Toronto, though at different residences. Aylesworth asked the Hyams for his $1,000 back because he and Annie needed if for "housekeeping." The brothers said he would get his money in January, as agreed. Aylesworth fumed at this, but he continued to work at the warehouse.

In September Harry approached young Willie with a proposition. He wanted Willie to take out a $30,000 life insurance policy and make Martha the beneficiary. Harry would pay the quarterly premiums. In five years they would cash in the policy, making a tidy profit on the interest. Harry would get most of the money, but he would give a percentage to Willie for the use of his name. By putting the policy in Willie's name, Harry explained, they would get a low premium because of Willie's age. (The Hyams twins were about thirty-one at this time.) The boy agreed to the plan and signed the necessary documents. Harry paid the first quarterly premium, the only one he would ever pay.

The Hyams brothers tried to talk Aylesworth into a similar scheme. He would have nothing to do with it. He no longer trusted Harry and Dallas. Annie tried to advise Willie against the venture, but the young man saw no reason why he shouldn't go in on a deal with the Hyams. After all, Harry was engaged to his sister.

Sometime late in 1892, Willie learned of another opportunity. His uncle, a farmer named Uriah Jones, told him of a farm near Pickering that was for sale. Willie decided to buy it. He didn't want to work it himself, but would rent it out. All he needed was a down payment of $1,000. Uncle Uriah made the arrangements for the sale, and Willie asked the Hyams for his $1,000. The twins said he could have his money back, but then came up with excuses for not having the cash on hand. They finally promised to repay him on January 14.

Willie arranged to meet his uncle in Whitby that day, so they could close the deal on the farm. On January 14, a Saturday, Uriah and his wife travelled to Whitby, but Willie didn't show up. When they returned home they found a telegram from Willie informing them that the money had been delayed and he would see them on Monday.

That weekend the Hyams brothers paid visits to the homes of Mabel Latimer and Ebeneezer Aylesworth. They gave Mabel letters that she was to deliver to three different Toronto addresses on Monday morning before going to the warehouse. Mabel had made such deliveries once or twice, so didn't think much of it. But Aylesworth was also given errands to run Monday morning before going to the warehouse. This was the first time he had ever been assigned a task that would take him out of the warehouse.

Willie and Martha also had a visit. Willie had a bad habit of showing up for work late. Now he was told that he must be at the warehouse, only fifteen minutes' walk from his home, at nine o'clock sharp Monday morning.

Willie was up bright and early on the morning of January 16. Martha gave him his breakfast, which he ate in a hurry because he didn't want to be late. At 8:45 she watched her young brother hurry out the door into a frosty Toronto morning. That was the last time she saw Willie alive.

At about ten o'clock that morning an expressman named Joseph Fox went to the Colbourne Street warehouse. Fox sometimes hauled furniture for the Hyams brothers and he wanted to see if they had any work for him that day. He was surprised to find both doors locked. He started to cross the street, but before he reached the other side he heard his name called. Fox looked back and saw Harry Hyams standing in the doorway, still wearing his hat and overcoat, as though he had just arrived. When the expressman went back to the doorway he saw that Harry's hands were bleeding.

"Hello! What's the matter with you?" he asked.

Harry, who looked very distraught, replied, "There has been an awful accident, and Willie is killed!"

Fox asked what had happened. Harry said, "He was doing something with the elevator and it broke loose and killed him."

Hyams and Fox both went down to the basement. There Fox saw Willie lying dead on the floor near the bottom of the elevator shaft, with the lead elevator weight on his head. The body was on its stomach, with the head turned sideways. Half of the head had been smashed to a pulp.

Harry told Fox he had come into the warehouse just after nine and found Willie like that, with Dallas sprawled over him in a faint. Dallas told him, Harry said, that he'd been working in the third floor office when he heard a great crash. He'd run down the stairs and then blacked out at the sight of Willie's pulverized head. Harry said he'd sent Dallas home in a hack. Then he'd cut his hands trying to remove the weight from poor Willie.

The burly expressman lifted the lead weight from the body. "My God, this is an awful thing!" he said.

"Yes," Harry replied. "It is an awful accident."

The Hyams' own physician, Dr. E. E. King, was brought to the scene. He became so nauseated that he made only a brief examination of the body. Then he sent for the coroner, Dr. W.H.B. Aikins. The coroner listened to Harry's story, then inspected the elevator. Both he and Dr. King concluded that Willie Wells had been killed in an accident and that an inquest was unnecessary. In an age when fatal industrial accidents were common, the incident received scant coverage in the press. The insurance company did not want to contest the decision of the two doctors, so they paid the $30,000 to Willie's grieving sister. When Willie was laid to rest in an Oshawa cemetery, Dallas Hyams did not attend the funeral.

Now, even with Mother still in the land of the living, Harry was anxious to set a wedding date. He and Martha were married in a quiet ceremony in May, though other members of her family were not convinced that Willie's death had been accidental. When Uriah Jones heard that Willie had been killed, he rushed to Toronto, burst into the warehouse and confronted the twins, demanding an explanation. He was ordered off the premises. Ebeneezer and Annie Aylesworth also suspected foul play, though Aylesworth continued to work for the Hyams for three or four months after the "accident."

As soon as Harry and Martha were married and he could get his hands on her money, Harry gave Aylesworth a few thousand dollars, apparently to placate him. But Harry would not allow Martha to visit her aunt and uncle. In one of her letters to her aunt, Martha wrote of her grief over Willie:

"Oh auntie, it just seems as though he must walk in! This is 5 o'clock Monday morning. I never can sleep when I awaken on Monday. I am always so glad when the day is over. Every night of my life when I awake poor Willie is on my mind."

The insurance money paid off the Hyams' debts, but it wasn't long before they were in financial straits again. Harry and Martha moved for a short while to Montreal. There Harry operated a pawnbroking scam. He opened an unlicensed pawnshop in which he paid small amounts of cash for jewellery. Then he took the items to legitimate pawnshops, claiming they belonged to his wife, and exchanged them for larger amounts of cash. By the time Harry took Martha back to Toronto in 1894, Montreal police were investigating him for fraud and for forging a cheque.

The Hyams brothers now decided to take out life insurance on Martha. Harry went around to various insurance offices and applied for policies totaling $250,000. Most of the companies turned him down. The insurance men had always thought there had been something fishy about the Willie Wells affair. Evidently they also asked Martha if she was aware her husband was trying to insure her life for a fortune. When Martha learned of this, she became suspicious. No one had consulted with her about life insurance. She knew Harry didn't have the money to pay the premiums on so many policies. She, too, began to have suspicions about Willie's death. Suspicion turned to fear when Harry wanted her to sleep in a newfangled bed that snapped up against the wall.

Martha left Harry about the end of 1894. She went to a lawyer to see about getting a separation allowance from her husband. When the lawyer heard her story, he used the threat of making the Hyams' affairs public in the press as a means of forcing Harry to provide an allowance for Martha. Then the lawyer dropped a hint about the sordid business to Hector Charlesworth, a rising Toronto journalist. Charlesworth smelled a story. He began to quietly investigate the Hyams brothers and the circumstances surrounding the death of Willie Wells. The insurance company that had paid out the $30,000 was especially happy to co-operate with the writer.

But for all Charlesworth's discretion, rumours circulated. The Hyams twins got wind that something was afoot. Dallas approached Charlesworth with the promise of $5,000 if his senior editor would keep the story out of the papers. Charlesworth ignored the bribe.

When Charlesworth's exclusive story appeared early in 1895, it turned out to be the scoop of the year. Authorities were suddenly interested in the "accident" that had killed Willie Wells and began an official investigation. On February 12, Harry and Dallas were arrested on a charge of murder.

The Hyams managed to have the judicial process delayed while they sent a distress call to New Orleans. A wealthy uncle, banker Chapman H. Hyams (who according to Charlesworth "didn't want any hangings in the family") didn't think any Canadian lawyer would be competent enough to defend his nephews. He got in touch with his brother Solomon "Hermit" Hyams, an elderly New York recluse who had made a fortune on Wall Street. Uncle Sol engaged the services of Francis Wellman, a former New York Assistant District Attorney and one of the most celebrated criminal lawyers in the United States.

Wellman arrived in Toronto expecting to impress the Canadians with a slick display of good old American legal know-how. However, because he was not a member of the Ontario Bar, he could not represent the Hyams in court. He was permitted to sit at the defense table as an advisor.

The trial began on May 9. Leading the representatives of the Crown was B.B. Osler, Q.C. The Hyams were defended by William Lount, Q.C. and E.F.B. Johnston, Q.C. The trial promised to be a hard legal battle, because these men were among the most distinguished attorneys in Ontario. Lending the defence his considerable experience from the sidelines was Wellman. Two exhibits in the courtroom added to the dramatic atmosphere: a nine-foot (2.7 m) model of the elevator, and Willie Wells' skull, which had been exhumed and wired together.

On the stand, Mabel Latimer testified that Harry Hyams had told her a different story than the one he had told Joseph Fox, Dr. King and Coroner Aikins. She said that when she arrived at work that day and heard of the accident, Harry told her that both Willie and Dallas had been repairing something on the elevator, when Dallas accidentally let the weight slip and it hit Willie. He told her he had come in to find Dallas "running around like a crazy man."

Several witnesses, including Dallas' housekeeper, testified to seeing blood *spattered* on his pants after the accident. The man who had occupied the warehouse prior to the Hyams said he had been there for six years, and the elevator weight had not come loose once. But another witness swore the weight had fallen once and squashed a cat "flat as a pancake." Engineers who examined the elevator said it was almost impossible for the weight to come loose on its own.

Then Robert Preston, a friend of Willie's, told a story that stunned the prosecution. The day before the accident, he claimed, he met Willie quite by chance outside the warehouse. Willie took him inside to show him the elevator. Willie demonstrated how he could change the weights. When Willie put the heavy weight back on, Preston said, the elevator got stuck. That was because Willie had not reattached the weight to the cable properly, and had to adjust it. Preston remarked to Willie that not doing the job right could be dangerous.

The greatest disagreement was over medical evidence. A team of doctors testifying for the Crown said the injuries to Willie's body could not have been caused by a single heavy weight falling on him. They based that conclusion on the absence of injuries to the neck and shoulders. In their collective opinion, Willie had received several blows to the head with an object such as a chisel, a hammer or an axe. Witnesses confirmed that there were indeed a chisel, a hammer and an axe in the warehouse.

Doctors called upon by the defence were just as adamant that the injuries to the skull had been the result of a single blow from a heavy object. The skull showed no signs, they insisted, of having been struck by a chisel, a hammer or an axe. The doctors on both sides explained their findings in medical terminology that would have sounded alien to the nine farmers, two tradesmen and one merchant who made up the jury.

Throughout the proceedings, Harry appeared cool and confident. A barber testified that Harry had been in his shop getting a shave at the time the "accident" was supposed to have happened, providing him with an alibi. The barber also said that sometimes the barbers he worked with couldn't tell the twins apart. For most of the trial, Dallas was the picture of nervous anxiety.

After two weeks of testimony the jury retired. The men deliberated for seven hours, but could not reach a unanimous decision. The judge dismissed them and ordered a new trial. Upon their dismissal, each member of the jury reported that the day before the trial began, he had been approached by a well-dressed man "with an American accent" who identified himself as a friend of the Hyams and who offered "material consideration" if Harry and Dallas should be acquitted. That July old "Hermit" Hyams died, allegedly crushed by the public shame his nephews had brought upon the family name.

The second trial began on November 5 and lasted four weeks. The twins were prosecuted and defended by the same teams of lawyers. Francis Wellman still sat as an unofficial advisor. The same witnesses were questioned and cross-examined, with the exception of Martha Hyams. While being questioned during the first trial she had suffered a nervous collapse. Her doctor considered her health too frail for her to go through the ordeal again. When all the evidence was in, Judge Thomas Ferguson instructed the jury in a manner that made it clear he favoured an acquittal. It took the jury only half an hour to reach a verdict of "Not guilty!"

The Hyams twins had stepped out of the shadow of the gallows, but they weren't entirely out of the woods. No sooner had they left the dock than they were placed under arrest and charged with conspiracy to defraud the insurance companies and conspiracy to murder Martha Hyams. Harry was also charged with forging a cheque and with a jewellery store theft that had happened the day before he was arrested for Willie's murder.

For several weeks the twins sat in jail, contemplating a possible stay in the Kingston Penitentiary. Then the Crown (which actually had little hard evidence to take to court, aside from Harry's forged cheque) made them an offer. They would be released from jail on the condition that they get out of Canada immediately. The charges would be pending if they ever set foot on Canadian soil again. As part of the deal, Chapman Hyams, the rich New Orleans uncle, agreed to pay Martha an allowance of $100 a month.

The brothers jumped at the chance. They were secretly put on a train for New York City, and disappeared from Canadian history. The day after their departure a Montreal detective arrived in Toronto with the intention of taking Harry back with him.

The public was generally dissatisfied with the verdict of the second trial. One Ontario newspaper after another complained that men with a lot of money behind them could get away with murder. "Not one man in a thousand believes Willie Wells' death was an accident," wrote one Toronto editor. Hector Charlesworth later wrote in his memoirs that one of the Hyams' own lawyers (he didn't say which one) told him:

"Of course Harry was guilty. But nobody will ever convince me that Dallas would hit anybody with an axe. If anyone accused Dallas of slipping poison in his tea, I would believe that, but he was too yellow to do anything violent."

It might well have been that the Hyams twins owed their lives and their freedom to that slick American lawyer Francis Wellman after all. When Wellman returned to Canada for the second trial, he brought along a New York *Herald* reporter whose job was to write articles about the two American boys who were being "railroaded" in a Toronto court. At the same time, the reporter flattered Judge Ferguson as the embodiment of the British sense of fair play. Wellman even had a picture of Ferguson in his judicial robes published in the *Herald,* and sent copies to His Honour. Wellman later boasted in his book, *Gentlemen of the Jury,* that these actions had influenced Ferguson to look favourably upon the American defendants. Hector Charlesworth dismissed this claim as an insult to the integrity of an honourable man.

The speed with which the second jury acquitted the Hyams twins might be more properly accredited to another man who accompanied Wellman to Toronto. Identified only as "Colonel Foster," this man had gained a notorious reputation as a "jury fixer" for the corrupt Tammany Hall gang of politicians in New York City. He and a team of men, posing as book agents, photographers and sewing machine salesmen, gained entry to the homes and hotel rooms of every member of the jury. Then they explained why Harry and Dallas should be freed. Considering the complaints made by members of the first jury about "material consideration," the explanations were no doubt accompanied by bribes.

Maybe Willie Wells died because of his own careless "monkeying" with the warehouse elevator. Or could it be that his youthful fascination with the machine played right into the hands of brothers who would kill to pull off an insurance scam? Mercifully, it's quite likely that Willie never knew what hit him.

THE SCOLLIE MYSTERY

Peterborough Horror

David Scollie—Old Davie, as his neighbours called him—lived alone on his farm at Otonabee, about two miles (3.2 km) from Peterborough, Ontario. He had never married, and his only living relative was a sister. Scollie had always worked hard, and his farm was prosperous. Because he had no family to support, he had saved a considerable sum of money. He was frugal, but no one could call him a miser. Old Davie was always willing to help out a neighbour in need.

In about 1888 Scollie's neighbour, John G. Weir, hired an Irish immigrant named Thomas Gray as a farmhand. He put Gray and his family up in a small cottage that was very near David Scollie's house. Thomas Gray was described as "stupid-looking, with small grey eyes, close-cropped black hair and a brown moustache."

However, his wife Hessie was said to be "a sharp, active little woman, bright as a new sixpence and sharp as a razor." She was good-looking, "with a bright, clear complexion." Those who knew Hessie said she was "a woman of strong passions and violent temper." Thomas and Hessie had five children: Thomas Jr., Annie, Hessie, Mary and George.

Old Davie became very friendly with the Gray children, especially little Tommy, a boy some called precocious but whom others found obnoxious. Tommy was often at Scollie's house. Sometimes his mother would go along with him to bake the old man's bread and tidy up for him.

After a few months, John Weir decided that he was not satisfied with Thomas Gray's work, and fired him. That meant the family had to vacate the cottage. Kind-hearted Scollie gave Thomas a job on his farm and said the family could live with him in his house. The Grays accepted without hesitation.

The arrangement worked well. The Grays had a fine house to live in, with room for the children. Thomas had work. Old Davie no longer had to worry about cooking and housekeeping. Most of all, he had people to keep him company in his old age.

Things went so well, in fact, that Scollie was receptive to an idea that was presented to him by Thomas, but quite likely was thought of by Hessie. If Scollie would sign his farm over to Thomas, he could continue to live there in comfort for the rest of his days as a virtual member of the family. Tom would take care of most of the work. Scollie had a lawyer draw up the appropriate papers for the two men to sign, and the deal was done.

For about two years there were no problems. Old Davie was like a grandfather to the children. The old man couldn't have been happier. He didn't realize that Thomas and Hessie were waiting impatiently for him to die. Scollie was in his early sixties—an advanced age at that time—but he showed no signs of failing health. Scollie was as fit and hale as he had ever been.

He even walked into Peterborough every day to buy his newspaper.

Hessie's sister Mary lived with her husband William McGregor on a farm about half a mile from the Scollie place. Hessie began to complain to Mary that it seemed as though Old Davie would never die. "He is as likely to live as long as I will," she said. She talked of shooting or poisoning the old man, then said that would attract the attention of the law. She needed some means of getting rid of Scollie that wouldn't leave any evidence. Mary told Hessie that such talk could get her arrested.

Then Old Davie had an "accident." He was standing in front of the house when a flowerpot fell—or was dropped—from a second floor window. It struck him on the head, and tore a bloody gash in his scalp. Scollie recovered from the injury, though under the care of neighbours, not his adopted family. Hessie blamed the accident on one of her children who, she said, had been playing with the flowerpot and clumsily dropped it.

Soon after that incident Hessie let Scollie know exactly where he stood. She told the old man that looking after him was more trouble than the farm was worth. Scollie subsequently told Thomas that he would pay any sum the Grays asked—within reason—to nullify their legal contract. Thomas demanded $1,300. Scollie considered that exorbitant and refused. Thomas went to see the lawyer in Peterborough. After listening to Gray's litany of woes, the lawyer advised him to honour the agreement he had made with Scollie.

For a time a semblance of normalcy seemed to return to the Scollie–Gray household. If there were quarrels, the neighbours didn't hear of it. But Hessie's impatience was growing. In

November of 1893 she told Mary that the winter to come would be "the old brute's last." She was going to cut off his head and then burn the house down with the body in it.

Mary said that if Hessie did such a thing, she would hang; or else some innocent person would be blamed for the crime. Hessie asked how the hell anyone would know what had happened, with the place in ashes. Then she said, "What the hell do I care who is blamed for it, so long as I keep Tom out of it!" That, at least, is what Mary McGregor testified later.

At about two o'clock on the morning of February 23, 1894, David Scollie's house caught fire. Thomas Gray was visiting his brother in Madoc, about forty miles (64.3 km) away. Hessie put her children, barefoot and barely clothed, out a window into the snow. Then she climbed out herself. At this time Hessie was pregnant with her sixth child.

Hessie told the children to hurry to the McGregor farm, half a mile away, and alert their aunt and uncle. The home of another farmer, Zaccheus Burnham, was only 120 yards (109.7 m) away, but she did not go there to call for help. She, too, headed for the more distant McGregor place.

Hessie met her brother-in-law part way. Roused by the children, McGregor had hurried toward the burning house. When he saw Hessie he asked her where Scollie was. She said she had shouted to him to get out, but she hadn't seen him. She thought he was still in the house.

When McGregor reached the house he kicked in the front door. The whole lower floor was ablaze. There was no chance of anyone getting out that way. McGregor knew that Scollie's bedroom was at the front of the house on the second floor. He looked up from the yard and saw that the flames had not yet reached that part of the house. He called Scollie's name. If he could get the old man to come to the window, he might convince him to jump into the snow. But there was no sign of Old Davie. Zaccheus Burnham came running over from his house, but there was nothing he and McGregor could do.

By dawn, as other neighbours gathered in the yard, the house had been totally destroyed. The men threw buckets of water on the smoking ruins, then began to probe through the debris in search of the charred remains of David Scollie. What they found wasn't what they expected.

They found Scollie's body under a pile of ash and wreckage, not at the front of the house, where it should have been if the old man had been in bed, but in the cellar that had been dug under the back part of the house. The body was lying on a straw mattress and was covered with two blankets and a quilt. It was dressed in underwear and a shirt. Old Davie's hands were folded over his breast, indicating that he had passed away painlessly in his sleep. Neither the bedding nor the clothing had been burned. Parts of the feet had been burned off, but otherwise the corpse showed little evidence of having been in an inferno. Not even the hair on the chest and arms was singed. What horrified those looking on was the fact that the head was missing. About six inches (15.2 cm) of bone, blackened at the end "like a piece of cordwood" protruded from the neck. The men sifted through the ashes, but could not find Old Davie's head, not even so much as a jawbone.

The coroner, a doctor and an undertaker all examined the body. Each noted that there was no blood on the clothing or bedding. The coroner's inquest concluded that the head had been separated from the body by action of the fire and had been completely consumed. The coroner's jury concluded that further investigation was unnecessary. David Scollie went to his grave in his shirt and underwear, without his head.

The Gray family lived for awhile with the McGregors. Thomas spoke of rebuilding the house on what was now his own property. But in spite of the coroner's finding, people in the area were whispering "murder." Four months after the fire, Thomas sold the farm. He packed up his wife and children and moved to the United States. But the departure of the Grays did not stop the gossip mills. Among those spreading tales were William and Mary McGregor.

Because the coroner in Peterborough had not reported anything unusual to the provincial government in Toronto, some fifteen months passed before the attorney general's office heard of the suspicious circumstances of the fire in Otonabee. When the story finally reached official ears, questions were raised. Why was the body in the wrong part of the house? How could the head have been separated from the trunk? Why hadn't Hessie Gray roused Scollie when she knew the house was burning? Why hadn't she gone straight to the Burnham house, only 120 yards away, rather than her sister's house, half a mile distant?

Old Scollie's body was exhumed and examined by Dr. John Caven, a professor of pathology at the University of Toronto. The professor was not at all convinced that Scollie was still alive when the fire started. A warrant was made out for the arrest of Thomas and Hessie Gray.

The task of locating the Gray family fell to Provincial Detective John Wilson Murray, the man who came to be known as Canada's "Great Detective." Murray was an outstanding investigator, though he embellished things somewhat in his memoirs. However, he was probably telling the truth when he described his experiences during the Gray case. Finding the family was easy. Bringing them back to Canada was an ordeal.

With William McGregor acting as driver and guide, Murray visited farms throughout the Otonabee area, gathering whatever information he could on the late David Scollie and the Grays. By good luck he found one household that had received a letter from the Grays. It was postmarked Ocala, Florida. Murray had extradition papers prepared, then boarded a train for the South.

Murray had no trouble finding Thomas and Hessie. They had squandered the money they'd received for David Scollie's farm, and were living in squalor in a shantytown shack. The children were hungry and half-naked. An infant several months old had increased the brood to six. Murray couldn't arrest the parents and leave the children on their own, so he took the whole family into custody and put them on a train. It would be the worst railroad journey of Murray's life.

"The moment the train started," Murray wrote, "Mrs. Gray began to boohoo, and the six little Grays burst forth into a chorus of caterwauling, and Thomas Gray blubbered, while Tommy Gray opened up his cave of the winds and poured forth loud howls...I have travelled many miles with many prisoners. But never did I have such a cargo and such a trip. It was a long series of snorings and shriekings. When they were awake, they howled, and when they were asleep they snored; and Tommy Gray kicked in his sleep and had dreams that called for wild acrobatic feats. It was stifling hot weather, too, and the presence of the Grays could be detected even by a blind man, if his olfactory organ did even half its duty."

A haggard and weary Detective Murray arrived with his charges at Peterborough on July 5, 1895. Eleven days later Thomas and Hessie were arraigned in police court on charges of murder, arson and fraud. Hessie had her baby in her arms. Thomas still appeared "stupid-looking," but Hessie seemed unconcerned, though attentive to the proceedings. She smiled and nodded to acquaintances in the crowded room, and nudged her husband with her elbow whenever a witness said something that caught her interest. A reporter for the Toronto *Globe* wrote: "... it was difficult to believe she had been guilty of the diabolical and deliberate crime charged." Nonetheless, the court decided that the Crown had a case for murder. The Grays' trial began on September 26 before Chancellor John Boyd. Farmers drove in from miles around to see the drama.

The couple were to be tried separately. Hessie's case came first. From the moment Hessie Gray appeared in the dock with a babe in arms, she had the sympathy of the audience—the very people who had gossiped about murder a year and a half earlier. Could a *mother* commit so bloody a deed as cutting off a man's head? It helped Hessie's cause, too, that she no longer had that defiant attitude she'd displayed in the police court. Now she looked pale and concerned.

At first things did not look promising for Hessie. Her sister Mary told the court about the threat to cut off Scollie's head and burn the house down. William McGregor said he had heard his sister-in-law talk "a thousand times" about poisoning "the old brute." McGegor further testified that Thomas once told him: "he

(Thomas) had the best little woman in Canada; she knew how to get rid of the damned old brute when he (Thomas) was out of the way." McGregor said that after the fire Thomas confided in him that when he set out for Madoc he never expected to see Scollie alive again, and if only the head hadn't been missing "it would have been all right." Mary McGregor hinted, perhaps unintentionally, that the relationship between the Grays and the McGregors was not exactly harmonious, when she said she would have visited her sister more frequently if William had permitted her to do so.

A boy testified that the day before the fire he had seen a lot of blood on the floor of Scollie's barn. The defence explained that some days prior to that, Thomas had been slaughtering hogs. Zaccheus Burnham stated that if Hessie had alerted him immediately, he probably would have been able to get Scollie out of the house. The strongest testimony for the Crown was that of Dr. Caven. He said it was not possible that David Scollie was still alive when the fire reached him. He did not believe it possible that the fire could entirely consume the head, yet leave the rest of the body relatively untouched—unless head and torso had been separated before the fire. But he had to admit there were no bloodstains on the clothing he'd seen on Scollie's exhumed remains, and he could not swear that the bones of the neck had been cut by a sharp instrument.

As far as the defence was concerned, the threats Hessie had made against Scollie's life—if, in fact, she had made them—were not proof she had murdered the old man. Nor did the discovery of the body in the wrong part of the house prove anything, counsel argued. There was absolutely no evidence that Scollie was actually in his bedroom when the fire started. If anyone wondered why Old Davie would have gone to sleep in the cold cellar on a February night, the question was not raised. It could only have led to speculation.

Hessie's oldest children, Annie, thirteen, and Tommy, eleven, won her case for her. Annie told the court that on the night of the fire, she had gone to bed between ten and eleven o'clock. She said the whole family slept in the same downstairs room. The last she saw of Mr. Scollie, he was sitting by the kitchen stove, holding one of the smaller children. She woke in the middle of the night in a room full of smoke. She awakened her mother, who opened the door to find the kitchen ablaze. Her mother found her father's axe behind a bureau and used it to smash the window. Her mother then put all of the children outside. Annie said they did not go to Mr. Burnham's house because, "he was a rich man and we didn't have much on."

Tommy's testimony supported Annie's. He added that the last he saw of Mr. Scollie, the old man was sitting in his bed, reading by lamplight. Both children spoke in a straightforward manner, with no sign of nervousness.

Chancellor Boyd was so impressed with what he considered the truthful accounts of the children, he stopped the trial. He told the defence it was unnecessary for them to call the seven or eight remaining witnesses. He then proposed that the jury enter a verdict of "not guilty." The gentlemen of the jury happily acquiesced. They were well aware that public sentiment was on Hessie's side. The murder charge against Thomas was dropped, as were all other charges against the couple. Several months later the Grays were still in the Peterborough area, trying to sue witnesses who had testified against them for slander. One can only wonder if they were once again guests in the McGregor home.

Did Old Davie die in the fire? Hessie's defence suggested that he could have been killed by poisonous fumes, which would account for the peaceful position of the body. As for the relatively intact condition of the corpse—aside from the head—stranger things had been found in the aftermath of fire.

Or did Hessie get up after the children had gone to bed, decapitate Scollie, and leave his body in the cellar, certain it would be reduced to ashes? If Hessie really intended to murder Scollie, would she actually have told her sister? If Mary was lying about the threats, what was her motive? Was McGregor telling the truth when he testified that Thomas said of Hessie, "she knew how to get rid of the damned old brute"?

THE WESTWOOD MYSTERY

Death at the Door

Frank Westwood didn't have an enemy in the world. The eighteen-year-old was well thought of by all who knew him. His parents, Benjamin and Clara, were pillars of the Methodist church. Mr. Westwood sometimes stood at the podium to address the congregation. His most recent topic in that October of 1894 had been, "If a man dies, shall he live again?"

The family was prosperous. Mr. Westwood owned a factory that manufactured fishing tackle and other sporting goods. The Westwoods lived in a fine house they proudly called Lakeside Hall, at the foot of Jameson Avenue in Toronto's Parkdale neighbourhood. The house overlooked Lake Ontario, and Frank, his older brother Bert and younger brother Willie were boating enthusiasts. Frank had his own canoe, and the brothers shared a yacht. There had recently been a problem with some trespassers hanging around a boathouse adjacent to their property where they kept their yacht. Benjamin had scared them off by firing a couple of shots from the .44 calibre British Bulldog revolver he kept in the house. Aside from that, all was well in the Westwood household. Tragedy, however, was about to strike swiftly and violently.

On the evening of Saturday, October 6, Frank went out to see some friends. He was home by ten-thirty. All of his family, except his mother, had already retired for the night. Frank and Clara sat talking in the dining room for about fifteen minutes, then they, too, went upstairs. Frank kissed his mother goodnight at the top of the stairs, then went into his room. Before he could even unbutton his shirt, the front doorbell rang.

Frank went back downstairs. He stopped to turn on the gas lamp in the hall. As Frank opened the door, he placed one foot against it in case the caller should try to force entry. One never knew who might be at the door at such a late hour.

Frank opened the door not quite a foot. He barely had a moment to look at the person standing there when his world exploded. The caller shot him at point blank range with a .38 calibre pistol. Frank slammed the door shut and cried, "Mother! I'm shot, I'm shot!"

Clara raced down the stairs and found Frank on the floor, the front of his shirt already soaked crimson. A cloud of gunsmoke still hung in the air. Clara shouted to her husband to get his gun, that there were burglars. Benjamin, who had been sick in bed with a cold, came down the stairs, armed. He took one look at his wounded son, then opened the front door. Clara cried to him not to go out. He probably didn't even hear her.

Whoever fired the shot had fled. Benjamin saw no one in the yard, and no one on the street. He discharged his pistol twice, to alert any constables who might be nearby and to warn his son's attacker that he was armed.

Back in the house Benjamin found that Clara had helped Frank up to his room and had phoned the doctor. He went up to Frank's room where the boy was lying on the floor with his head on a pillow. He was conscious and in extreme pain. Benjamin knelt beside him and asked, "Do you know who shot you, Frank?"

"No, Father."

"Are you sure?"

"Yes, Father."

A doctor arrived fifteen minutes after Clara Westwood's call. Benjamin helped him lift the boy onto his bed. Soon a second doctor came to the house. The physicians could tell from the blood that oozed out of the wound that Frank had serious internal injuries. The bullet had slammed into his chest, travelled downward and pierced his liver, and was lodged in muscle tissue in his back. Frank's situation was hopeless. There was little 19th-century medicine could do for a victim whose liver had been perforated by a bullet.

By this time the police were on the scene. They searched the area and questioned neighbours. A Mrs. Card, who lived across the street from the Westwoods, said she had been on her way home from the theatre shortly before 11:00, and had seen a strange man loitering in front of Lakeside Hall. She said he was clean-shaven and wore a light-coloured coat. She'd thought it was Frank, and wondered why he was just standing on the street in front of his house.

In the morning police detectives came to speak to Frank and the rest of the family. Reporters showed up with them, but Benjamin ordered the newsmen out of his house. For the time being, the reporters had to be satisfied with whatever information they could get from neighbours.

Frank had caught only a momentary glimpse of his attacker. He said the man was of medium height and stout build. He had a moustache, and wore a fedora hat and a drab, dark-coloured coat. Frank insisted he had never seen the man before, and didn't think he could identify him if he ever saw him again.

The detectives wondered if Frank was telling them all he knew. For some reason he didn't want them to search his clothes. They did, but found nothing unusual. They asked about his relationships with his friends. Frank reluctantly said he'd had some trouble with a friend named Gus Clarke. Gus was a young man who was known to the police as a small-time thief. Frank said he had warned the owner of the boathouse that Gus planned to break into it. Gus found out, and he and Frank had words. Frank didn't want Gus to know that he had mentioned his name to the police, because if he got better, Gus might "lay for me."

Then the detectives asked Frank if he'd been in any "scrapes" involving girls. He said he had not. When the officers pressed the question, Frank grew agitated and said, "You can't pump me." He had no trouble with any girl, he repeated.

Frank said he had told them absolutely everything he could. The detectives questioned Benjamin about his gun. He showed it to them and explained his reason for firing it. The officers were satisfied it was not the gun used to shoot Frank. They asked Bert Westwood if he had a gun. He did, but it was only a .22 calibre pistol. Moreover, there had been no quarrel of any kind among the Westwood family members. The detectives asked the doctors if Frank's wound could have been self-inflicted. The doctors said that was highly unlikely.

The police were stymied. A young man had been gunned down at his own front door, and for no apparent reason. They had few clues to go on, except Frank's vague description of the gunman, which did not fit that of the man Mrs. Card had seen loitering in front of the house. To make matters worse, the newspapers had learned that there were no constables on patrol in Parkdale at the time of the shooting. Toronto editors demanded to know why the community's citizens were left unprotected. The police had to find a suspect, and quickly.

Frank lingered for four days. He knew he was dying. He fought hard to live, but even a strong will couldn't fight the damage done by a .38 slug. When the end was near, Frank made an *ante-mortem* statement.

"I, Frank Westwood, believing that I am about to die, desire to state the facts connected with my being shot." Frank described everything that happened from the moment he heard the doorbell ring until he was gunned down. Then he said, "I had some trouble with Gus Clarke. The man who shot me, I think, looked like a man who chummed with him. Possibly it might have been him. Lowe, I think, is his name. He is in the nail works. His Christian name is James."

An officer asked, "Do you think Gus Clarke shot you?"

Frank replied, "No. I don't know."

The police investigated Clarke and Lowe. Both had airtight alibis for the night of the shooting. Frank died without telling the police another thing that might help them find his slayer. The coroner's inquest held later in October reached an open verdict: that Frank Westwood had died as the result of a wound inflicted by a bullet fired from a gun in the hand of an unknown person. The press speculated that perhaps the bullet had been intended for someone else in the Westwood family, and that Frank had been a victim of mistaken identity. But police could uncover no evidence that any of the Westwoods had done anything to bring about such severe retribution.

Then, on November 20 the Toronto police made a startling announcement. On a tip provided by none other than Gus Clarke, they had brought a suspect in for questioning. That suspect had voluntarily confessed to shooting Frank Westwood. The killer was not a man, but a woman named Clara Ford!

Thirty-three-year-old Clara Ford was of mixed racial background. The newspapers of the time described her as a "light-skinned mulatto." She was born in Toronto but had lived for a while in the United States with a husband who had eventually deserted her and their daughter, Florence McKay, now 14.

Gus Clarke told the police that Clara once lived in a cottage on a property behind the Westwood house. He said she had known Frank and had tried to become intimate with him, but Frank had rejected her. The information most interesting to the police was that Clara often carried a gun, and she frequently dressed in men's clothing. The latter would have been considered scandalous behaviour at that time.

Detectives looked into Clara Ford's background. They learned that even though most people who knew her spoke highly of her as an independent, hard-working woman, she was also known to have a quick temper. She had once lost a job in a Toronto restaurant when, in a fit of anger she pulled her gun and threatened fellow employees after a petty argument.

Now Clara worked as a seamstress in a tailor shop on York Street. She had a room above a "Negro restaurant" in a poor part of town. Her daughter Florrie was employed as a domestic in a private home.

According to the story the Toronto police told the newspapers, Detectives Reburn, Sleman and Porter went to the tailor shop and told Clara that Inspector William Stark wanted to talk to her at the police station. They said she knew right away that it was about the Westwood murder. At the police station Inspector Stark asked Clara where she was on the night of October 6. Clara said she and her daughter had been to the theatre to see a play called *The Black Crook.* After the show she went straight home because her landlady would be waiting up to lock the door.

However, when Florrie was questioned she said she was supposed to meet her mother at the theatre that night, but Clara hadn't shown up. Then a friend of Clara's, a Mrs. Crozier, told the detectives that Clara had been at *her* house that night, and had been drinking. She had a gun in her coat when she left, supposedly to meet her daughter at the theatre. The following day, when the shooting was the talk of the town, Clara remarked to her, "Well, I'm glad I wasn't in Parkdale last night, or I'd be blamed for it."

The police took Clara to her room where they found a suit of men's clothes, a fedora hat, and a cheap .38 calibre pistol. She said she kept the gun for protection, and it wasn't a crime for a woman to wear men's clothes. She denied having a false moustache, and the officers couldn't find one in her lodgings.

Back at the station, the police said, Clara suddenly decided to tell the truth. "There is no use in misleading you any longer," she said. "I shot Frank Westwood."

At this point the officers warned her that anything she said could be used against her in court, that she could hang. But Clara insisted on telling all. Detective Reburn told her that if she was going to talk, "You had better tell no lies." Clara told one of the men that if what had happened to her had happened to his sister, he'd have done the same thing she did.

Clara's story, as related to the press by the police, was that Frank Westwood and his friends would often ridicule her because of her colour. They also threatened to expose her for "parading around" in men's clothing. Then Frank did the unforgivable. In July or August of 1894, Frank sexually assaulted Clara. He knocked her down and tried to have his way with her. Clara was a strong woman and was able to fight him off. But she swore she would make him pay for the outrage.

On the night of October 6, Clara got her revenge. When she left her friend's house she was wearing men's clothing under her female attire. She stopped in a secluded place and took off the women's garb so she was dressed as a man when she went to the front door of Lakeside Hall. After she shot Frank, she retrieved her clothing and fled the neighbourhood by taking a route along the shore of the lake. She later told her daughter that if anyone asked questions about that night, she was to lie and say they had been at the theatre together. But for some reason Florrie did not back her mother's story. Clara had no regrets about shooting Frank. He deserved to die after what he had done.

Toronto was electrified! People didn't know which side to take in the sensational drama. If Frank Westwood had indeed tried to take indecent liberties with a woman, he certainly wasn't the good Christian boy everyone had thought him to be. But if Clara had shot him, why didn't he tell the police? Had he been trying to spare his family the shame of knowing what he'd done? Or had he been so remorseful of his terrible mistake, that he knew the woman was justified in her act of vengeance, and could not say the words that would send her to the gallows? Had Frank not, in the end, died gallantly?

As for Clara Ford, what decent woman who had no man to defend her honour would not take action herself against a man who had tried to inflict upon her "a fate worse than death"? It was reported that she did not tell the police about the assault because they would not be likely to believe "a woman of colour," so what options were left for her? Of course, Clara's colour provided plenty of grist for the rumour mills of white Toronto. People said she smoked a pipe (most unseemly at that time), that she once knocked down two big men in a brawl and took a shot at a third, and that she drank bull's blood. Some even said she shaved!

At the preliminary hearing in police court, when Clara was asked how she pleaded, she immediately said, "Guilty." The magistrate and Crown Attorney explained to her that in a homicide trial, a guilty plea was inadmissible. Clara changed her plea to "Not guilty." Her trial was set for the spring assize.

Clara Ford's trial for murder took place over five days in the first week of May 1895. Prosecuting for the Crown was B.B. Osler, one of the most formidable criminal lawyers of his time. Partway through the trial, Osler had to withdraw due to the death of his wife, and leave the case in the hands of his assistant, Hartley Dewart. However, so great were the odds against Clara Ford when the trial opened, it appeared that a first-year law student could have gained a conviction.

Clara was defended by E.F.B. Johnston. He was a rising star in the legal world, but at the time was not considered to be in the same league as Osler. He took Clara's case *pro bono.*

The trial began with the Crown building up what appeared to be an insurmountable wall of evidence against Clara. They had her gun, a .38 that fired bullets identical to the one removed from Frank Westwood's body. They had evidence from Gus Clarke—who had to be brought in from Toronto's Central Prison where he was doing time for burglary—that Frank and Clara were well-acquainted. They had Clara's own daughter's denial that Clara had been at the theatre with her that night. There was the testimony of a Mrs. Libby Black who said that on one occasion she had spoken to Frank Westwood, and a jealous Clara told her, "If you ever speak to him again, I will do for you." Libby described Frank as having a moustache at that time.

Most importantly, the prosecution had Clara's "confession." The detectives who had allegedly heard the confession took their turns on the stand to repeat what they claimed Clara had told them, in spite of the heated objections of Mr. Johnston. The defence lawyer argued that the so-called confession was inadmissible. Detective Reburn telling Clara, "You had better tell no lies," constituted a threat, he said, rendering the confession involuntary. But the presiding judge, Chancellor Sir John Boyd, chose to allow the detectives to give their evidence. By the time the officers had finished their testimony, no one in the courtroom would have bet a dollar on Clara's chance of an acquittal—with one exception.

Through his methodical line of questioning witnesses, E.F.B. Johnston made it clear to the jury that Gus Clarke was a convicted criminal whose word could not be trusted. At the time Frank Westwood supposedly rejected Clara Ford's affections, he would have been but a boy of thirteen. Libby Black was an alcoholic who had already been jailed three times for public drunkenness.

Frank Westwood never had a moustache. The type of gun Clara owned could be purchased for $1.50; there were hundreds of them in the city, all made from the same mould. They would all make the same marks on bullets. Then Johnston sent murmurs through the courtroom by calling Clara Ford to the stand.

Only recently had Canadian law permitted defendants charged with first-degree murder to testify on their own behalf. Prior to the Clara Ford case, only one defence lawyer in a murder trial had put his client on the stand. Clara's fate was now in her own hands.

Speaking confidently and without a sign of nervousness, Clara said she did not shoot Frank Westwood. She had known him only as a casual acquaintance when they were neighbours. The "confession," she said, was a lie.

Clara testified that when the police took her to the station, she told them she had been at the theatre that night, and then had gone home. When Florence and Mrs. Crozier did not corroborate her story, the detectives began to press her. They spoke "sharp and rough," and left her sitting alone in a room for long periods of time between sessions of intense questioning.

Clara admitted Frank Westwood had never laid a hand on her. That tale, she said, was part of the story the detectives wanted her to tell.

"Sergeant Reburn continued to press me to confess, and said that if I said Frank Westwood insulted me, nothing would be done to me. No one, he said, will know to the contrary; he is dead, and won't come back again. If I would confess, Reburn said I would be a free woman and walk the streets again. When in Inspector Stark's office he said that if I were a man, he would lock me up without a moment's hesitation. He took his watch out, looked at it, and said it was time I said something. He kept repeating I was in a net and could not get out. The more I denied, the more he pressed me to confess. At last, I said I did it."

Clara made up the story of the assault, the shooting and of her escape along the lakeshore. She said Detective Reburn then told her, "Now stick to this story. Be sure and do not alter your story."

Clara's testimony was compelling, to be sure; but it was her word against those of the detectives. Mr. Johnston still had aces to play. He brought in the theatre's box office manager, an usher and a constable who had been on duty there that night. All testified that they had seen Clara Ford in the theatre. She had watched the play alone.

Clara's landlady testified that she had arrived home at eleven o'clock that night. She could not have been at the Westwood house, several miles away, at the same time. Other witnesses testified that Clara could not have taken the lakeshore route she was supposed to have used to flee from the scene of the crime, because the water was too high.

In his summation, Johnston presented Clara as a helpless "coloured woman" who'd been ensnared by detectives who were anxious to get a conviction for a heinous crime. He spoke deploringly of the "sweatbox tactics" the police employed. He praised Clara for the courage she'd shown in taking the stand to fight for her own life.

The Crown's body of damning evidence was now in tatters. Hartley Dewart tried to rescue the case in his own summation. He reminded the jury of the thankless job police detectives had, and how the peace and security of the community lay in their hands. Of Clara Ford's performance on the witness stand he said:

"You may have admiration for a woman who gives her evidence in the manner Clara Ford did; but it is the admiration you have for the daring and recklessness of the Mexican bandit, who, careless of his own life, goes to any length, or the admiration of the Indian stoic who, knowing no fear, would go so far as to shoot a man down, though he knew his life might pay the penalty the next moment. You may have that admiration, but it is only admiration for a spirit of bravado."

It took the jury only an hour to reach a decision: "Not guilty." When the foreman announced the verdict, the crowd in the courtroom cheered and applauded. Clara had not only saved her own life, she had also rescued the reputation of the slain youth.

Now that she was free, Clara unwisely took advantage of her celebrity by appearing in a theatrical sideshow dressed in the clothes in which she had allegedly killed Frank Westwood. E.F.B. Johnston was appalled when he heard of this indiscreet behaviour. He called Clara to his office and reminded her that had it not been for him, she would be keeping an appointment with the hangman. He suggested she leave Canada. Clara did just that. She joined Sam T. Jack's Creoles, a company of black burlesque performers and toured the American West as "a damsel who had killed a man in pursuance of 'The Unwritten Law.'"

No other person was ever charged with the murder of Frank Westwood. Frank's apparent relationship with the likes of Gus Clarke indicates that the young man did not always keep good company. Perhaps therein lay the key, now gone forever, to the mystery of the killer at the door.

THE MEADOW BROOK MYSTERY

"Go Away, John Sullivan!"

In the late 19th century a widow with a family to support had very limited options if her husband had not left her well provided for. That, quite likely, was why Eliza Dutcher began selling whiskey in violation of the Scott Act, a law that placed restrictions on the sale of alcoholic beverages. Mrs. Dutcher lived in Meadow Brook, a small community nineteen kilometres (twelve miles) east of Moncton, New Brunswick. She had a modest two-storey house that her husband had built himself. But when he died suddenly in 1893 he left Eliza with two small children to care for. Their two older sons were grown up and out on their own.

Eliza might have been introduced to the illegal liquor and beer business by her brother Hugh Green, who had been involved in bootlegging for a while. She turned her home into a "roadhouse" where she sold alcohol. Railway men and workers from the local sawmill went there on Saturday nights and Sundays to drink and socialize.

The police prosecuted Eliza several times for Scott Act violations. She once spent forty-five days in the county jail at

Dorchester for refusing to pay a fine. She also had a falling-out with Hugh, apparently over a case of whiskey. For reasons unknown Hugh got out of the bootlegging business and then became self-righteous. He accused Eliza of keeping a "rough house" and would not allow his children to go there. Brother and sister were no longer speaking to each other.

Besides the working men who were her regular patrons, Eliza's place would also have been attractive to the many tramps who passed through Meadow Brook. The village was on the Intercolonial Railway line, and the Dutcher house was right beside the tracks. The railroads were highways for transients who travelled around by hopping freight trains. These drifters, who passed information among themselves about the communities they visited, would have known that Eliza's house was a place where a man could get a drink. Some of them might have been aware of a fact that seemed to be common knowledge in Meadow Brook: Eliza, like many people in those days, did not trust banks. She kept her money in a trunk in her bedroom. It was said she had between four hundred and five hundred dollars, a lot of cash at that time. For protection Eliza kept a watchdog named Kiss.

Eliza's brother James and his wife Jane lived across the road from her. On the night of September 10, 1896, James was away and Jane lay awake, unable to sleep because of worry over some tramps that had been in the area. At about 2:00 a.m. she heard a wagon crossing a nearby bridge. Curious as to who would be out and about at that hour, she got out of bed and looked out the window. She saw a light in the bedroom window of Eliza's house. At first Jane thought nothing of it. Then the light suddenly flared brighter. Jane was immediately alarmed, because that could mean only one thing. She awakened her children, then ran out to the street yelling, "Fire!"

Hugh Green, also a neighbour of Eliza's, dashed out of his house and saw the flames in the second-storey window of his sister's home. He shouted to Jane, "For God's sake, get an axe!"

Hugh tried Eliza's front door, but it was locked. When Jane arrived with an axe, Hugh smashed the door down then rushed inside. He went straight to the stairway where he encountered thick smoke. In the bedroom at the top of the stairs, he knew, were Eliza and her two children: eight-year-old Maggie and seven-year-old Harris.

Hugh groped his way up through the smoke to the bedroom. He could not see a thing. Then he heard Maggie cry, "Mamma! Mamma!" Hugh followed the sound of the voice until he found the little girl. He raced down the stairs and outside with her in his arms, passed her to one of the people there, then turned to go back for Eliza and Harris. By this time the second floor was an inferno. Rescue was impossible. Heat and smoke drove Hugh back outside.

People from all over the village had gathered in front of the house, but there was no hope of saving the building or anyone still in it. Maggie had some minor burns and her hair and eyebrows had been singed. Then she was found to have other injuries Hugh had not noticed in his haste to get her out of the house. Maggie's left ear was split open and there was a bloody laceration on her scalp. Hugh took her into his house and sent for the doctor. The doctor soon discovered that the little girl's head injury was serious. She had a fractured skull!

As the doctor worked, the child cried, "Oh, don't kill me anymore!" He didn't think her chances were very good. Meanwhile, the house, with her mother and brother inside, burned to the ground.

In the morning men sifted through the ashes. They found part of the trunk of Eliza's body. Her head and limbs had been completely consumed. Nothing was found of Harris but a piece of skull and a few blackened bones. There was no sign whatever of the dog, Kiss. Everyone knew that the dog was kept in the yard, not in the house. Someone had evidently gotten rid of it.

Maggie's injuries were a strong indication that the fire had not been accidental. The girl was in no condition to be questioned, but people speculated that a robber had forced his way into the house, probably killed Eliza, then realized he would have to kill the children and burn the house down to hide his crime. This theory was supported when someone found an iron railway-coupling pin in the ashes. There was absolutely no reason for Eliza to have such a thing in her house. The intruder had undoubtedly used it as a weapon. It could easily crack a child's skull.

Shortly after the fire, Eliza's son William Dutcher arrived from Nova Scotia. He searched the ruins of his mother's house and found $45 in gold coins. The coins showed little evidence of having been through a fire. Had they somehow been protected? Or had the killer returned and planted them to dispel the suspicion of robbery, thus making it possible the fire had been accidental?

The pathetic remains of Eliza and Harris had not yet been interred in the village's Catholic cemetery when suspicion fell on John Sullivan. There had been bad blood between the Sullivans and Eliza and her in-laws, the Greens, ever since John's mother had reported Eliza to the police for selling liquor on the Sabbath. That had resulted in Eliza's stint in the Dorchester jail.

Sullivan worked at various times in the sawmill and as a brakeman for the railway. He was known to be a hard drinker. But Sullivan, thirty-six years old at the time of the fire, had led an adventurous life.

As a youth he'd found life dull in his corner of New Brunswick, so he went to Maine and joined the United States Navy. He sailed around the world twice. In New York he was assigned to a torpedo boat as a deckhand, and rose to the position of pilot.

Growing weary of "harbour life," Sullivan transferred to the United States Army and was sent to Arizona to fight the Apaches with the Second Cavalry. He served as a bugler and courier. "I had quite a varied experience," he wrote later, "and witnessed a great deal of brutality and genuine butchery. I stuck to the cavalry till the Indians were subdued and returned to their respective reservations. Then we were sent back to New York, where I gave up the trumpet and shipped on board one of the Anchor Line boats running between New York and England. I made two voyages, after which I shipped on a small steamer named the *Dundee,* running between England and the East Indies and China. I made four voyages in her, when I was taken ill with the fever and sent to the hospital. After my recovery I returned to my home, and being advised by my parents to reside in Canada, I went to work in the mills in Westmorland County and in Nova Scotia."

Sullivan had never had any kind of trouble with the law. But people thought it suspicious that he had suddenly disappeared from Meadow Brook. Jane Green told a reporter from the Moncton *Daily Times* of an incident Eliza had discussed with her, that happened the day before the fire. Sullivan had allegedly been at Eliza's house.

"He asked her if she had anything to drink, she replied that she had not a drop in the house. He then asked her if she had any cigars and she said yes. He told her to come down and give him some and he would pay her a little debt he owed her. She went into the bedroom and he asked her if she had any ale and she said she thought she had one bottle; he got the bottle and two cigars and paid her for them, but he did not pay the debt. He took one cigar and left the other on the counter. He said he was going to George McPhee's to stay all night. She next saw him coming down the track Thursday morning. She said she didn't care much about him; that was the reason she did not let him in. She was that afraid of him that she took her pocket book out of her pocket and put it under her children's feet before she came downstairs. She was afraid he might knock her down and take it away from her."

This statement by Jane Green was pure hearsay, but the *Daily Times* printed it.

Sullivan's father, Daniel, a resident of Moncton, said his son had been at his house the night of the fire, but had since left town. He claimed he did not know where John had gone. Meanwhile, other citizens of Moncton were going out to Meadow Brook to look at the ruins of Eliza Dutcher's house and to peek into the room where Maggie lay clinging to life.

Moncton did not have a hospital, so the child was placed in the care of two nursing sisters, Anna and Muriel Croasdale. One of the women told the *Daily Times,* "When she (Maggie) awakens, she evinces great terror and will cling to the person trying to soothe her imploring her to be protected from some monster. In her delirium she has given utterance to a few things which the crown consider to be of great importance. Recently she startled those in the room by crying out, 'Go away John Sullivan!' At other times she shrieks, 'Don't kill me!' At such times she is very much agitated and terrified."

This, too, appeared in the newspaper. The immediate, dramatic impression is that of a badly injured, frightened girl suffering nightmares about the fiend who attacked her. But Maggie was drifting in and out of consciousness, and might also have been reacting to the conversation of the adults around her.

Another newspaper story that drew a lot of attention said that Sullivan had been in Moncton the day after the fire and he appeared to be "flush" with money. He treated some friends to rounds of drinks and bought himself a new pair of pants. Then he and a companion went to David Richard's barbershop where Sullivan paid for shaves for them both. Sullivan even paid the barber in advance for a month's worth of shaves. The author of the article offered his own speculation that Sullivan was trying to establish the alibi that he had been in Moncton the whole time.

Sullivan was said to have had in his possession some American coins, including two fifty-cent pieces. William Dutcher took that as proof Sullivan had been in his mother's house. There had been two American fifty-cent pieces in Eliza's stash of money. The Toronto *Globe* added that American fifty-cent pieces were rare in New Brunswick. But were they? There was considerable cross-border traffic and commerce between New Brunswick and Maine. Canadian and American currencies were in circulation on both sides of the border. Also, John Sullivan had relatives in

Maine and evidently visited them from time to time. It would not be unusual for him to have American coins in his pockets.

Sullivan's parents insisted he had been in Moncton the night of the fire. His mother said she heard him come into the house in the middle of the night. The elder Sullivans admitted that when they'd heard the rumours connecting John with the fire and the murders, they'd told him to go and stay with an uncle in Maine. He left town, they said, but they weren't sure where he'd gone.

The Moncton sheriff, a man named McQueen, found Sullivan at his uncle's home in Alexandria, Maine. Sullivan said he had gone there to see about the division of some property, not because he was running from anything. At first he refused to accompany Sheriff McQueen back to New Brunswick. McQueen had him arrested and held in the jail at Calais, right on the border. Then Sullivan received a letter from R.B. Smith, a lawyer his father had engaged for his defence. Smith advised Sullivan that it would not help his case if he put the Canadian government to the trouble of extraditing him. Sullivan reluctantly agreed to go back with McQueen. He believed—with good reason—that the people in New Brunswick were prejudiced against him.

When the sheriff and his prisoner got off the train in Moncton a large crowd was on hand to get a look at the accused murderer. Sullivan stepped onto the platform with a jaunty air. He smiled cheerfully, nodded to acquaintances and walked—without handcuffs—to the police station. The crowd of several hundred people followed him as though he were leading a parade.

At the coroner's inquest Sullivan refused to testify. After listening to the testimonies of many witnesses, the coroner's jury took just under an hour to conclude "that Eliza Dutcher and

Harris Dutcher came to their deaths by foul means and we have reasonable grounds to believe and do believe from the evidence that John E. Sullivan was implicated in the same."

The preliminary examination was held in Moncton's police court. As with the coroner's inquest, this hearing was well-attended. For many of the good people of Moncton, this was their first visit to the local jail, and they were shocked by its filthy condition. The *Daily Times* reported:

"Those who have had occasion to visit the lockup and police courtroom of late could not have failed to notice their filthy condition. The stench in the lockup is almost unbearable and in the police courtroom it is little better when crowded as it has been of late. The building is unfit for occupation of man or beast and the most ill-kept stable would be a rose garden in comparison with the lockup. It is a shame to put the most debased criminal in the lockup in its present condition while the health of the magistrate and court attendants generally must be seriously imperilled by the atmosphere of the courtroom. The city fathers should be confined for at least a quarter of an hour within the precincts of the Duke street edifice."

Officials mercifully decided that Sullivan would be held in the county jail at Dorchester.

The first witnesses testified that Eliza Dutcher habitually kept large sums of money in her house, the proceeds from her "disreputable business." Employees from the mill frequently got drunk there. Then court had to be adjourned for a day because Sullivan suddenly became ill and began to vomit, quite likely because of the foul state of the premises.

When the hearing resumed, the court heard more circumstantial evidence against Sullivan. A hotel keeper from Saint John testified that he had met Sullivan several days after the fire and that John had a large roll of bills. Sullivan said he'd been on a train that arrived in Moncton on the evening of September 10, but the conductor who'd been on duty at that time testified that Sullivan had not been on his train. Then a woman named Ardina Howell told the court that Daniel Sullivan had urged her to swear she had met John at the train in Moncton that night. She also said John Sullivan told her he'd been in Meadow Brook the night of the fire.

Sullivan's parents insisted he'd been at their house that night. Mrs. Sullivan believed the Greens were responsible for her son's trouble. "They had a spite on me," she said, "and they would have revenge on the family." She said she especially mistrusted Jane Green.

The witness who was the key to the whole case was still unable to testify. Maggie Dutcher had been taken to Moncton and lodged in a room of her own in the almshouse (county poorhouse). Her condition was still serious, and her doctors said it could be weeks before she was well enough to appear in court. A would-be intruder allegedly tried to break into the almshouse one night. It was never determined if this was a kidnapping attempt or the work of a burglar or common drunk. The police assigned a constable to guard Maggie. She was said to express fear of being left alone because, "He might come upstairs again." It was never reported if she said who "he" was.

The Crown prosecutor wanted the case postponed until the following January when it could be put before the Supreme Court of New Brunswick, and Maggie might be well enough to appear. Mr. Smith did not think this boded well for his client. He asked for a postponement of eight days. "If the girl is able to give evidence then we will call her. If she is not fit, then we won't call her."

He also wanted Maggie to be examined by another doctor besides "the Crown doctor" to determine if she was well enough to appear in court. Smith argued, "There are more lies to the square inch being told about John Sullivan than about any person living. I mean to put a stop to some of them if I can."

The prosecution and the judge himself responded by suggesting Mr. Smith put his client on the stand right then and there. Smith said he wasn't ready to do that. His requests were all refused. John Sullivan was scheduled to go on trial for his life on January 12, 1897. Bail was denied.

Sullivan's trial, held in Dorchester before Justice Hanington, lasted two weeks. A.S. White, Solicitor General for New Brunswick, represented the Crown. At first Sullivan appeared unconcerned, as though certain he would be acquitted. Mr. Smith proved that several statements Jane Green had made were false. David Richard, the Moncton barber whose shop Sullivan had visited, testified that he gave him a shave only hours after the time of the fire. He also said that later the same day, Sullivan came back and asked for the money he'd paid in advance for shaves, because he said he was going to Nova Scotia. That seemed an odd thing for a man who supposedly had several hundred dollars in his pockets. Then a neighbour who'd searched the ruins of Eliza's house testified that he'd found thirty dollars in the drawer of a dresser that had somehow survived the blaze. Had the robber simply overlooked the money? Or had there been a robbery at all? Neither Canadian nor American police had found the bundle of money Sullivan was supposed to have stolen.

The high point of the trial came when the Croasdale sisters brought Maggie Dutcher into the courtroom. The little girl had recovered sufficiently to testify. Smith had been anxious for the girl to appear because he was sure her testimony would exonerate his client. The judge impressed upon her the importance of telling the truth and being absolutely sure of what she said. Then he allowed White to question her.

Maggie said that she, her mother and brother were in the same bed. She was awakened by a noise.

"There was a man in the room. Mamma said, 'John, don't hit.' The man had hold of Mamma. He struck Mamma two times. Mamma laid back on the bed still. The man hit Harry. He then hit me and I cried. He hit me two times."

White asked Maggie if she knew who the man was. She replied, "Yes. John Sullivan." Then she pointed at Sullivan and said, "That is him."

Under Smith's gentle but searching cross-examination Maggie contradicted herself a few times, but in general she stuck to her story.

"I knew John Sullivan well. He was often at our house. I liked him. He used to nurse me often. That night he hit me on the head. I cried. He hit me again. We had a dog. I did not see him that day nor the day before. I don't know what money Mamma had. I did not see John Sullivan take any."

When Maggie was finished one of her nurses took her back to her room.

Things had not gone at all as Smith had expected. He charged the prosecution with coaching the child on what to say. Miss Croasdale denied anyone had been coaching the girl while she was in the care of her and her sister. (There were allegations later that William Dutcher had told people *before* Maggie testified that he knew exactly what his little sister was going to say.)White countered by accusing Sullivan's family of threatening Crown witnesses. Sullivan's brother Charlie had, in fact, physically assaulted one Crown witness. Justice Hanington warned that any further behaviour of that kind would earn the guilty parties two years in prison.

Besides Sullivan's parents, who testified again that John had been at their house that night, Smith brought forth two witnesses to support that alibi. Under cross-examination, however, both admitted they had been lying. They said the Sullivan family had put them up to it. The Sullivans' reckless efforts to save John were only pushing him closer to the gallows.

Finally Sullivan himself took the stand. He testified that on September 10 he was in Memramcook. He took the train to Moncton, arriving about 8:15 that night. He spent some time down at the docks with two girls, but said "nothing improper happened." Then he went to his parents' house because he was sick from drinking too much. He denied being anywhere near the Dutcher house on the tenth or the day after. He admitted he had gone to Maine because of the stories connecting him to the fire and the murders. The newspapers said Sullivan was very composed and spoke well. Nothing, however, was going to shake from the jury members' minds that image of little Maggie Dutcher pointing her finger and saying "That is him."

Smith made a five-hour summation to the jury. He told them Sullivan had no motive for killing Eliza and her son. The Crown had failed to prove there had even been a robbery. He put forth the possibility that in Hugh Green's haste to get his niece out of the burning house, Maggie's head had struck something.

Smith said again that Maggie had obviously been coached. If anyone had broken into the Dutcher house, he insisted, it was a passing tramp.

Then White delivered his rebuttal. The man's eloquence so moved Justice Hanington, that when he addressed the jury he made it clear that he expected a guilty verdict. A little over an hour later, he got it. He sentenced Sullivan to be hanged on March 12. There was no recommendation for mercy. An appeal to the Supreme Court of Canada failed. Some people signed a petition for government clemency. That, too, was futile.

Sullivan was kept in solitary confinement while he awaited execution. He spent much of his time writing letters. One that was addressed to a friend in Calais might well have been for the general public.

"I am here for a few days only and I can count the hours when I will be taken from here and asked to say goodbye to all the world and then mount the scaffold and die. Judge Hanington says so, the order must be obeyed. I am as innocent as a child unborn of the crime of murder, but what does that matter? The crown wanted a victim, and I was the only available man. Concerning my trial I have only to say that if public opinion ever took a hand in a public prosecution, it did in my particular case. However, as I write from behind these dark stone walls, I only do so to let the public know that I am not satisfied with the manner in which the criminal law of Canada is administered in this country. I make this complaint, as one who has been tried and found guilty of murder in the Supreme Court of Westmorland County. My complaint will not alter the present state of affairs, but it will go down to future generations as a sort of protest against the mock trial system which is such a curse to our country at this time... Since my arrest I have not asked for public sympathy, nor have I any idea of doing so now. Moreover, I know that the whole force of public opinion is against me and that it militated against me at my trial, and that even the judge who presided over the court was prejudiced against me."

Because Sullivan had served in the American navy and army, Washington made some inquiries about him. But Sullivan had been legally tried, convicted and sentenced in a Canadian court of law. It was none of Washington's affair.

A few days before Sullivan was to hang, a reporter from the Saint John *Globe* visited him. The newspaperman was surprised to see the condemned man so remarkably composed. Sullivan said, "Well, I've only a short time to live now, but I've nothing to fear."

"Nothing to fear?" the reporter asked.

"No, nothing," Sullivan replied. "Nothing. I've faced death a hundred times and I'm not going to flinch now."

Sullivan spent many hours talking with Father Cormier, the prison chaplain. The priest told the Saint John *Globe,* "That man is not a criminal. He has not the nature of a criminal. During all the time I have been with him I never heard him say a harsh word about anyone. He is thoughtful and kind and his is not the nature of a man who would commit a cruel murder. I cannot and will not believe that he committed such a crime as the circumstantial evidence against him showed."

The night before the execution, John Radclive, the hangman, came to Sullivan's cell to measure and weigh him. "Well, John, you know who I am," he said. "I am sorry for you, but cannot help you. I am only the instrument of the law."

"I know," Sullivan replied. "You can't help it. After all, it might as well be you as anyone else. I was really glad when I heard you were to do it. I was afraid the sheriff might undertake it and he is old and fussy, and there might have been a bungle that would have caused me torture. I have no fear of that now."

Sullivan was hanged at 7:45 the next morning before a crowd of fifty to sixty people, including his two brothers. Two minutes later he was pronounced dead. Father Cormier gave him a Catholic funeral.

Though John Sullivan went to his grave a convicted murderer and the Meadow Brook case was officially solved, the crime is still considered by many to be a mystery. Sullivan had been found guilty in the court of public opinion long before he ever stepped into a court of law. The local press participated in gossip mongering and spreading innuendo, making the selection of an impartial jury all but impossible. Sullivan's fate was sealed by the testimony of a severely traumatized child.

It is possible, of course, that Sullivan *was* guilty. But the evidence that sent him to the gallows in 1897 would hardly be considered sufficient for a conviction in a modern court. A jury charged with determining the guilt or innocence of a person on trial for murder is supposed to reach a guilty verdict only if every member is certain of that guilt *beyond the shadow of a doubt.* The shadow over John Sullivan's case was very long indeed. It could well be that the killer of Eliza and Harris Dutcher hopped the first freight train that passed through Meadow Brook, and allowed an innocent man to take the blame.

THE MYSTERY OF HEADLESS VALLEY

Deadly Shangri-La

The easy pickings of the Klondike gold fields had petered out by the turn of the 20th century. Most of the adventurers who had made the arduous journey north to Canada's Yukon Territory turned around and went home. But some diehard sourdoughs wouldn't quit. They were certain there were other bonanzas in the northland, just waiting to be found. Many of these optimists joined the next big rush, this time to Alaska. Others still believed their fortunes lay on the Canadian side of the line.

In the summer of 1900 an aged Slavey Native called Little Nahanni walked into the Hudson's Bay Post at Fort Liard, just north of the British Columbia border in what was then part of the Northwest Territories. The old man astounded all present when he tossed a small bag full of gold nuggets on the counter. Naturally, they wanted to know where the gold came from. Just as naturally, Little Nahanni was reluctant to tell them. He just pointed north—toward the Mackenzie Mountains.

The men were dumbstruck, for Little Nahanni's gesture indicated the valley of the South Nahanni River, which lay just below the waterway's junction with the Flat River. This was wild, mysterious, and practically inaccessible country. There, in a corner of the Northwest Territories bordered by the Yukon Territory on the west and British Columbia on the south, are some of the most spectacular vistas on the continent. The South Nahanni River boils and foams for some 480 kilometres (300 miles) between steep canyon walls sometimes 457 metres (1500 feet) high. At magnificent Virginia Falls the water drops 96.3 metres (316 feet), twice the height of Niagara Falls.

So remote was this valley that few people had actually seen it. Of those, fewer had lived to tell about it. To the local Natives, whose word "Nahanni" roughly translates as "the people over there," the valley was cursed. The curse was a strange one that combined the beauty of paradise with the horrors of hell.

Somewhere within the confines of the valley, the Natives said, lay another hidden valley where the climate was warm all year and the land lush with greenery. Hot springs bubbled up from the ground, filling the valley with a magical mist. Whites who heard the story envisioned a Shangri-La in the middle of the Canadian subarctic and wondered if such a place might actually exist.

But if the hidden valley was indeed a Shangri-La, it was a deadly one. The Natives said the valley had once been fought over by rival tribes, and the ghosts of slain warriors haunted it. Worse, it was the home of human-like creatures the Natives called Mountain Men—tall, hairy creatures that Natives in British Columbia called Sasquatch. These creatures ate human flesh, the legends claimed, and would kill anyone who trespassed on their land.

The whites no doubt laughed at these Native superstitions, but prospectors who wanted to explore the valley for gold could not convince Native guides to take them. In 1898, a Native had taken prospectors Jack Stanier and Joe Bird as far as a place called Rabbitkettle Mounds, just above Virginia Falls. Then he was warned in a dream not to take the white men any farther. In spite of Stanier and Bird's protests, the trio had to turn back. Over the years Stanier would try many times to find gold in that valley, without success.

There were more wild tales about this isolated place; stories of demonic possession, of a Lost Tribe ruled by a White Queen—and of riverbanks glittering with gold. Quite likely the valley's very remoteness gave rise to these yarns. Even today the place is difficult to reach except by air. There are, in fact, several hot springs, but not enough to create a tropical oasis in the midst of cold desolation. As for a fabulous gold mine…

When Little Nahanni wouldn't tell anyone the exact place where he had found the gold, hopeful prospectors kept a careful watch on him. If he headed back into the Mackenzie Mountains, they intended to follow him. But Little Nahanni made no such move. When he'd spent all his gold, he went back to trapping.

Then in 1903 another Native came into Fort Liard with gold—nuggets the size of eggs, it was said. His name has not been recorded, but he evidently was a friend of Murdoch McLeod, the factor at the Hudson's Bay post there. McLeod had married a Native woman and had three grown-up sons: Willie, Frank and Charlie. The boys had been "raised as Indians," according to one veteran prospector, and knew how to handle themselves in rough country. The unidentified Native told them he had found the gold near Bennett Creek, a tributary of the Flat River.

The McLeod Brothers decided that, curse or not, they were going after the gold. However, they did not strike out directly from Fort Liard. First they went to Edmonton, perhaps because they had to work at temporary jobs to earn enough money to grubstake their operation. In January 1904 they were ready to go.

They went to Vancouver by train, then by steamer to Wrangell, Alaska. There they bought a sled and a team of dogs. Mushing their way up frozen rivers, over land and across iced-in lakes, they left the Alaska Panhandle behind and drove on into Canadian territory. Where the snow was deep, two brothers would walk ahead on snowshoes to break trail for the dogs, sled and driver behind.

The long route took the McLeods past places that had figured in the tales of earlier gold seekers: Telegraph Creek, Tanzilla Butte, Dease Lake. A forty-eight-kilometre (thirty-mile) trek down the length of Dease Lake brought them to the Dease River. Another 161 kilometres (100 miles) along its twisting, frozen surface took them to the Cassiar Mountains.

By now the brothers had lost track of time and were living on what they could shoot. If one of them brought down a moose, they and the dogs ate well. If there was no game, the men tightened their belts and the dogs just had to whine. At times Willie, Frank and Charlie weren't even sure where they were, because the maps available to them were not always accurate. At last they came to the upper reaches of the Flat River. It was spring by now, but Charlie, who later gave an account of the journey, did not know the date.

The boys found a few Cassiar Natives sluicing at the mouth of a small creek. The Natives had found some coarse gold. Charlie said it was "big stuff, up to $2 and $3 a nugget." The Natives were probably not pleased with the sudden arrival of the "half-breeds," but Charlie made no further mention of them or the dogs and sled. Quite possibly some sort of deal was struck which allowed the McLeods to take over the claim while the Natives took the dogs and sled. The brothers set up camp and began panning and sluicing. They called the stream Gold Creek.

It seemed the Natives had picked the creek clean, because the McLeods didn't find much gold, just enough to fill a small medicine bottle. With summer almost over and a 480-km (300 mile) journey downriver back to Fort Liard ahead of them, they decided to call it quits for the season. The brothers used rough-hewn planks from some of the sluice boxes the Natives had constructed to build a crude, box-shaped boat. They pushed off in this contraption to navigate some of the meanest white water rapids in the Canadian North.

They were probably lucky to be swamped in the very first drop in the rapids. Had it happened farther down that furious stretch of water, between unscalable cliffs, they all might have drowned. As it was, they got a thorough soaking and lost most of their property, including the bottle of gold. They hauled themselves ashore with nothing but the clothes on their backs, a rifle and thirty cartridges.

The McLeods trudged back to Gold Creek. One of them shot a moose, so they wouldn't starve. As they built yet another ramshackle boat, the brothers did some more panning and sluicing, and found a small amount of gold. No doubt they were relieved they wouldn't be completely broke when they returned to Fort Liard. Ironically, those few flakes of gold would lead two of the brothers to their deaths, and would be a catalyst in the mystery of Headless Valley.

The McLeods' second attempt to reach Fort Liard was successful. This time they used a line made of moosehide to ease their craft through the rougher stretches of the river. All they had to show for their efforts was a small sample of gold. But it was part of the prospector's creed that where there's a little, there might be a motherlode. Using their glittering sample as "evidence," Willie and Frank talked a Scotsman into joining them in a new expedition.

The Scot is a shadowy figure in the story. Some people said his name was Weir; others called him Wilkinson. Why the McLeods asked him to be their partner is also uncertain. Perhaps they did so because Charlie didn't want to go back, and his brothers felt they needed a third man. Or it could have been because the Scot was supposed to be an engineer. Maybe he was. He might also have been just another drifter looking for an easy mark. If so, he found one in the McLeods.

In the spring of 1905 the two McLeods and their Scottish pal headed up the South Nahanni River. They were never seen alive again. When his brothers did not return to Fort Liard in the fall, Charlie went looking for them. Not until 1908 did he learn his brothers' tragic fate.

A search party found the bones of Frank and Willie in a riverside camp at an isolated location about eighty km (fifty miles) upstream from Fort Liard. Evidence indicated they had been on their way home. The brothers had been shot, and their heads had been surgically removed from their bodies. The skulls were never found. Charlie named the place Deadman's Valley, for which many people would substitute Headless Valley. The name was eventually attached to the entire South Nahanni Valley.

There seemed little doubt that the two McLeods had been murdered, but from that point on the stories vary. Near the campsite there was a wooden sled runner with a message carved in it: "We have found a fine prospect." This was an indication that the party had struck it rich. Had the boys' Scottish partner murdered them in their sleep and then absconded with the gold? One report says that his remains were found not far from the camp, and that he had evidently starved to death. But another story says he was seen in Telegraph Creek with a lot of gold in his possession. The Mounties supposedly traced him to Vancouver before the trail went cold.

Years later, when interviewed by journalist Pierre Berton, another Willie McLeod, nephew of the murdered men, said that his uncles had not been decapitated, and had been identified by their teeth, "The Indians here told me the real murderer of my uncles was a bad Indian who had a trapline in the country and killed them for their food."

At the same time another nephew, G. M. McLeod of Calgary, was telling another journalist "...Charlie buried them without their heads...One brother was found lying in their night bed face up, and the other was lying face down, three steps away, with his arm outstretched in a vain attempt to reach his gun which was at the foot of a tree, only another step from where he fell. The blankets were thrown across his brother as if he'd left the bed with a leap." By "face up" and "face down," McLeod evidently meant one body was on its back and the other on its stomach.

Not everybody agreed that the heads had been removed by the killer. Some said the heads had most likely been dragged away by animals. One trapper said there were wolves "the size of ponies" in that part of the country, as well as grizzly bears. Either predator could have made short work of a human head.

Why then, were the trunks of the bodies still wrapped in blankets? If they had been scavenged by wolves or bears, wouldn't the bones have been scattered around? This was the case with other human remains that animals had come across in the wild.

Whoever had killed the McLeods, and whatever had happened to their heads, the news quickly spread that they had found gold. Some men would be brave enough—or foolhardy enough—to go looking for it, in spite of a growing legend about "headhunting Indians." Over the years the "haunted" valley's list of victims would grow.

In 1910 Martin Jorgenson, a Swede who had been in the Yukon Gold Rush, went into Headless Valley alone. For two years no one heard a word about him. Then a Native showed up at the Hudson's Bay post at Pelly Lakes, about 320 km (200 miles) from the valley. He was looking for Poole Field, an ex-Mountie who was Jorgenson's friend and one-time business partner. When the Native found Poole he told him that Martin had struck it rich near the mouth of the Flat River and wanted Field to join him right away. He gave Field a map showing the way to Jorgenson's cabin.

Field left for the South Nahanni as soon as he could. When he arrived at the mouth of the Flat River he found Jorgenson's cabin burned to the ground. The Swede's skeleton lay halfway between the cabin and the river... minus its head! Jorgenson had been shot in the back. A new Savage rifle Jorgenson had taken with him was missing. Field allegedly saw it sometime later in the trading post at Fort Simpson, where a stranger had swapped it for some goods.

That, at least, is *one* story. Another said that Jorgenson's rifle lay beside him. Two empty cartridges were evidence that he had tried to shoot it out with his assailant. Again, some people attempted to explain the missing head as the work of scavenging animals.

The map Jorgenson had drawn for Field showed the location of the cabin, but not the gold mine. There was no indication if it was the same "prospect" the McLeods had found. In spite of Jorgenson's sorry end, others took up the search.

In 1926 a woman adventurer named Annie Laferte went into the valley alone and was never heard from again. There was a story about another woman who tore off all her clothes and ran up a mountainside, naked and screaming, never to be seen again. The Natives said the spirits of the valley had taken her.

Shortly after Annie Laferte's disappearance, a man known as Yukon Fisher tried his luck on the South Nahanni. For a while it seemed that he had broken the curse of Headless Valley. Yukon showed up a couple of times at trading posts where he bought supplies with gold nuggets. His luck didn't last. In 1928 his bones were found near Bennett Creek. This time the head was not missing. There was some suspicion that he had been murdered, but the twisted shape of his rifle also suggested he had been killed by a grizzly bear.

In 1929 a seven-man party that included a fellow named Angus Hall penetrated the valley. Hall quarrelled with the other men, and struck out on his own. His companions searched for him, but found no trace except the print of a hobnailed boot in the mud. These men found what might have been the site of the McLeods' diggings, but there was little gold in it. As for the missing Angus Hall, people would later say, "He was just swallowed up."

Phil Powers went into Headless Valley in 1931, not to seek gold, but to trap. Since other trappers, Native and white alike, were afraid to go into that notorious valley, he probably thought there would be a fortune in furs, just waiting for the man who had the nerve to go and get them. When Powers did not come out the following spring, the Mounted Police sent four men in to look for him. The Mounties found Powers' charred body in his burnt-out cabin. His gun lay beside him. The police suspected he had been murdered while defending his cabin. The killer then set fire to the building to cover up the crime. But they did not have enough evidence to pursue an investigation.

In 1936 Poole Field and his partner J.H. Mulholland organized an expedition that was to be accompanied by thirty Native packers and guides. They started off with high hopes of finding the elusive gold mine. But the Natives' fear of the place was too great. They said only death awaited prospectors who went into that cursed valley. The expedition had to turn back.

Not long after, Mulholland and his friend Bill Epler set out for Headless Valley by themselves. They, too, vanished and were believed murdered. While searching for them the police found a body, but it was not that of Mulholland or Epler. It had to be reported as "unidentified."

On Christmas Day, 1945, a French Canadian prospector named Ernest Savard emerged from the South Nahanni country and announced he had found gold. He bought supplies and headed right back to Headless Valley. The following summer a man named Walter Tulley reported to police that he had found Savard dead in his sleeping bag. His head had been "all but severed."

A story about Savard's death in infamous Headless Valley appeared in the newspapers. Police soon learned, however, that Savard was alive and well in Yellowknife. Apparently his gold strike hadn't been such a big one after all. Whose then was the body Tulley had found? The answer might have been in the next story to reach the police.

A man named Frank Henderson and an unidentified partner had gone into the South Nahanni country in 1946. Only Henderson came out. He had thirty ounces of gold. He said he and his partner had split up, and were supposed to meet at Virginia Falls. The partner had not shown up. Henderson—if that was his real name—was gone before the police could follow up on the story.

Sometimes the dreaded valley was wrongly blamed for a death or a disappearance. A prospector named Andy Hays was said to have been killed in Headless Valley. But he, like Savard, had simply moved on to Yellowknife without telling anyone. Ollie Holmburg was also listed as a victim of Headless Valley. Actually, Holmburg disappeared in the Smith River country, 240 km (150 miles) away.

The South Nahanni Valley is extremely rough country even by subarctic standards. Quite likely most of those people who disappeared suffered accidents (a broken leg would doom the most experienced woodsman), encountered wolves or grizzly bears, or perished from the cold. One such victim was trapper John O'Brien. His frozen body was found kneeling beside an unlit fire, his last match clutched in his rigid fingers.

W.J. McDonough, a veteran bush pilot, scoffed at the idea of Headless Valley being cursed. He told a Toronto *Globe and Mail* reporter in 1947:

"It is a hard thing to say of men who are dead, but their deaths were due to nothing but sheer stupidity. They went in without proper equipment and sufficient food, and were caught by the freeze-up in the middle of September."

Another Northerner told the reporter, "Headless Valley is no place for anyone interested in escaping, but only men of the hardest character and physical toughness. It probably wasn't Indians who killed off previous prospectors, but nature in the raw."

But there were still the suspicious deaths of the McLeods, Martin Jorgenson and Phil Powers, not to mention three curiously missing heads. If those men were indeed murdered, who did it? No one knows. There was speculation in 1932 that the Mad Trapper of Rat River, slain in the Yukon in a gunfight with the RCMP, might have been the Headless Valley killer, but police could find no evidence connecting the unidentified trapper with those deaths.

In 1947 Pierre Berton visited Headless Valley by ski plane and wrote a series of articles in which he dismissed as nonsense the tales of Sasquatch, Shangri-La and headhunting Indians. Moreover, though traces of placer gold were found in the streams, there was no gold mine. Mr. Berton's articles were quite a sensation and stirred up interest in that wild corner of Canada. After that, Headless Valley was forgotten by all but a few adventurers who wanted to pit themselves against one of the most dangerous rivers in the world.

Then, in 1960, Headless Valley was in the news again. Five prospectors, Alex Mieskanen, Tony Pappas, Orville Webb, Dean Rosswarren and John Richardson, had gone into the valley in October 1959 to look for gold. A plane was supposed to pick them up early the following March. For some reason the plane did not arrive. The men were out of food and their situation desperate. They ate their dogs, then survived on a few squirrels they managed to shoot. Finally they had nothing to eat but a paste they made by cracking open the dogs' bones and boiling them together with a moose hide. This sustained them for weeks.

Pappas and Webb finally set off on foot to get help. They were never seen again. Driven insane by hunger, Mieskanen lit a stick of dynamite and blew himself to kingdom come. In early May a bush pilot went looking for the men and found Rosswarren and Richardson still alive—barely. He put them aboard his plane and took them to the hospital in Yellowknife. The story had nothing to do with spirits, monsters or bloodthirsty killers, but mysterious Headless Valley had claimed three more lives.

THE GUN-AN-NOOT MYSTERY

"Some Day I'll Fix You Good!"

In the latter part of the 1890s two Native outlaws, Almighty Voice in what is now Saskatchewan and Charcoal in what is now Alberta, shot their way into legend when they killed Mounted Police officers and then led the NWMP on chases that lasted months. In the end each of them lost his race with the law. Almighty Voice was killed when the police used cannonfire to bombard the grove of trees in which he was holed up. Charcoal died on the gallows.

Another Native who was suspected of murder and branded an outlaw baffled the forces of law and order not for a matter of months, but for *thirteen years*! The final chapter of his story was not as melodramatic as those of Almighty Voice and Charcoal. Yet, in many ways it was just as tragic. His name was Simon Gun-an-noot.

He was born Zhum-min-hoot (little bear that climbs trees) to the Kispiox clan of the Carrier Nation in 1874, near the junction of the Skeena and Kispiox rivers, about 804 km (500 miles) north of Vancouver. Roman Catholic missionaries called him Simon Peter, and corrupted his Native name to Gun-an-noot. Young Gun-an-noot grew up in a time of great change for his people. White settlers were moving in to take away the land, and Christian missionaries were working hard to banish traditional concepts of spiritualism. The way of life that had served Gun-an-noot's people for thousands of years was giving way to "progress."

As a boy and youth, Gun-an-noot hunted and trapped over a vast area of wild country 160 km (100 miles) to the east of Bear Lake. His domain covered some ten thousand square miles, and over the years he came to know it the way an urbanite knows his city. Rivers and almost invisible trails were his streets. Promontories, ancient trees and long-abandoned village sites no white man would recognize were his signposts.

By the age of twenty-one, Gun-an-noot was 1.8 m (6 feet) tall, with a muscular 90.7 kg (200 pound) body. He was as quick and agile as a gymnast and as strong as a weightlifter. He was a crack shot with his Winchester rifle, and it was said he had killed a bear with his hunting knife.

But for all that, Gun-an-noot did not fit the white stereotype of a "typical Indian." He liked an occasional drink, but generally was not much taken with alcohol. He was not an easy mark for the white men who ran the trading posts. He wanted cash for his pelts, and if he didn't get what he considered a fair price, he took his business elsewhere, even if he had to go all the way to Vancouver. What money he made, he saved.

In 1901, Gun-an-noot married a woman named Sarah. Shortly after their first child was born, they went to Vancouver to buy supplies for a venture most whites of the time would have thought astounding. Gun-an-noot was opening his own store in his home village of Hagowilgate (now Kispiox).

The store did well, and for a few years Gun-an-noot prospered. He bought part interest in a sawmill, and started a ranch on which he raised cattle and horses. The white man's way of living was working for this Carrier Native, and he grew a moustache so he'd fit in more with the other ranchers and businessmen. But the good times were not to last.

In the winter of 1905-06 Gun-an-noot left Sarah, who had just given birth to their second child, to look after the store. He and a nephew by marriage, Peter Hi-ma-dan, went on a trapping expedition. The men did well, and the following June they exchanged their pelts for cash. On their way home they stopped at the settlement of Two Mile House to celebrate.

Two Mile House, near Hazelton, was a rough-and-tumble place. Trappers, hunters and prospectors congregated in the saloon there to drink, pick up information, and sometimes fight. There was still a law against selling alcohol to Natives, but the bar's owner, Jim "the Geezer" Cameron, paid little mind to it. If Simon Gun-an-noot and his nephew wanted a drink, what did it matter? Their money was as good as anybody else's. Unfortunately, a man named Alex McIntosh was also in the bar that night. Gun-an-noot, who had made a gallant effort to live by the white man's rules, was soon to find himself on the run from them.

Alex McIntosh, of mixed white and Native blood, was a known troublemaker, ever ready to pick a fight. He and some other men had a mule train camped nearby and had come into Two Mile House for some two-fisted drinking. A little after midnight McIntosh began to make loud, crude remarks about "squaws." He was obviously trying to provoke Gun-an-noot. McIntosh had a reputation for molesting Native women and had even been jailed for it. Nonetheless, Gun-an-noot ignored the loudmouth. McIntosh wouldn't shut up. He said that every woman had her price, even "Christian squaws." This was clearly intended to mean Sarah, who was a devout Christian. Still, Gun-an-noot kept his temper.

Then McIntosh stepped well over the line. He boasted that he had slept with Gun-an-noot's wife. That was a remark Gun-an-noot could not let pass.

Gun-an-noot sprang to his feet and lashed out at McIntosh, driving him into a corner. McIntosh came roaring back, but if he'd expected to have an easy time beating up a drunken Indian, he quickly discovered he'd picked the wrong man. The fight was short but vicious. Gun-an-noot was no brawler, but he gave as good as he got. Both men were bloodied by the time the Geezer and other men pulled Gun-an-noot off his opponent. McIntosh had a badly mangled finger. As the men dragged Gun-an-noot out the door, he shouted at McIntosh, "Some day I'll fix you good!" Those were to be fateful words.

Gun-an-noot and Peter Hi-ma-dan mounted their horses and rode toward Hagowilgate. A fifteen-year-old Native named Peter Barney saw them go, and would remember later that neither man had a gun. A little while later the boy saw Alex McIntosh leave the bar and ride off in the opposite direction toward Hazelton, quite likely to have his injured finger treated at the hospital there. He never made it.

At dawn a party of Natives on the trail to Hazelton found Alex McIntosh lying dead. He had been shot in the back. They hurried on to town to report their discovery. British Columbia Provincial

Police Constable Jim Kirby and coroner Edward Hicks-Beach went out to investigate. As they were looking over the crime scene and arranging for a wagon to take the body to Hazelton, they learned of a second killing. A man was dead on the trail about a mile and a half from the other side of Two Mile House. He had also been shot in the back.

The second victim was identified as Max Leclair, a relative newcomer to the area. He lived quietly on his ranch and worked as a woodsman and guide. Leclair been bringing a packtrain into Hazelton when he was inexplicably murdered in an ambush.

The post-mortems suggested (but did not prove) that the same killer had shot both men. They had both died between six and seven a.m. The bullet holes were in almost the same place. In both killings the shooter seemed to have waited for the victim to pass, and then fired from a kneeling or prone position.

Historians have questioned Constable Kirby's investigation of the crime scene. They say he did not look for bullets, cartridges or tracks. Others defend Kirby, saying there just wasn't much evidence to find and record. Whatever the case, the questions Kirby asked the few available witnesses took him to the bar in Two Mile House. There, from a hungover, groggy lot, he heard of the fight between Gun-an-noot and McIntosh, and of Gun-an-noot's threat to "fix" McIntosh. A coroner's jury, acting on Kirby's report, came to an easy conclusion:

"We, having heard the evidence relating to the above case, have come to the conclusion that Alex McIntosh was killed by a gunshot wound between Ten Mile Creek and the hospital, and are agreed that it was a case of wilful murder by a person by the name of Simon Gun-an-noot (Indian)."

The jury also named Gun-an-noot and Peter Hi-ma-dan as the probable killers of Leclair. Nobody seems to have thought of what motive they would have for killing this man. He hadn't been anywhere near the bar when the fight broke out.

Meanwhile, a summons was issued for Geezer Cameron on a charge of selling liquor to Natives. But the saloon keeper had mysteriously disappeared. Nobody sought to make any connection between that and the killings. In fact, Cameron was never seen in those parts again. The police did not investigate why, after two murders had been committed, Cameron had abandoned his place of business and vanished. They wanted Gun-an-noot.

By this time, news had reached Gun-an-noot at his ranch that he was wanted for murder. His father, Nah-gun, advised him to get away and hide in the bush until the trouble blew over. Nah-gun had been jailed a few times for petty offences, and did not trust the white man's ideas about "justice." Gun-an-noot and Hi-ma-dan packed up some supplies and headed for the hills.

Constable Kirby and four men sworn in as special constables rode out to Gun-an-noot's ranch. The wanted man was not there, and Sarah would tell them nothing. In the corral they found four dead horses. Kirby decided Gun-an-noot had fled on foot because hoofprints would leave an easy trail, and had killed his horses so the police couldn't use them. There was a possibility, though, that Alex McIntosh's relatives had killed the horses as an act of revenge against the man they believed had murdered their kinsman.

Kirby's posse rode on to Peter Hi-ma-dan's home. He, too, was absent. Kirby had no more luck in getting answers from Peter's wife than he'd had with Sarah.

On their way back to Hazelton, Kirby and his men encountered Nah-gun. They arrested the old man and clapped him in jail, even though there were no charges against him. This was an old tactic white policemen used on Natives, dating back to the earliest days of the North West Mounted Police. Lock up a fugitive's family members, and you just might draw him out into the open. It gave the lie to the notion that whites and Natives were equal in the eyes of the law. Nah-gun did not remain in jail long. He escaped by removing some boards from the back wall of a privy, while a guard waited patiently at the door.

Kirby and his men searched far and wide for Gun-an-noot. They found nothing but a team of Gun-an-noot's pack dogs—all of which Kirby shot. While Kirby was venting his frustration on the dogs, Gun-an-noot was back in his unwatched home, collecting his family and some supplies. He headed back into the bush with Sarah and the children, Hi-ma-dan and his wife (reputed to be the best shot in the party), and his mother and Nah-gun.

The two suspected killers, the aged jailbreaker, the women and two small children headed north into mountainous, heavily forested country. They passed through the tiny settlement of Kisgegas, east of the junction of the Babine and Skeena rivers. They pressed on to Bear Lake, where they stayed two days with the Bear Lake Natives. Then they continued north to the head of the Nass River. There Gun-an-noot had cached a large amount of food, ammunition and equipment, including three canoes. He had intended to use these things in the next winter's trapping expedition. Now they would help sustain him and his band while they stayed out of the clutches of the law.

Kirby and his men gave up the hunt after two fruitless weeks. After he returned to Hazelton, Kirby went out to Gun-an-noot's store and confiscated all his stock. This was not legal, but perhaps he thought Gun-an-noot might sneak back for supplies.

Throughout that summer, police parties tried to pick up clues as to the fugitives' whereabouts. They learned Gun-an-noot had been to Kisgegas and Bear Lake, and sent men to those places. Nobody would tell them anything except that Gun-an-noot and his people had been and gone. Not even the promise of a $1,000 reward loosened any tongues.

Back in Hazelton children were playing a "cops and Indians" game that ridiculed the police. People jokingly said the outlaws had "Done-a-scoot." That wasn't the worst, as far as the police were concerned. Other Natives, heartened by Gun-an-noot's continued defiance of the law, were showing rebelliousness of their own in matters totally unrelated to the killings of McIntosh and Leclair.

The Babine Lake Natives had been involved in a bitter dispute with the government and canneries over fishing rights in their region. When government officials tore down barriers the Natives had erected, the Native put them up again. They roughly handled a special constable sent out to stop them. The Kamloops *Standard* complained: "Because of the non-capture of the murderers Simon Gun-an-noot and Peter Hi-ma-dan, the Indians in this district are becoming very cheeky and defying the law." The *Standard* ignored the fact that the "murderers" had not yet been convicted of anything.

Gun-an-noot had nothing to do with the fishing dispute. But his being at large was a source of embarrassment for the police.

They were not moved at all when a trapper named McPhail reported that he had met Gun-an-noot in the woods, and the man had tearfully told him he'd had nothing to do with the deaths of McIntosh and Leclair.

The country into which Gun-an-noot and his band had fled was truly a howling wilderness, much of which was not yet even charted. It was a land of wild rivers, unnamed lakes, muskeg, mountains and canyons. At the best of times even white men skilled in woodcraft travelled through it only with difficulty. In winter it was among the most inhospitable places on earth. Once the snows came, the police were obliged to postpone the manhunt until spring.

The winter of 1906–07 was one of the cruellest on record, with heavy snow and temperatures dropping as low as –45° C (–50° F). As Native trappers came out of the bush to Hazelton, police questioned them. The officers heard many conflicting reports of Gun-an-noot being seen in locations hundreds of miles apart. There were tales of the outlaws being destitute, and even one that Gun-an-noot and Nah-gun had died. But nobody brought in an iota of information the police could consider reliable. Promises of rewards still went for naught. One Indian agent complained, "The Indians are not making the slightest effort to locate Simon. They are going about their usual rounds and keeping away from any place where they think Simon might be."

By the spring of 1907 the government in Victoria was becoming concerned. British Columbia was booming and the men in the capital were pulling out all the stops to lure new settlers west. But would people want to come to a wild country where renegade Indians got away with murder? Stories about the woods being full of dangerous outlaws were hurting the tourist business, too.

That summer, Sergeant Otway Wilkie of the B.C. Provincial police took up the chase. He was a woodsman of considerable experience. His party included Sergeant F. R. Murray, a pair of ex-Mounties, and several packers and guides. Throughout the summer and into fall and winter they made several excursions into Gun-an-noot's seemingly boundless hideout.

Sometimes travelling together, at other times split into two groups, this posse searched the country of the Stikine, Skeena, Sustut, and Ominica rivers, Bear Lake, and White Wolf Pass. They hiked mountain trails and fought blinding snowstorms. On Bear Lake their raft overturned, sending their supplies and equipment to the bottom. Guides who were supposed to be reliable men turned out to be incompetent, with the result that the posse would be lost for days on end. At least one guide deserted. On one occasion their food ran out and they almost starved. Yet for all this ill luck, perhaps the worst of it was that—without knowing it at the time—they almost stumbled upon their elusive quarry.

By this time, after being on the run for over a year and a half, the fugitives had exhausted their supplies and were living off the land. Gun-an-noot and Hi-ma-dan were in a canyon near the headwaters of the Skeena River setting rabbit snares. Suddenly they saw Wilkie and another man coming up the trail that led to the canyon's mouth. A few more steps, and the white men would come upon the Native's snowshoe tracks. The canyon was a dead end, which meant the outlaws had nowhere to run.

Hi-ma-dan raised his rifle, aimed it at Wilkie, and cocked the hammer. Without a word, Gun-an-noot stuck his thumb between the hammer and the firing pin, preventing Hi-ma-dan from shooting. Seconds later, Wilkie and his companion stopped. They spoke briefly, then turned and went back the way they had come.

Gun-an-noot felt that had been too close. The best way to avoid detection, he thought, was for him to keep the manhunters in sight. As Wilkie and the other man trudged back to their camp, Gun-an-noot and Hi-ma-dan followed them.

It was now the end of January 1908. Wilkie and his men were exhausted and had made up their minds to return to Hazelton. They wanted to travel light, so when they packed up their camp they left behind a quantity of food they wouldn't need.

From concealment in a frigid cave, Gun-an-noot and Hi-ma-dan watched the white men head down the trail. They couldn't believe their good fortune when they saw the supplies the men had abandoned. But was it a trap? The hungry men stayed in their hiding place the rest of the day and all night. They did not dare make a fire. The next morning they cautiously climbed down to the camp. No constables jumped from behind the trees with guns drawn. The fugitives gratefully gathered up the parcels of bacon, rice, flour, beans, sugar and tea. Gun-an-noot swore he would not be so careless again.

Back in civilization, newspapermen who had no idea what it was like to hunt for a skilled woodsman in thousands of square miles of frozen wilderness, charged Wilkie with spending most of his time in a cabin by a warm fire. They nicknamed him "Wrong Way Wilkie." Several prospectors claimed to have seen Gun-an-noot. If those men could find the outlaw, why couldn't the police? Senior police officials thought that perhaps it was because the fugitives were kept informed of police movements via the "moccasin telegraph." Prospectors and white trappers going about their own business did not receive such scrutiny.

A prospector named Frank Watson was in Vancouver, telling people he had met Peter Hi-ma-dan on several occasions. The wanted man had even given him gifts of caribou meat. Believing a man like Watson could move about more freely than police officers could, the authorities swore him in as a special constable. They sent him after Hi-ma-dan, and hoped that arrest would lead to Gun-an-noot. Watson took along Joe Belleway, a guide who claimed to know where Hi-ma-dan could be found. To allay Native suspicions, they travelled as prospectors. But the two men were striking out into the wild country in the dead of the winter of 1908-09. Men hunting gold and silver usually stayed close to the settlements during the cold months.

In the first week of January 1909, Watson and Belleway tramped on snowshoes into a Native camp on Kitsumkalum Lake. There were about two dozen men, women and children. Watson saw Peter Hi-ma-dan, but the man didn't seem to want to talk to him. The other Natives received the white men hospitably, but eyed them with suspicion. They wanted to know what the visitors were doing in that country in the middle of winter. Watson wrote later:

"They were armed with Winchester repeating rifles, and their cartridge belts were fairly bulging. We told them we were on a prospecting mission to the head of the Nass River and inquired about the most direct route. This reply was received with derision, especially by the squaws. 'It is queer that you should be hunting for gold in the depth of mid-winter. We don't believe your story,' remarked one of the young bucks around the campfire the evening of our arrival as he gently handled his rifle."

Watson and Belleway stayed in the camp for three days. Peter Hi-ma-dan ignored them. Then, as the Natives packed up to move to a new location, a deputation approached them. Watson wrote:

"The Indians, armed with rifles, waited on us in a body and told us they did not want our company any longer and asked us to return the way we had come. Their threats were covert ones. Not once were we threatened with harm, but the Indian is too smooth a customer to act that way. One of the Indians, acting as a spokesman, once more assured us that they did not believe our story, and with no little eloquence said that white men had been known to penetrate that region and never return alive. All the while the other Indians fondled their rifles in a manner to indicate we would receive summary treatment if we persisted in remaining any longer. So we saw their argument, and, packing our outfit, said goodbye and started south, while the Indians with their tents already packed, struck off in the direction of the Nass River."

Watson returned to Vancouver empty-handed. He said he was finished with tracking down "Indian murderers." The odds were too unfair. He said it would take "a very considerable force to capture fugitives who had 'numerous friendly allies ready to risk their time and if necessary their lives to prevent a capture.'"

Another year gone, and still the phantom outlaws were secure in their craggy, forested stronghold. The British Columbia government's next move was a strange one. Watson had advised sending in a large force that could track the outlaws down, surround them, and finally capture them. This plan was dismissed as too costly—though there was some weight to the argument that it might also have angered the Native population in general. The last thing the Natives would have stood for was an army of constables bullying their way through camps and villages.

But the government's decision to hire the American Pinkerton detective agency seemed to fly in the face of logic, especially since the Pinkerton men came at the hefty cost of $11,000. The government was desperate, however, and the Pinkertons certainly had a stellar reputation. Over the past quarter-century they had hounded such infamous desperados as Jesse James, Butch Cassidy and the deadly Harry Tracy.

Pinkerton agents arrived in Hazelton in the summer of 1910. They swaggered around town asking questions. Then they plunged into the forest, confident of accomplishing what the bumpkin Canadian police could not, the capture of Gun-an-noot. They returned in the fall, footsore and unsuccessful. There were even stories (unproven) that Gun-an-noot had played tricks on the Americans, like sneaking into their camp at night and hanging their rifles from trees.

While the stories of Gun-an-noot bedevilling the Pinkerton men may be tall tales, there were times when he did, in fact, pilfer food from his pursuers' camps. He would also "tease" the manhunters by carving his initials on trees they had blazed. Not once, however, did Gun-an-noot shoot at the men who were trying to run him to earth, though he had many opportunities.

Gun-an-noot and Hi-ma-dan hunted, fished and trapped. Friends and relatives took their pelts to trading posts and returned with food, clothing, ammunition and other supplies. Whatever extra cash they had, they put away for the day they would need a good lawyer.

In all the years Gun-an-noot was on the run, no Native betrayed him. They allowed him to hunt in their territories, refused to help the police, and protected him in any other way they could. The few Natives who were tempted to deliver him to the police in return for a reward demanded sums of money several times the amount of the reward. They knew they would have to live elsewhere after such an act of treachery. The government that had paid $11,000 to Pinkerton's was not willing to shell out a few thousand dollars to a Native.

On numerous occasions white prospectors and hunters saw Gun-an-noot in the woods. They did not dare try to apprehend him in country in which every Native was his friend. All they could do was report the sighting when they returned to civilization weeks or months later.

In March 1912, a prospector named Frank Chettleburgh was approached in his camp by a Native who asked if he was the owner of a cache he'd found nearby. Chettleburgh said the cache was his. The Native asked if he could take a jar of jam, and Chettleburgh said he could. Days later Chettleburgh visited the cache, and found a message written in pencil on a piece of wood: "I take one jar of jam." About a week after that, the same Native returned to Chettleburgh's camp and gave him a haunch of caribou in payment for the jam. The prospector's Native guide told him the man was Gun-an-noot.

Gun-an-noot even visited friends and relatives in Hazelton and other communities, right under the noses of the police. His sympathizers hid him. No one breathed a word to the law.

But although Gun-an-noot had widespread support and was as much at home in the woods as his ancestors had been, the long years of outlaw life took their toll. Both of Gun-an-noot's parents died in the wilderness—his father about a year after breaking out of jail. Gun-an-noot carried Nah-gun's body sixty-four km (forty miles) to bury it beside a lake the old man had loved. In 1916, Hi-ma-dan's wife came out of the bush and rejoined her people near Hazelton. She was ill, and had not long to live. On her deathbed she allegedly confessed that she had shot Max Leclair because he had made sexual advances on her. Gun-an-noot had come upon the scene and told her to keep quiet about it; he would take the blame for the killing.

There were other privations for those who were left. Sarah bore four more children, three of whom died. Their two older children had no schooling, and were growing up without any of the benefits of civilized society. Sarah was ill and needed medical attention. Gun-an-noot himself was weary of being a hunted man.

The one thing that kept Gun-an-noot from surrendering was his lack of faith in the white man's justice. Several times the authorities in Hazelton—and later Smithers, when the Provincial Police District Headquarters was moved there—let it be known that if Gun-an-noot would give himself up, he'd be provided with a court-appointed attorney. Of course, Gun-an-noot received this information. But he was not about to put his life in the hands of just any lawyer the court decided to pick for him. He wanted the best legal help he could afford. That meant trapping more furs and converting them to cash.

In 1917 Gun-an-noot met an old prospector named George Beirnes, who was currently a supply contractor for the Yukon Telegraph line. The two became friends, and Gun-an-noot told Beirnes of his willingness to surrender once he could afford a lawyer. Beirnes suggested that he personally "capture" Gun-an-noot and claim the reward, then use the money for legal expenses.

Gun-an-noot would have none of it. He would make his own money. When the time came he would not be "captured," but would walk into Hazelton and surrender himself. He went back to his traplines, while Beirnes looked for a reliable lawyer.

The man Beirnes found was one of the best criminal lawyers in British Columbia. Stewart Henderson had a law office in Victoria, and had once worked for the Federal Justice Department in Ottawa. Among his clients were Indian and Chinese immigrants, people much discriminated against at that time. It mattered not a whit to Henderson that Gun-an-noot was a Native. When he heard Gun-an-noot's story, Henderson said he was certain he could win an acquittal. But Henderson was expensive. Not until 1919 did Gun-an-noot have enough money to cover his legal bills.

On June 24 of that year, George Beirnes and Stewart Henderson walked into the Hazelton police station with a greying, worn-out looking Native man. They told the officer on duty, Constable James Kelly, that Simon Gun-an-noot was voluntarily surrendering to him. When Kelly locked Gun-an-noot in a cell, the prisoner suddenly broke into a cold sweat that soaked his clothes. Gun-an-noot had become severely claustrophobic. Kelly left the cell door and the back door of the jailhouse open, on Gun-an-noot's word of honour that he wouldn't run.

News of Gun-an-noot's surrender stirred up some old animosities in Hazelton, so the venue was moved to New Westminster. Gun-an-noot had to languish in a cell in Oakalla Prison. There the door was not left open. Claustrophobia reduced the man who had lived outdoors in rough country for thirteen years to a trembling shadow of himself.

It would take officials most of the summer to haul out old documents related to the case, and to locate and summon witnesses. The trial did not get underway until October. The outcome was practically a foregone conclusion.

James Kirby was the principal witness for the Crown. Stewart Henderson made him look like a fool on the witness stand. He asked why Kirby hadn't investigated the sudden disappearance of Geezer Cameron. Kirby said he wasn't aware Cameron had disappeared.

"Then why did you say that Simon Gun-an-noot had disappeared?"

"Because I searched for him."

"Then there was a hunt for just one man, not an investigation of the state of affairs?"

"I was hunting just one man."

"Your mind was made up that Simon was guilty?"

"He was the only one I looked for."

Henderson also tore to shreds the testimony of two men who claimed to have heard Gun-an-noot confess to shooting McIntosh. Then he put Peter Barney on the stand. This was the man who, as a boy, had seen Gun-an-noot and McIntosh ride off in opposite directions when they left Two Mile House.

In his summation Henderson told the jury: "The prisoner has already been punished for a crime he did not commit by thirteen years of exile in a harsh northern wilderness. Throughout that time he provided for his family. He endured an exile because he was afraid he would not receive justice in a white man's courtroom. It remains for you, the jury, to prove his fears were groundless."

The jury took only fifteen minutes to reach a verdict of not guilty.

Gun-an-noot could at last walk in the open as a free man. But the months in jail and the three-day trial had taken more out of him than the thirteen years in the bush had done. He had to spend several days recovering in a Vancouver hospital before he could go home.

In 1920 Peter Hi-ma-dan surrendered. He, too, was defended by Stewart Henderson and acquitted. No one else was ever charged with the murder of Alex McIntosh.

Gun-an-noot went back to trapping, but his heart was no longer in it. He had spent his prime years simply trying to survive. Now he was just a tired old man. Foolish people who thought he had discovered a gold mine pestered him with silly questions. One of his sons broke his heart by getting into constant trouble with the police. Sarah died, and Gun-an-noot was more alone than he had ever been as a fugitive.

In 1933, at the age of 60, Gun-an-noot collapsed while working his trapline. He died in October of that year from tuberculosis, a malady that had carried off so many of his people. He was buried next to Nah-gun.

Gun-an-noot, like Almighty Voice and Charcoal, passed into Native legend. His extraordinary thirteen-year run from the law puts him in company with other Canadians who have served lengthy prison sentences for crimes they did not commit. Had Gun-an-noot been apprehended earlier, he might well have been hanged.

Questions remain unanswered. If Gun-an-noot didn't kill Alex McIntosh, who did? Did Geezer Cameron do it, and if so, why?

What became of Cameron? Did he depart for places unknown? Or was he, too, ambushed on a lonely trail, and his body never found? Did Gun-an-noot and Hi-ma-dan go to their graves actually knowing more than they had ever told?

THE KINRADE MYSTERY

The Tramp at the Door

Certain elements of the Kinrade murder, which stunned Edwardian Canada, paralleled the infamous Lizzie Borden case that shocked Massachusetts in 1892. Lizzie was the only person home with her father and stepmother when they were brutally murdered with an axe. She blamed the murders on an intruder who was never found. Many people believed Lizzie had committed the crime, but investigators could not find enough evidence to gain a conviction.

The Kinrade family lived at 105 Herkimer Street in an upscale part of Hamilton, Ontario. The front of the large, two-storey brick house was graced by a wooden verandah and balcony. Thomas L. Kinrade was principal of the Cannon Street Public School. He and his wife Isabel were well-respected in the community. Kinrade owned between twenty and thirty houses in the city, which he rented out. His son Ernest, twenty-three, who was in the construction business, lived in one of the houses with his wife. The Kinrade's other son Earl, nineteen, worked at a bank in Montreal. Their daughter Ethel, twenty-five, was by some accounts the couple's favourite.

She helped with her father's business by collecting rents. Sixteen-year-old Gertrude still attended her father's school.

Florence, twenty-three, reputedly the most attractive Kinrade sister, aspired to be a singer. She had sung locally in churches and private homes, with the consent of her father. Thomas believed the young woman had talent. Then in early 1908, while singing in a Toronto church, Florence caught the attention of a well-to-do English woman named Marion Elliot. Miss Elliot, who was somewhat older than Florence, and whom the rest of the family never met, was impressed with the young singer. She took her on a tour that included Galt, Guelph, Stratford, Kincardine and Goderich, where Florence sang for church congregations. Miss Elliot paid all travel expenses.

Florence thought that she could make a career of singing. (In those days people were paid to sing in church.) She accompanied Miss Elliot on a trip to Virginia. Evidently her father approved, but Isabel and Ethel opposed the idea. Soon Florence was writing to her family about her position as a soloist in a church in Richmond. She returned to Hamilton in June due to a bout of illness, but in the first week of October she was off to Richmond again. A week before Christmas, Florence was back home. She said she'd grown weary of the life she'd been leading in Virginia. She also complained about an American actor named Jimmy Baum. She said he had been making unwanted advances, and had even asked her to marry him. At the time Florence was engaged to Clair Montrose Wright, a theology student from Palmerston, Ontario. She spoke disparagingly of Baum's proposal, calling it "a joke." She said the young Virginian knew she was already betrothed, but persisted in his attempts to "win her."

Thomas Kinrade was something of a philanthropist. He told his wife and children they should share their good fortune with the needy. In those days, unemployed homeless men, commonly called tramps, would knock on people's doors looking for handouts of food. It was a rule in the Kinrade household not to turn away anyone who came to the door. The family usually had meal tickets on hand, which could be redeemed at cheap restaurants. Thus, the house at 105 Herkimer Street became marked by transients as a soft touch. Unfortunately, not all of those who lived the hobo life were honest men down on their luck.

In the early weeks of 1909 Isabel began to feel nervous about the numbers of strange men coming to her door. In the first week of February, Ethel and Florence came home from a church social one stormy Sunday night and were badly frightened by a stranger lurking in their yard. Isabel wanted to report the incident to the police, but Thomas told her to just tell the people in the restaurants to stop sending so many beggars looking for meal tickets to their house.

On Wednesday, February 24, Isabel told a man who'd asked for a handout that she had no meal tickets and he must ask somewhere else. The man left, but a little while later he was back, ringing the doorbell. Isabel wouldn't answer the door. By the time Thomas came out of his study, the man was gone. After this was repeated once or twice more, Isabel turned out the lights to make it appear that the family had retired for the night. She did this reluctantly because they had had a letter from Earl in Montreal, saying he was sick, and she was concerned that a telegraph messenger might come to the door with further news. She and Gertrude went to bed.

Sometime later Thomas was back in his study when he heard a shriek. He hurried out to the parlour and turned on the light.

Isabel, Ethel and Gertrude were there, all very frightened. They said they had heard a noise, as though someone had tried to get in through the parlour window. The next morning, before he left for school, Thomas inspected the outside of the window. Marks in the frame showed that someone had tried to force it open with a crowbar. He told Isabel to go to the police station to report the attempted break-in and ask the constables to watch their house.

At noon Thomas, Isabel and the three daughters were all home for lunch. Isabel had not yet gone to the police station, but said she would do so that afternoon. Thomas and Gertrude went to school. At about 3:10 Isabel headed downtown, leaving only Ethel and Florence in the house. One of them would be dead within an hour. The account of what happened next would be given by the surviving sister, and the details would vary with each telling. This is the core of the Kinrade mystery.

Shortly after their mother went out, Ethel and Florence decided to go for a walk. Each went to her bedroom on the second floor to dress for the outdoors. Florence found a tear in one of her gloves and went downstairs for a needle and thread. The doorbell rang and she answered it. The man who was there asked for food. Florence said, "Certainly." She started to close the door, intending to go for a meal ticket. The man suddenly pushed it open and forced his way inside. "I want all the money you have in the house!" he demanded.

Florence remembered she had a ten-dollar bill in her room. She hurried up the front stairs to get it. As she passed Ethel's closed door she said, "Lock yourself in your room." She didn't know if her sister heard her. In her own room Florence picked up the ten-dollar bill, then opened her window. She thought of climbing out on the balcony and jumping to the ground, but decided it was too high. Then she heard a noise "like the house going up." It did not occur to her that it was the sound of gunfire.

Florence raced down the front stairs and saw that the intruder had advanced down the hall almost to the dining room. She gave him the money. She would not remember later if, at that moment, he had a gun in his hand.

Now overcome with fear, Florence dashed into the parlour and opened the window about three feet. She climbed out into the side yard and ran through the snow to a fence that ran along the side of the property. The fence was only about three feet high; a child could have climbed over it. Instead, Florence turned around and went back to the house. She said later that she wondered where her sister was, and she thought the robber would be gone.

Florence entered the house through the kitchen door. In the dining room she ran right into the intruder. That was when she saw Ethel lying on her back in a pool of blood at the foot of the back stairs. The robber pointed a gun at Florence and said he would shoot her if she opened her mouth.

Florence panicked! She ran toward the man, somehow pushed past him, and fled the house through another door. The man fired a shot at her but missed. Florence ran across the street to 106 Herkimer and cried out to her neighbour, Mrs. Hickey, "Ethel is shot—six times!"

It was now two or three minutes before four o'clock. At first Mrs. Hickey did not believe what the frantic young woman was telling her. She finally accompanied Florence to a nearby grocery store where they phoned the police. An inspector, two detectives and several constables were immediately dispatched to the

Kinrade house. Only a few minutes earlier Isabel had been in the police station to report the previous night's incident.

Even as police officers arrived at the crime scene, news of the murder was racing through Hamilton. An anonymous person phoned Thomas Kinrade at school and said, "A tramp has got into your house and shot your daughter and she's dead." The horrified principal bolted from his office, not knowing which of his daughters the tactless caller had meant. When he arrived home the body had been covered with an oilcloth. He lifted the cover, saw that it was Ethel, and said in a choked voice, "I have expected this would happen for a long time." He embraced his murdered daughter, and it was only with difficulty that the constables made him release her.

Isabel, meanwhile, saw the patrol wagon parked in front of her house as she walked home. Her first thought was that something terrible had happened to Earl and the police had come to inform the family. She fainted in the street. When she was revived, she learned the terrible truth.

While policemen searched the house and property, and doctors examined the body, Thomas and Isabel were taken to Mrs. Hickey's house where Florence was. When she saw her father, Florence said, "Oh Papa, you must keep up. I'll keep up if you do. It might have been worse because he threatened to shoot me, too."

Ethel had been shot twice in the mouth, once in the cheek, once in the temple and three times in the left breast. The gunshots to her breast had been at point-blank range, close enough for the gunpowder to set her clothes smouldering. The doctors believed she had been shot once as she came down the stairs. Then the killer had stood over the prone figure and emptied the revolver into her.

A sobbing, hysterical Florence gave the police a description of the murderer. She said he was about thirty-five years old, five-foot-seven or -eight, stout, of dark complexion, with a long, waxy, drooping moustache. He wore a dark overcoat and a slouch hat. She said he was better dressed than a tramp, but not as well-dressed as a gentleman. Florence swore she had never seen him before, but was certain she would know him if she saw him again. When a constable muttered that whoever had done the foul deed would be conscience-stricken for life, Florence screamed, and then swooned. Someone had to catch her to prevent her from falling.

Police searched all over Hamilton for the man Florence had described. They had a report that a man who fit the description and who appeared to be very agitated had been seen on a street-car in the Kinrade's neighbourhood. But that man was clean-shaven. Could the killer have disguised himself with a false moustache? People speculated that a patient from the Hamilton insane asylum was the culprit, but no evidence supported that. Hamilton police sent information to other police departments in the U.S. and Canada. A $2,000 reward was posted. Whoever the killer was, he'd made a clean getaway.

While the police conducted their investigation, Thomas Kinrade took his family to a Toronto hotel to escape the crowds of the morbidly curious. People were coming right up on the verandah of their house to peer through the windows. He also hired a nurse to care for Isabel and Florence, both of whom were on the verge of nervous breakdown. At Ethel's funeral, when the coffin lid was opened so her family could have a last look, Florence became hysterical. She cried, "Ethel, lock yourself in your room!" and fainted.

Police made a thorough search of the Kinrade home and property. They found no gun, no spent cartridges, and no evidence of the shot Florence said had been fired at her. The only footprints in the snow around the house were hers, so the killer had to have left by the front door and gone down the walk. They could not find anybody who had seen a stranger enter or leave the house at the time in question. A coach driver said he had been parked in view of the house at the time Florence claimed to have run out, and had seen nothing. A neighbour said she had seen Florence run out, but at a different time. The police did, however, find some letters that piqued their interest enough for them to send a detective to Virginia.

Another neighbour said she had been looking out an upstairs window when she saw a strange man enter her yard. The man walked around the house, then knocked on her door. She did not go down to answer. The man then went away. This neighbour said the man at her door resembled the one Florence had described.

Investigators knew that a person who had just been through a traumatic experience would likely have a garbled memory of just what had happened. But some things about Florence's story didn't make sense.

Why didn't Florence go into Ethel's room, where they could have locked themselves in, gone out onto the balcony, and called for help? Why didn't she climb out her own window and call for help? Why didn't she go over the low fence and run to a neighbour's? Why had the intruder shot Ethel at all, let alone riddle her? Petty thieves generally were not murderers. Was the man a desperate criminal, already wanted for something much worse than a ten-dollar robbery, and afraid of being identified? If so, why didn't he shoot Florence when he had the chance?

The autopsy report made the case all the more mystifying. Basing their findings on the manner in which the wounds had bled, the doctors concluded that Ethel was shot in the breast *fifteen minutes* after she had been shot in the head! And why, when Florence first encountered Mrs. Hickey, did she say that Ethel had been shot six times?

Each time Florence retold her story there were inconsistencies. In one version she grabbed the intruder's gun and struggled with him. In another he grabbed her when she tried to go out the parlour window. She said at one time that she saw Ethel on the stairs. But at other times she did not mention seeing Ethel from the time her sister went into her room to dress until she saw her on the floor at the foot of the stairs.

A clairvoyant named Anna Eva Fay was in Hamilton at the time, and she said that she "saw" a gun in a drainpipe near the Kinrade house. Police looked there and did find a revolver. This was clearly a hoax, however, as the gun was brand new and had never been fired. There were other charlatans at work. Police received a letter that said, "Dear Sir.—You needn't bother looking any more for the murderer of Ethel Kinrade. I done it and you can't catch me. I fired eight shots at her and got away." The officers didn't take the letter seriously. They had a dozen more just like it from several Canadian and American cities.

The coroner's inquest into the death of Ethel Kinrade began on March 10. It required fifteen sessions, held mostly at night, over a period of fifty-six days. Reporters representing fifty newspapers, from as far away as New York and Chicago, covered the event. Hamilton's police court was packed for every session. Crowds of people who couldn't get tickets waited in the street for word of what was happening within. People paid twenty-five cents to sit at windows overlooking the police station so they could catch a glimpse of witnesses and court officials as they came and went; perhaps even Florence Kinrade herself, whose name rapidly became famous. At one point during the hearings, Florence and Isabel refused to appear, pleading poor health, and had to be subpoenaed.

One of the most prominent Canadian criminal lawyers of his day, George Tate Blackstock, K.C., was appointed Crown investigator. The Kinrades were represented by George Lynch-Staunton, K.C., who would one day be a senator. The inquest was not a trial, but a hearing officiated by a coroner before a jury to determine if there was sufficient cause and enough evidence to proceed with a trial. Nonetheless, it had all the drama of a major murder trial.

Thirty-two witnesses were questioned, including all of the surviving members of the Kinrade family. Thomas Kinrade could not remember saying, "I have expected this would happen for a long time." He stated that if he did say it, he must have been thinking of the trouble they'd been having with tramps. But people wondered if there was another reason. The Kinrades all insisted there had been no family difficulties. Earl, who had come home from Montreal right after the murder, said that Florence and Ethel had been the best of friends, practically inseparable.

Blackstock was gentle with the grieving parents, but he grilled Florence relentlessly. A magistrate probably would have restrained him, but the coroner overseeing the inquiry did not, and Lynch-Staunton's objections were ignored. Blackstock zeroed in on the numerous flaws in Florence's story. When he tried to browbeat explanations out of her, the harried girl would say, "I cannot remember," or simply, "I don't know." She was frustratingly evasive with many of her answers. Blackstock insinuated that Florence knew more than she was telling, perhaps even the identity of the intruder. Florence said repeatedly that she had never seen him before.

One session became melodramatic when Blackstock inferred that there had been no intruder at all.

"Do you now tell us, in this solemn moment, under these solemn circumstances, that you do not know who killed your sister Ethel?"

"I do not."

"Do you know anything more than what you have told us?"

"I do not."

"Then that man did it, or else the only persons in the house were you and your sister Ethel, and if no man was there then only you two girls would be left?"

"Yes."

"That will do, Miss Kinrade."

At that implication, Florence fainted. A constable and Florence's fiancée, Clair Montrose Wright, dashed to her aid. As they carried her out, Florence ranted hysterically, "That man! I see that man! He will shoot me! He will shoot me!"

The men took Florence to an anteroom where a nurse tried to calm her. But she continued to rave. "Oh, Ethel! Ethel! They think I did it! I! I! Oh Ethel! Oh, he will shoot me!" Lynch-Staunton angrily condemned Blackstock's "American sweatbox style" of questioning.

Blackstock argued that he was trying to get to the truth and, for Miss Kinrade's own sake, eliminate all possibilities. He was not through with Florence. He had letters she had written home during her sojourns in Virginia. Moreover, the Hamilton police detective who had gone to Virginia had returned with Jimmy Baum, a Pinkerton detective named Pender, and letters Florence had written to Jimmy from Canada. Evidently, all was not as harmonious in the Kinrade home as the family maintained. Through the reading of letters in court, from the testimonies of Pender and Baum, and from admissions grudgingly made by Florence, Blackstock gradually revealed an intriguing story.

Florence had not been singing in churches, as she had told her family. She had been singing and acting on stage at the Orpheum Theater in Portsmouth, Virginia, with Jimmy Baum's theatrical company. She went under the name Mildred Dale. In those days actors and actresses—aside from a small elite—were regarded by polite society as vagabonds and riff-raff. They would not have been considered suitable company for a young lady from a respectable Ontario family. Florence's letters told her family of the churches she was singing in and the name of the good Christian family with whom she'd been staying. Agent Pender, who'd been assigned to trace Florence's movements in Virginia, learned that the pastors of those churches had never heard of her. The good Christian family didn't exist. Florence had an inscribed bracelet that she'd said was presented to her by the choir of a church in Richmond. She had bought the bracelet herself.

In an apparent attempt to further her theatrical career, Florence had made up a scrapbook of fake newspaper articles about performances she had never given. One article described a reception held in her honour, that had never taken place. Marion Elliot, Florence's benefactress, had been angry about her involvement with the theatre. Miss Elliot withdrew her financial support and threatened to tell Florence's parents. She had apparently returned to England. At the time of the inquest, Florence had no idea where she could be reached.

Thomas Kinrade had testified that no one in his family owned a gun, and that none of his children had any familiarity at all with firearms. Then the court heard that Florence had carried a revolver during a visit to Savannah, Georgia. She explained that in the South white women often carried firearms "for protection from Negroes." She said she had fired a gun only once, and that had been a prop used in a play.

Florence's relationship with Jimmy Baum had not been at all what she told her family. Jimmy testified that Florence told him her parents and sister had forced her to marry an older man whom she "hated, feared and despised." She had divorced that man, she said, but was afraid he would come after her. Jimmy said he had indeed proposed to Florence, and she had accepted.

Jimmy and Florence corresponded while she was in Hamilton, and this was the undoing of her secret love affair. Isabel intercepted some of Jimmy's letters. She was shocked to discover that her daughter was involved in the theatre and that she intended to marry an actor. She returned a pearl and diamond brooch Jimmy had sent in the mail with a letter telling the young man that her daughter was already engaged.

Isabel and Ethel confronted Florence with what they knew. They told her they disapproved of her singing onstage. Furthermore, she would marry Clair Montrose Wright, and not some American actor. Thomas was also dead set against a marriage to a lowly actor.

Florence quickly wrote to Jimmy, telling him to address his letters to Mildred Dale, care of the Hamilton post office. But her family must have prevailed upon her to sever all ties with Baum. She finally sent him a letter breaking off the engagement. She said she was marrying Wright. This was just two weeks before the murder. Ethel allegedly told Florence that she had gotten rid of one husband, but she would not get rid of another.

Jimmy Baum, who seems to have been truly in love with Florence, had yet another story to tell, about something more sinister than the lies Florence had told her family—and him. Somebody, Jimmy testified, really had been "following" (today we would say "stalking") Florence in Virginia. He had seen one of the threatening letters she'd received, though he couldn't remember if it had been signed.

On one occasion, Jimmy said, Florence had been presented with a bouquet of flowers onstage. It wasn't until later that she read the card. She told him that if she had read that card onstage, "You would have had to carry me off." Another time an anonymous admirer sent Florence a box of candy. She was afraid they'd been poisoned.

Jimmy was convinced that Florence had an enemy somewhere; someone who told her in letters that he would shoot her onstage, "drag her over the footlights," or tell her family that she was working in a "dive." He testified (and Pender's sleuthing supported this) that before returning to Hamilton, Florence appeared to be under great strain. She spent ten days shut up in a cottage at Virginia Beach, afraid even to step outside.

Jimmy did not know who this "enemy" was. He said at first he thought it was her ex-husband. But when he learned there was no ex-husband, he though it might be Claude Elliot, Marion's brother. Florence had met him and taken an instant dislike to the man.

Before Jimmy Baum left the stand, he gave the Canadians a little display of Southern gallantry. He asked permission to make a statement, and when it was granted he said: "I just want to say that if any of the jury here thinks Miss Kinrade murdered her sister, he is making a big mistake. Find the person who chased Miss Florence Kinrade out of Portsmouth, and you will find the person who killed her sister Ethel."

On May 5, after ninety minutes of deliberation, the jury reached an open verdict: "...that the deceased met her death by shot wounds inflicted by some person or persons unknown to the jury." They requested that the Crown continue its investigation. There was simply not enough evidence to charge Florence with murder. When Jimmy Baum was told of the verdict, he said, "God bless them." He shook Clair Montrose Wright's hand, bid his farewell to Florence, and boarded a train for Virginia.

Thomas Kinrade soon resigned as school principal and moved his family away from Hamilton. Florence married Wright, who dropped his theological studies and took up law. They moved to Calgary, where Wright died of pneumonia in 1918. To support her two children, Florence did what she had always wanted to do and became an actress. She earned some fame as Florence Wright and even performed in Hamilton. She eventually went to California.

Like the Lizzie Borden story, the Kinrade murder remains an enigma. Quite possibly things happened more or less as Florence said they did, making some allowance for error in memory. Medical science wasn't very exact in 1909, and the doctors could have been wrong in their conclusion about the passage of fifteen minutes. The police might simply have failed to find the bullet that was fired at Florence as she ran from the house. Neither Florence nor the killer behaved rationally, but rationality is usually absent where murder is concerned.

Was Jimmy Baum correct in his belief that someone Florence feared from the South had followed her and awaited an opportunity? Had the killer thought Florence was alone in the house? If the killer was her tormentor from Virginia, why wouldn't she give that information to the police?

To speculate that Florence killed Ethel raises a whole crop of questions, the first being one of motive. Would Ethel's interference in Florence's choice of a career and a husband be reason enough for her to murder her own sister in cold blood? Or did sibling jealousy that had been smouldering for years suddenly erupt in searing rage? After the shooting, what did she do with the gun? Police searched the house from top to bottom, as well as the grounds, and found no murder weapon. Also, why would she describe the killer as dressed better than a tramp but not as well-dressed as a gentleman if she intended to blame the crime on an imaginary tramp? If Florence Kinrade *did* in fact kill her sister, one thing is certain: the performance she gave during the coroner's inquest was the greatest of her acting career.

MYSTERY ON THE GALLOWS

Who Hanged Gary Barrett?

Before this little-known tale is told, perhaps it would be worthwhile for the reader to know something of the history of capital punishment in Canada. In the earliest colonial days, death was the official penalty for more than two hundred crimes. These capital offences ranged from treason, murder and rape, to livestock rustling and armed robbery, to petty theft. In Halifax in 1785 a man was hanged for stealing a bag of potatoes. Children charged with crimes were often treated as adults. In 1803 a thirteen-year-old Quebec boy identified only as B. Clements was hanged for stealing a cow. The authorities of those times often expressed reluctance to hang women, but they did it anyway. The first person known to have been hanged in Upper Canada (Ontario) was Mary Osborn, who went to the gallows c.1791 for killing her husband. From the time of Confederation in 1867, until capital punishment was formally abolished in 1976, thirteen women were hanged in Canadian jails.

Over the years most crimes were dropped from the list of capital offences until only treason and first-degree murder remained.

The last person in Canada to be hanged for treason was Louis Riel after the 1885 Rebellion. After that time, all executions were for murder. Once a jury found a prisoner guilty of murder, the presiding judge was obliged to pronounce the death sentence. This did not necessarily mean the condemned person was hopelessly doomed; he or she had the right to appeal. Also, if the jury believed there were extenuating circumstances in the case, they might come to a verdict of guilty, but with a recommendation for mercy. Then it was up to the federal government in Ottawa to review the case and decide if the sentence should be commuted to life imprisonment. A recommendation for mercy did not guarantee a commutation. Many such recommendations were denied, even when accompanied by petitions signed by thousands of citizens. But the condemned person's chances were better with the recommendation than they were without it. Between 1867 and 1962—the year of Canada's last hanging—710 people were executed, while 438 sentences were commuted. Because pre-Confederation records were poorly kept or have been lost, nobody is certain how many people were hanged before Canada became a nation.

In the early days, a hanging was a public event. People came from miles around to watch an execution. Hawkers went through the crowds selling food and drinks. Pickpockets did a brisk business. Children perched on their father's shoulders so they could get a good look. Men who owned wagons sold standing space in them to spectators who wanted a better view. Newspaper editors routinely lamented over the large number of women who turned out to watch executions, but that did not stop the ladies from joining the menfolk in the throng around the gallows. At the double hanging of John Blowes and George King for murder at Cayuga, Canada West (Ontario), in 1855, when some women could not see past the men in the front ranks, a gallant constable asked the gentlemen to please step aside so the ladies could see. In 1861 a crowd of Montrealers had gathered in eager anticipation of a double hanging. When only one prisoner was brought out because the other man had been granted a last-minute reprieve, the crowd rioted. The people felt they'd been cheated!

Eventually executions were moved to within jailyard or prison walls. Attendance was by invitation only. Canada's last public hanging took place at Hull, Quebec, in 1902. But even when the executions were carried out behind walls, uninvited spectators climbed telegraph poles or paid to watch from upper-floor windows that overlooked the jailyard.

The kind of "show" that people saw at a public hanging depended upon the prisoner, the method of hanging, and the skill (or lack of it) of the executioner. Most of the condemned tried to meet death with a show of bravado. They would walk to the gallows unassisted, make a speech to the crowd (sometimes a very long one) in which they confessed their crimes and forgave their enemies, or protested their innocence and damned their accusers. Some fainted at the sight of the scaffold and had to be carried to it. A few, like Marie Anne Crispin of Montreal, condemned to hang for murder in 1858, put up a desperate fight. Crispin was a big woman, standing over 1.8 metres (six feet). When the hangman came to her cell, she punched him in the face. Female guards who were to have accompanied her to the gallows fled. Burly male guards had to drag her, kicking, biting and screaming all the way. She managed to throw several of them off the scaffold before someone finally got the rope around her neck and the hangman dropped her to her death.

Most hangmen were amateurs. Officially, the local sheriff presided over an execution. But few of them wanted to do the actual dirty work. Whenever possible, the sheriff would find someone else to do the job. Sometimes it would be another condemned prisoner whose life would be spared if he performed the execution. Or the hangman might be a private citizen who was willing to do the job for a fee. He would usually wear a mask or a hood to protect his identity. The pay wasn't much, but the hangman could claim the dead victim's clothing. He could also cut up the hanging rope and the death hood worn by the victim, and sell the pieces as souvenirs. An enterprising hangman would make the best of the occasion by chopping up and selling several ropes and hoods, including the ones he had actually used.

The first hangings were carried out simply by putting the noose around the prisoner's neck and then hoisting him up by means of a beam supported between two uprights, or swinging him from the branch of a sturdy tree. The victim's hands would be tied or his arms pinioned, but his legs would be free so he could kick as he strangled. Executioners believed the kicking helped tighten the noose, so death would come more quickly. But it also added to the thrill for the spectators to see the hanged man "dancing on air" as he died. If the hangman was a compassionate sort (or if he'd been bribed by family and friends of the condemned) he would pull on the victim's legs to bring a hasty end to the struggle.

"Hoisting" the victim was eventually replaced by the "drop," which meant the condemned had the noose placed around his neck and then stepped off the scaffold, was pushed off, or had a trap door open beneath his feet. The "drop" was considered humanitarian. The sudden plunge down, and the abrupt halt, was intended to break the victim's neck, killing him (or her) instantly. A problem arose, however, concerning the length of the drop.

Some hangmen experimented with the short drop, which required just a few feet of rope and a low scaffold. They found that the neck often did not break. The victim might hang for up to twenty minutes before the attending physician announced the heart had stopped beating. Even then, there were times that the doctor detected a pulse after the body had been cut down. Then all involved with the due process of law had to wait for that glimmer of life to go out before they could say that the convicted murderer had been "hanged by the neck until dead." One man actually had to be hanged a second time.

The alternative to the "short drop" was the "long drop." This required a higher scaffold and a longer rope. It supposedly guaranteed a quick death from a broken neck. Most hangmen, however, were not students of physics. Executioners had to take into account the prisoner's weight, the length of the drop and the tension of the rope. In a good, clean hanging, the prisoner's neck was broken without messy bloodshed. When all worked well, a prisoner who was taken from the death cell at 7:55 a.m. on the appointed day was pronounced dead a few seconds after eight o'clock. Fast, clean and painless! But it didn't always work that way.

If the hangman miscalculated one way, the prisoner's neck did not break and he slowly strangled. If the hangman miscalculated the other way, the victim was decapitated, as happened to murderer Thomas Cook when he was hanged at Woodstock in 1862.

Since few people at that time would even consider the idea of abolishing capital punishment, the solution was clear. The judicial system needed a professional hangman. The government found its man in John Robert Radclive (often misspelled in the newspapers of the time as Radcliff).

Radclive had served in the Royal Navy, where he learned all there was to know about ropes and knots. It was in the navy, too, that he learned something about hangings. Royal Navy discipline had always been almost Spartan in its harshness. By the latter half of the nineteenth century some of the more brutal practices had been discontinued, but sailors guilty of serious offenses were still hanged from yardarms. Radclive quite likely witnessed, and perhaps even was obliged to assist in shipboard executions.

Radclive became fascinated with hanging, so when he left the navy he went to London to meet William Marwood, England's official hangman. To Marwood, hanging was a science. He discarded the traditional thick, stiff rope with the bulky "hangman's knot." Instead, he used a thinner, softer rope that he stretched by repeated drops with cement bags. He also designed a noose that was more likely to snap the victim's neck. He replaced the series of slipknots that hangmen had been using for centuries with a metal ring that had a leather washer to prevent slipping. Conventional hangmen placed the knotted part of the noose behind the victim's left ear. Marwood placed the ring of his noose under the victim's chin. This resulted in a cleanly broken neck almost every time.

Marwood favoured the long drop, but was well aware of its potential for a bungled hanging. He designed a mathematical table that correlated the length of the drop to the weight of the condemned person. Prior to execution the prisoner was weighed; Marwood then simply had to consult his table to know how far the person should drop.

Radclive became Marwood's apprentice. He soon knew as much about the art of hanging as the master, although oddly enough, he preferred the old-fashioned noose to Marwood's innovation. In 1887 Radclive immigrated to Canada.

Radclive settled in Toronto and got a job as a steward at the Sunnyside Boating Club. The pay was low, so he informed several Ontario sheriffs of his experience as an executioner. In addition to his proven skill, Radclive had a hanging device of his own design. Instead of dropping the victim through the floor of a scaffold, Radclive would have the person stand on the ground with the noose around his neck. The other end of the rope was attached to a 159-kg (350-pound) iron weight. When Radclive pulled a pin, the iron weight dropped and the victim was jerked up into the air with sufficient force to dislocate the neck. The device was painless and efficient, and required only two upright posts and a crossbeam. It spared the county the cost of building a scaffold. Radclive believed his new method would spare the doomed prisoner the awful experience of climbing the steps to the gallows. Jail guards would call Radclive's system the "jerk 'em up gallows."

In February 1890 Radclive got his chance. Thomas Kane was to be hanged in Toronto for the murder of his wife. Kane had the dubious honour of being the first man executed by Radclive's invention. The execution went so smoothly that in June of that year Radclive was sent to Belleville to hang a convicted murderer named Peter Davis. Once again his device worked like a charm.

Then in November 1890 Radclive went to Woodstock to hang Reginald Birchall. The Birchall case was the most sensational news event of the time. Birchall was a former Oxford University student who had worked out a plot to lure wealthy young Englishmen to Canada where he could rob and murder them. He shot a youth named Frederick Benwell to death, but was thwarted in his attempt to murder a second lad. John Wilson Murray, Canada's "Great Detective," tracked Birchall down and arrested him.

Everything connected with the Birchall case made headline news, so his execution was well-attended by the press. Radclive's gallows now drew national attention. But when the moment arrived, it didn't work properly. Birchall strangled for eighteen minutes before he was pronounced dead.

Reginald Birchall was undeniably an evil man, and there were no tears shed over his ghastly end. But Radclive was shaken by this botched execution. He felt it was his duty to ensure that the sentence of the court be carried out in as humane a manner as possible, no matter whose neck was in the noose.

Some accounts have it that the messy Birchall hanging meant the end of Radclive's gallows. Actually, Radclive used the device in Sherbrooke, Quebec, just a month later to hang René Lamontagne. He was still using it in 1895 when he hanged Almeda Chatelle in Stratford, Ontario, for the rape, murder and mutilation of a thirteen-year-old Listowel girl named Jessie Keith. Throughout this time the "jerk 'em up gallows" did its grim duty well. Radclive was finally obliged to pack it away and go back to the conventional gallows because of bad publicity. A hanging victim who shot up into the air was just too spectacularly visible. Better to drop them—the skirting around the base of the scaffold hid the last spasms from view.

Unlike most executioners, Radclive did not wear a hood or mask. He showed up for work formally dressed in a black Prince Albert coat. He also used his own name professionally. In his private life he went by the alias Thomas Ratley to protect his wife and children. Eventually, however, his wife could no longer bear being married to a hangman. She left him, taking the children and changing their last name.

Radclive also lost his regular job at the Sunnyside Boating Club. A visiting Mounted Police inspector recognized him and complained. The policeman did not want his drinks served by a common hangman. Radclive had to pick up whatever odd jobs he could find between hangings.

In his career as executioner, Radclive would hang 132 men and women in jails all across Canada. They included some of the most highly publicized criminals of the time. Early in 1897, Radclive went to Fort McLeod in what is now Alberta to hang the Blood Native, Charcoal. This once-renowned warrior had murdered a Native named Medicine Pipe Stem, and then had killed North West Mounted Police Sergeant William Brock Wilde. Charcoal went on a hunger strike before his execution. He was too weak to stand on the scaffold, and had to be hanged sitting in a chair.

Later that year, in St. Scholastique, Quebec, Radclive hanged Samuel Parslow and Cordelia Viau back-to-back. The pair had murdered Viau's husband. Two hundred invitation cards were issued for the execution, but a mob of two thousand tried to break down the prison doors to get in. Police had to disperse them with gunfire. Inside the prison yard, as soon as the condemned couple dropped, the two hundred guests surged forward and tore down the blankets that skirted the scaffold so they could see the twitching bodies. They, too, had to be forced back by police.

In 1899 Radclive was the hangman at one of the most tragic executions in Canadian history. An English servant girl named Hilda Blake, twenty-one, had killed her master's wife in Brandon, Manitoba. Hilda had been orphaned as a child and sent to Canada to go into service. She'd been passed from one indifferent family to another before arriving at the home of Robert Lane. Like most servants at that time, Hilda received little more regard than a piece of furniture. Out of envy for the affection shown to the Lane children—the kind of affection she'd never known—Hilda shot Mrs. Lane. She told police a passing tramp had done the deed, but when constables arrested a vagrant and accused him of the crime, Hilda exonerated him. She confessed to the murder when police found her gun.

A jury found her guilty, with a recommendation for mercy. As her execution date drew near, public sympathy for her grew and many Manitobans signed a petition asking that her death sentence be commuted. But the government would not grant her clemency. Persons of the serving class could not be allowed to get away with shooting their social betters. The crowds stayed away from Hilda's execution. The newspapers called it "lawful murder."

The Blake hanging bothered Radclive considerably. Many years later he said in an interview, "I argued with myself that if I was doing wrong, then the government of the country was wrong. I held that I was the Minister of Justice at a hanging, and that if I was a murderer, then he was also a murderer."

Radclive's travel expenses came out of his pay, so early in the twentieth century he took on an assistant who worked under the name J.H. Holmes. Because Holmes lived in Regina, Radclive allowed him to handle some of the executions in the western provinces. There was one western execution, however, that would add a mystery to the dark legend of Radclive the hangman.

In October 1907 Gary R. Barrett tried to kill his wife on their farm near Prince Albert, Saskatchewan. Barrett had been suffering from depression, and one day he picked up his revolver and pointed it at his wife. Their ten-year-old son Burnett jumped in front of his mother. When Barrett fired, the bullet struck the boy in the arm, severing an artery. Ten days later he died.

Barrett was tried for murder and found guilty, but with a recommendation for mercy. He was sentenced to hang, but the government commuted the death sentence to one of life imprisonment. Barrett was sent to the Alberta Penitentiary in Edmonton.

Barrett continued to have fits of depression, but prisons at that time were not equipped to deal with inmates' psychological problems. One April morning in 1909 Barrett was sharpening a hatchet in the prison shop, under the supervision of Deputy Warden Richard Stedman. Without warning Barrett whirled around and struck the guard down with the hatchet, killing him on the spot.

Barrett probably should have been sent to an asylum. Instead, he was tried again for murder. The jury took only five minutes to reach a guilty verdict. There was no recommendation for mercy, no reprieve from Ottawa. Barrett was sentenced to hang on July 1. The Edmonton sheriff, a man named Robertson, sent for Radclive—or so he said.

Radclive usually arrived in a town the day before a scheduled execution. Edmonton reporters hoping for an interview searched the hotels, but could not find the hangman. They thought that perhaps Holmes had been sent instead, so they did the rounds of the hotels again. They could not find Holmes, either.

The newspapermen went to Sheriff Robertson and asked him who was going to hang Barrett. First Robertson said Radclive was going to do the job. A few minutes later he said it would be Holmes. Finally he refused to answer any more questions.

Hard-nosed reporters generally knew when someone wasn't being straight with them. These men thought there was something fishy about Sheriff Robertson's evasiveness. Why didn't he seem to know which of the hangmen was coming to drop Barrett? The reporters found themselves pondering a rather alarming possibility. Could it be that the sheriff hadn't sent for a professional at all, and was about to put Barrett in the hands of an amateur?

Their suspicions were confirmed the next morning when they went to the prison to witness the execution. The hangman who brought Barrett from the death cell was hooded. Everyone knew Radclive didn't wear a hood. Some of the newspapermen had seen Holmes work before, and they knew the hooded man was not he. They looked at the executioner's shoes and saw they were regulation prison boots—the type issued to guards with their uniforms.

Whatever the identity of the man under the hood, he was not a professional hangman. When Barrett stepped on the trap door, he began to make a farewell speech. The hangman immediately put the hood over his head and the noose around his neck, choking off his words. The noose had to be loosened so Barrett could speak his last.

When the prisoner had said his piece, he began to recite the Lord's Prayer with the attending priest. The hangman was so anxious to pull the lever, he almost did it while the priest was still standing on the trap. The worst was yet to come.

The obviously inexperienced hangman had not set the noose in the proper position around Barrett's neck. When Barrett dropped, the noose slipped around so it was in his face. The neck did not break, and Barrett slowly strangled. The hangman's clumsiness did not end there. Twice he tried to cut Barrett down, and had to be stopped by the attending doctor because there was still a heartbeat. When the doctor finally pronounced Barrett dead, the hangman cut him down. He immediately sliced the rope into pieces and distributed them to the guards.

Radclive is credited with Barrett's execution. But Radclive was definitely not the hangman that day. Nor was Holmes. The reporters were certain that the guards, seeking vengeance on the man who had killed their colleague, selected one of their own number to dispatch him. Sheriff Robertson was certainly in on it. How he arranged to prevent Radclive or Holmes from doing the job is not known. One of the reporters later thought he saw a guard wearing the same shoes as the man who had done the hanging. But the identity of the man under the hood remained a secret. One can only wonder what Radclive would have thought of such a messy hanging being done in his name.

By this time Radclive himself was suffering psychological problems because of his profession. He was drinking heavily, especially after a hanging—though he never drank before one. He once told a reporter, "The remorse which comes over me is terrible and my nerves give out until I have not slept days at a time. I used to say to condemned persons as I beckoned with my hand, 'Come with me.' Now at night when I lie down, I start up with a roar as victim after victim comes up before me. I can see them on the trap, waiting a second before they face their Maker. They taunt me and haunt me until I am nearly crazy with an unearthly fear."

In 1912 Radclive died in Toronto from the effects of alcoholism. Only after he was gone did the Canadian government understand what a craftsman he had been, because he was not easy to replace. There were several badly botched hangings before they finally found another professional hangman in 1913. Like Radclive, he was from Britain. His name was Arthur Bartholemew English, but Canadians would know him as John Ellis. Condemned murderers could take some comfort, perhaps, in knowing they would be in the hands of a hangman as competent as Radclive.

THE OAKES MYSTERY

Who Killed Sir Harry?

As a young man Harry Oakes dreamed of being wealthy. But he was not a dreamer who passively waited for fortune to come his way. Oakes was an adventurous, driven man who went after fame and wealth with confident determination. He would finally seize his golden prize in the Canadian wilds, and in so doing make his name a legend. However, fortune of another kind would ultimately find Harry Oakes and strike him down, far from Canada, leaving behind a mystery that is nonetheless Canadian.

Unlike many fortune hunters, Harry Oakes did not come from poverty, though he would certainly know hardship during his years of struggle. He was born in Maine in 1874, the third of five children in a middle-class family with strong Christian values. Lessons in philanthropy he learned from his devout mother stayed with him all his eventful life.

Oakes received a good education at the finest schools his parents could afford. Upon graduation from Bowdoin College in Brunswick, Maine, he attended medical school in Syracuse, New

York. His ambition to become a doctor diminished considerably when he realized most doctors did not make much money—at least, not the kind of money Harry Oakes wanted. That ambition succumbed completely during the epidemic of gold fever that gripped the world with news of the big strike on the Klondike River in Canada's Yukon Territory. Young Harry wanted to quit medical school, pack up his gear, and join the thousands who were heading north by whatever means possible to prospect for gold. Even though Oakes was obsessed with getting rich, he did not want to do it by exploiting other people, as so many of the industrial barons of his time were doing. Yukon gold seemed the perfect solution.

Harry's family was behind him all the way. This might have surprised people since so many young men went north in defiance of parents and other relatives. But in the Oakes family there was a "one for all and all for one" attitude. Harry's mother spent a large portion of her personal savings to equip him for the adventure. His brother Louis promised to send him $75 a month until he struck it rich. His sister Gertrude, a lowly bank stenographer, said she would send him whatever she could, as long as he needed it.

In 1897, twenty-three-year-old Harry Oakes struck out for the Klondike, certain he would return home rich. He didn't. Like most of the *cheechakos* who braved the hazards of the journey to the Canadian El Dorado, Oakes found only cold, hardship and disappointment. But he was beginning to learn some things about the nature of elusive gold and the men who sought it.

Oakes followed the next big rush to Alaska. Hard luck followed him. He did not strike pay dirt, and had to earn his daily bread by working as a medical assistant treating frostbite victims. He himself almost froze to death. One story has it that he was briefly a prisoner on a Russian ship.

If people who knew Harry Oakes in those heady days thought him a dreamer, they would also have had to call him a survivor. Harry's quest for wealth took him around the world, often working his way as a deckhand aboard a ship. He visited places that anyone back home in Maine would have considered exotic: the Pacific islands, the Philippines, New Zealand, Australia, Central Africa, Mexico, then back to the United States to California's Death Valley.

Oakes packed more adventure into a few years than most people would in a lifetime. He endured Arctic cold, desert heat, a shipwreck, a cave full of rattlesnakes, and often the company of men who could best be described as hard cases. But still he had no gold. A lesser man would have cut his losses and given up. Harry Oakes was more determined than ever to realize his dream. He was not just pushing ahead on raw stubbornness. He studied geology. Wherever he went, he made notes about the kind of ground in which men luckier than he had found gold.

In 1911 Oakes was in the American West, thinking of trying his luck again in the Yukon, when he heard of some small gold strikes in the Porcupine and Cobalt regions of Ontario. He decided that the Yukon had had its chance. Still in his prime at thirty-six, Oakes boarded a train for Canada. He got off in the town of Swastika in Northern Ontario. Harry didn't know it yet, but he was finally on the road to destiny.

Oakes boarded at a house owned by a Hungarian woman named Roza Brown. Roza generally considered prospectors a lazy, unimaginative lot who tended to move on when the easy pickings were gone. But she liked Harry because he was determined to find the gold the others had overlooked. She had some knowledge of the region and told him which sites she considered worthy of investigation. One promising location, she said, was Kirkland Lake.

When Oakes went to Kirkland Lake in January 1912 he had his prospecting tools and $2.65. All of the ground there had been staked, he was told. By this time Harry knew the ways of prospectors. He looked through the files of the local mines office and found that several claims were about to expire; some in a matter of hours. This was because the men who had filed the claims had not worked them the required minimum of forty days a year. To Harry's experienced eye, some of the locations looked promising.

Oakes had no money, but he talked four brothers named Tough into a partnership. If they would put up the money, he would show them where the most likely claims were. If they found gold—and Oakes was certain they would—they would share the rewards.

The men set out in weather so intensely cold, Harry wore five pairs of pants. They drove their claiming stakes into frozen rock, and ground frozen so hard it might as well have been rock. But they found gold!

The strike was no bonanza, but it paid enough to finance other explorations. Eventually Oakes and the Tough brothers had a falling out. Harry sold his share in the partnership and set out once again on his own.

Prospectors had searched most of the country around Kirkland Lake, but they had ignored the region at the lake's southern bay.

They said it was not promising ground for gold. Oakes staked out that ground. He wasn't going to explore just the shore of the lake; he was going to dig *under* the lake. Because the project would cost more money than Harry could raise himself, he went looking for backers.

There was a saying in Northern Ontario at that time: "A gold mine is a hole in the ground with a fool at the top." People thought Harry Oakes was just such a fool. Nobody would risk a penny on his venture.

Finally Harry's mother sent him what money she had left. A Chinese boarding house operator named Charlie Chow also gave Oakes some financial help in return for shares in the mine. That would turn out to be the smartest financial decision the man ever made.

Harry Oakes started digging in 1918 and struck gold almost immediately. This time it *was* a bonanza! Harry's gold mine turned out to be the richest in Canada and the second most productive in the world. After a lifetime of hard work, danger and disappointment, Harry Oakes was a multi-millionaire. By 1920 he was considered to be the richest man in Canada. Harry's family and his friend Charlie Chow were also very wealthy people.

Harry Oakes' dream had come true with a vengeance. At a time when the average working man was lucky to make $1,000 a year, Harry was pulling in $60,000 a *day*. He quickly adapted to a life of wealth and luxury. Oakes built a lovely chateau overlooking the site of his Lake Shore Mine. He constructed his own private golf course. He generously gave shares in his mining company to friends. Then, when his mother died in 1923, the grieving Harry sought consolation in a world cruise.

In Sydney, Australia, Harry met Eunice MacIntyre, a bank stenographer. It was love at first sight, and the two were soon married. Eunice was twenty-four, Harry was forty-nine. She was tall, graceful, and gentle in her ways. He was short, stocky, and presented a gruff exterior that masked the kinder soul within. The couple would eventually have five children.

Back in Kirkland Lake, Harry built an even bigger house. He also had two houses in England and one in Palm Beach, Florida. But though Oakes liked to show off his wealth, he was by no means selfish. He built a skating rink for the children of Kirkland Lake. He financed a tree-planting program to provide work for unemployed men. He bought and donated land for parks, and gave the city of Niagara Falls the beautiful Oakes Garden Theatre. Many schools and charities benefited from the largesse of Harry Oakes.

Bringing Eunice to Canada created an unforeseen problem. She had forfeited her Australian passport when she married an American. In Canada, Harry was a foreigner. This made Eunice technically a woman without a country. To solve the problem Harry became a Canadian citizen, which automatically made his wife a citizen, too.

For several years the Oakes family lived happily in Canada. Oddly enough, considering his generous ways, Harry was not terribly popular with the locals. This may have been because of the uncouth exterior he always presented to the world. He was also known to have a volcanic temper. Harry could be vindictive with people he thought had wronged him, but he was not known as a man who held a grudge. The resentment some people felt might simply have stemmed from envy and the fact that Oakes had proven so many of them wrong.

Harry now wanted something more than money; he wanted prestige. With the 1930 federal election approaching, Oakes actively—and generously—supported the incumbent Liberal Party, quite sure that Prime Minister William Lyon Mackenzie King would win. Harry expected a grateful King would reward him with an appointment to the Senate.

However, the Liberals went down to defeat at the hands of R.B. Bennett's Conservatives. With malicious glee the Tories slapped an exorbitant tax on Harry's huge income. They even taxed him for the parklands he had donated to various municipalities.

Oakes actually became physically ill when he received the news of what amounted to punitive measures because of his support of the Liberals. He was confined to his bed for two weeks. When he felt well enough to travel, he went to his house in Palm Beach. There he learned that a wealthy man could live almost tax-free in the Bahamas. Oakes went back to Canada, packed up his family and moved to Nassau.

Oakes still made regular trips to Canada, but by 1935 he was a full-time resident of the Bahamas, which was still a British colony. He took out Bahamian citizenship. He and his family lived in a beautiful mansion he called Westbourne. And once again Harry was generous to his new adopted country.

Oakes was a one-man boost to the struggling Bahamian economy. He financed a milk program for poor school children. He built a new wing on Nassau's general hospital. He paid for seaplanes and other light aircraft to bring patients from the colony's many islands to the hospital. At Eunice's suggestion, Harry brought in Italian craftsmen to teach local people how to carve artifacts from conch shells, so they could sell them to tourists. He introduced new agricultural products like strawberries, and imported sheep to improve the local stock.

Harry's money developed Nassau's first airport and started a new airline. Oakes built a hotel, a country club and a seaside golf course. When he learned that the local population lacked skilled workers, he set up training programs so they could learn the skills necessary for them to work on his many projects. He even provided free transportation to and from work. He gave large sums of money to the cash-strapped colonial government to help ease the burden of unemployment. Harry was glad to share his good fortune with others. In Canada he had simply objected to having his pocket picked by the short-sighted Tory bureaucrats who had taken charge in Ottawa.

Harry Oakes' philanthropy did not go unnoticed. In 1939 King George VI knighted him in recognition of his good works in the Bahamas. Harry Oakes from Maine was now Sir Harry. He had money *and* prestige. That did not mean he suddenly closed his wallet. No sooner had he been made a member of the aristocracy than the Second World War broke out. Harry did his bit for the Allied war effort.

He paid for three Spitfire fighter planes that saw action in the Battle of Britain. He bought a boarding house in Nassau and had it converted into a home for children evacuated from Britain during the blitz. He constructed airfields for the use of Allied aircraft. Etienne Dupuch, editor and publisher of the *Tribune,* Nassau's main newspaper, said of Sir Harry Oakes:

"By contrast with the activities of so many wealthy people in the community, Sir Harry's investments were not made with any regard to his personal future. They were made with the sole idea of helping others."

Sir Harry Oakes had it all. He was one of the most influential men in the Bahamas. Some of the more genteel folk probably didn't approve of his unpolished social manners, but aside from some disgruntled politicians back in Canada, Oakes should not have had an enemy in the world. But he did!

Harry and Eunice's eldest daughter, Nancy, was born in Toronto. After the move to Nassau her parents sent her to schools in Britain and New York. She spent her summers with the family at Westbourne. By the time Nancy turned seventeen in 1941, she was a strikingly beautiful young woman. That year, at a dance in Nassau, she met thirty-two-year-old Count Marie Alfred Fouquereaux de Marigny, known to his friends as Freddie Marigny.

De Marigny was from the French colony of Mauritius. He was a son of aristocrats but had turned his back on his family and his title. He was twice-divorced and had known some hard times. Since his arrival in Nassau he had prospered in the poultry business. Though de Marigny no longer used his title, he mingled with Nassau's high society and so met Sir Harry Oakes. He had even been a guest at Westbourne.

Standing six-foot-five, handsome, charming and sophisticated, de Marigny had a reputation as a playboy and a womanizer. This earned him the resentment of many of the men in Nassau's elite social circles. He was also a sailing enthusiast, and entered his yacht in numerous racing competitions, winning most of them. This, too, became a source of jealousy. The fact that he named his yacht *The Concubine*, which was considered highly inappropriate in a society still mired in Victorian morality, did not help matters.

Nancy Oakes and Freddie de Marigny fell in love and were secretly engaged. When Nancy returned to New York for school, Freddie followed her. On May 19, 1942, two days after her eighteenth birthday, Nancy and Freddie were married. Nancy phoned home to tell her parents the news.

Harry and Eunice were shocked and hurt. Freddie de Marigny was not the man they wanted for a son-in-law. Nonetheless, they tried at first to accept him into the family. Harry offered Freddie money and a job, which de Marigny politely declined. He was doing well enough on his own.

Try as he would, Harry could not hide his anger over the marriage for long. As far as he was concerned, de Marigny was a contemptible cradle-robber. He was certain, too, that the dashing playboy was still cavorting with other women. He let his friends know in no uncertain terms that he disapproved of the marriage. Soon Sir Harry and Freddie were quarrelling publicly. The ongoing feud drove a rift between Nancy and her parents. The situation deteriorated further when Nancy became pregnant and had to have an abortion for health reasons.

His daughter's marriage was not the only source of turmoil in Sir Harry Oakes' world. He was involved—possibly without being fully aware of it—in Byzantine plots that involved the Mafia, Nazi agents and the British Royal Family. A key figure was the Duke of Windsor, formerly King Edward VIII, the man who caused the scandal of the century when he abdicated the throne so he could marry a divorced American woman, Wallis Simpson.

At the outbreak of the war, Edward was sent to the Bahamas as Royal Governor. Supposedly this was to keep him out of the reach of Nazi kidnappers. But there were suspicions, too, that he had Nazi sympathies and was sent to the Bahamas to get him out of the way. Harry Oakes came to know the Duke of Windsor well. They often played golf.

Among the Duke's associates in Nassau was Axel Wenner-Gren, a Swedish-born industrialist. He was known to have close ties with top Nazi Hermann Goering, and boasted of a friendly relationship with Italian dictator Benito Mussolini. Wenner-Gren established a bank in Mexico, which Allied intelligence suspected of financing weapons and petroleum deals for the Axis powers. The Duke of Windsor and Sir Harry Oakes were clients of that bank.

The Allies believed Wenner-Gren was a Nazi spy. While he was on vacation in Mexico they blacklisted him and froze his assets. He had to stay in neutral Mexico or risk being arrested.

Then there was Sir Harry's good friend Harold Christie. He was a native white Bahamian who had been born poor but made a fortune in real estate. He owed much of his success to Harry Oakes, who bought numerous properties from him. Christie wanted to help the Bahamas develop as a tourist destination. He believed that quality hotels and reliable transportation between Miami and Nassau were vital to the colony's economic future. He was enthusiastic when a man named Frank Marshall approached him in the early 1940s with a plan to build gambling casinos. Marshall said he represented a cartel of American businessmen. He knew that Christie had influence with two very important men, the Duke of Windsor and Sir Harry Oakes.

At that time gambling was illegal in the Bahamas. Marshall wanted Christie to use his winning ways to convince Sir Harry and the Duke to help change the law. The Duke was certainly interested; he was always looking for money to support the extravagant lifestyle he and the Duchess lived. But Oakes was dead set against casinos.

By now Christie was aware that the "businessmen" Marshall represented were Meyer Lansky and Charles "Lucky" Luciano, two of America's most notorious and powerful gangsters. Just how deeply Christie became involved with them was never fully ascertained. One thing was sure: Lansky and Luciano were not known for taking no for an answer.

On the night of July 7, 1943, Sir Harry was the only member of the Oakes family home in Westbourne. Eunice was at their summer home in Bar Harbor, Maine, where Sir Harry was to join her in a couple of days. The Oakes children were at various places in Canada and the United States. However, there were guests at the house that evening. Harold Christie was there with his niece and one of her friends. Harry's neighbours Charles Hubbard and Dulcibelle Henneage were also paying a visit.

The two young women left early, but the other guests stayed to have dinner and play Chinese checkers.

Hubbard and Mrs. Henneage left at about eleven o'clock. The story of what happened over the next eight hours was told later by Christie.

Christie decided to spend the night in the guest bedroom, as he often did. He and Oakes went upstairs to Sir Harry's bedroom where they talked for about fifteen minutes. Then Sir Harry put on his pajamas and got into bed. He was reading a newspaper when Christie left him.

Christie went to his room and read a magazine for half an hour before going to sleep. He woke up once when he was being bothered by mosquitoes and again when the noise of a rainstorm disturbed him. Aside from the sound of the rain, he heard nothing unusual.

Christie awoke at dawn and went out onto the balcony where he and Oakes usually had breakfast. Sir Harry wasn't there, so he went to the screen door of Oakes' room and called, "Hi, Harry." Later, Christie described what happened next.

"There was no reply, so I opened the door and went in. I noticed that the mosquito net had disappeared and the wooden frame was charred. I rushed to the bed and saw Sir Harry lying diagonally across it, his head about a foot from the south side. I was greatly shocked, naturally, because we were so friendly. I can hardly describe the feeling.

"I lifted his head, shook him, and poured some water from a Thermos bottle, on a table between the two beds, into his mouth, and held his head up so that he would not choke. I wet a towel and wiped his face. I believe the towel came from my bathroom. Sir Harry's body was warm, and I felt there was still hope. It was approximately seven o'clock. I moved a pillow from the other bed and put it under his head. I rushed onto the north porch and shouted for help."

Sir Harry Oakes, sixty-nine, was dead. On the left side of his head were four triangular indentations, each less than half an inch across, set about two inches apart in the form of a square. Whatever had caused these wounds had cracked his skull. Christie found Oakes lying on his back, but blood from the wounds had run down across his face. This indicated that Oakes had not been on his back when struck. He had either turned over himself or the body had been moved.

The killer had then started a fire, quite likely hoping flames would engulf the house and destroy all evidence. The body had been soaked with gasoline, as had the bed, the mosquito netting, the rugs and curtains. An electric fan was set on the floor beside the bed, evidently to accelerate the fire's spread.

But the rainstorm that had briefly awakened Christie had blown through the screens into Sir Harry's room and doused the fire. There was fire damage to the netting and bedding, and Oakes' pajamas were half-burned. The dead man's face was blackened with soot, and feathers from a pillow were stuck to it. Heat blisters had arisen on various parts of the body. That meant Oakes had been alive, though not necessarily conscious, when the fire started.

More than one person had been involved in the murder. Handprints were all over the walls. An ornate Chinese screen near the bed was covered with fingerprints and spattered blood. Mud, sand and footprints on the stairs leading up to the bedroom clearly indicated this was not the work of a lone assassin. Whoever had done the deed had no trouble getting into the house. Like most Nassau residents, Oakes did not lock his doors at night. Theft was almost unheard of in the Bahamas.

After finding the body, Christie phoned his brother Frank and told him to fetch a doctor. Frank did so and also called the police. Then Etienne Dupuch, the newspaper editor, phoned Westbourne to confirm an appointment he had with Oakes. The distraught Christie told him Sir Harry was dead. Dupuch was stunned. But he was a newsman, and he got off a cable that went around the world. Almost everything about the Oakes murder case that happened after that reeked of cover-up, frame-up and deception.

When the Duke of Windsor, who was scheduled to play golf with Sir Harry that very day, received the news he immediately took "a personal hand" in the investigation. He placed a forty-eight-hour publication ban on any news about the death. This was done too late to stop Dupuch's cable, resulting in much misinformation being spread verbally and even published outside the Bahamas.

Then the Duke used his authority to keep the local police department, which was run by experienced British officers, from investigating the crime. He sent for two Miami detectives, Captain James Barker and Captain Edward Melchen. Captain Melchen had once served as a personal bodyguard for the Duke, and Edward liked him. These American policemen, operating in a British colony, conducted an investigation that has gone down as one of the most completely botched in the annals of crime. Why the Duke brought in these men, when he could have put Scotland Yard or even the FBI on the case was never explained. It would be revealed much later that Barker was a crooked cop in the pay of the Mafia.

The Miami detectives arrived without vital equipment for taking forensic evidence. They allowed curious civilians to walk through the crime scene. They instructed local police officers to wash away handprints and fingerprints they considered unimportant to the investigation. Some evidence they did collect, including fingerprints, was mysteriously lost.

Thirty-six hours after Oakes was found dead, the Americans arrested Freddie de Marigny for the murder. They claimed to have found Freddie's fingerprint on the Chinese screen. "It is a ridiculous charge," Freddie said. He insisted he hadn't spoken to Sir Harry in over three months, and hadn't been to Westbourne in two years. But there were people on the island who very much wanted Freddie de Marigny to be found guilty. He would be hanged, and the case would be closed forever.

As soon as Freddie was arrested he told the police he wanted to speak to Alfred Adderley, a black Bahamian who was considered the best lawyer in the colony. He wanted Adderley to defend him. But Adderley never received the message. Instead, he was chosen to represent the Crown as prosecutor. De Marigny hired Godfrey Higgs as his defence counsel.

When word of the arrest reached the streets, an angry crowd formed in front of the jail. Sir Harry had been very popular with the common people because of his generosity. Now his ungrateful son-in-law, a foreigner, had murdered him. Fearful that a lynch mob might storm the jail, the Duke sent out the fire brigade to turn their hoses on the crowd if things got ugly. The crowd dispersed. The Duke had merely maintained law and order, as a governor should. He was not doing any favours for Freddie. He had already told Eunice there was no doubt her son-in-law had killed her husband.

Barker and Melchen told Nancy, who'd been in Vermont, the same thing. They were absolutely certain her husband had murdered her father. Nancy grieved for her father, but she thought the charge against Freddie was absurd. She hired an American private detective named Raymond Schindler to conduct a separate investigation. Schindler got no cooperation from the police. His phone was tapped. But a test Schindler gave Freddie with an early version of a lie detector indicated Freddie was innocent.

Police took Freddie's chauffeur to the jail and told him to make a statement that he had driven Freddie to Westbourne the night Sir Harry died. The driver refused. Police officers beat him up, but he still refused.

Police also visited several of de Marigny's friends who had agreed to testify for the defence. These friends were accused of speaking for Freddie only because they were being paid to do so. They were warned about the consequences of perjury and told not to consort with a murderer. A Nassau police official who could have been an important witness for the defence was suddenly given a post outside the Bahamas.

Some of de Marigny's friends thought the level of hostility against him in Nassau was too high for him to have a chance for a fair trial. They wanted the venue moved to Jamaica, Bermuda or Canada. It was decided, however, that this would be too costly.

Freddie de Marigny's trial in the Supreme Court of the Bahamas began on October 18, 1943. It was a sensation not only in the Bahamas, but also around the world. News of the trial actually knocked reports of the war off the front pages of major newspapers. The Duke and Duchess were conveniently away on an extended vacation at the time of the trial, so Edward could not be summoned as a witness.

Godfrey Higgs subjected an extremely nervous Harold Christie to a harrowing cross-examination. The lawyer said witnesses had seen Christie leave Westbourne the night of the murder. Furthermore, he had been seen in the company of some unidentified strangers who entered Nassau's harbour in a motor launch under cover of darkness. That launch had been gone in the morning. Higgs' line of questioning inferred that Christie had a hand in the murder.

Christie insisted he did not leave Westbourne that night. However, the only man who could have confirmed whether or not Christie had been with the strangers from the launch was a night watchman. That man's body was hauled out of the water shortly after Freddie's arrest: victim of an "accidental" drowning. But Harold Christie was not on trial for his life. Freddie de Marigny was. As the trial proceeded the noose seemed to be tightening around his neck.

Oakes' displeasure with the marriage was no secret. Many people in Nassau believed Freddie had married Nancy only so he could get his hands on her father's money. One witness for the prosecution testified that Freddie had told him, "That guy, Sir Harry, the old bastard, should have been killed anyhow."

Another said he had witnessed a quarrel between Oakes and de Marigny in which Sir Harry told Freddie, "You had better not write any more letters to my wife. You are a sex maniac!" Yet another swore he had heard Freddie threaten to crack Sir Harry's head open.

Bad as the situation looked for de Marigny in the early stages of the trial, things began to change when James Barker and Edward Melchen had their turns in the stand. Little by little the jury learned how those two men had totally bungled the investigation and even manipulated evidence. Their admission of mistakes and their inability to answer key questions severely undermined the Crown's case.

Freddie had always claimed he had been in his own home the night of the murder. The prosecution attacked that story vigorously, and seemed to have disproved it. But then Georges Visdelou, who had been de Marigny's guest that night, confirmed that Freddie had indeed been home.

If the jury had any doubts about Freddie's innocence, those were dispelled when Nancy de Marigny testified. Nancy told the court about the difficulties the marriage had caused. She said she had disapproved of her parents' attitude toward Freddie and had refused to accept money they tried to give her as "gifts that have the smell of charity to a poor relative."

Nancy said she and Freddie did not need her father's money. Freddie had never asked her for money. She had invested a few thousand pounds of her own savings in his poultry business as an equal partner. Freddie had never asked her about her parents' wills. He had never spoken ill of her father in spite of the "disagreeable episodes." She had never been "cut off" by her parents. She had only ceased to communicate with them in the hope they would change their attitude toward Freddie. Nancy's testimony concerning what Barker and Melchen had told her about the supposedly incriminating fingerprint seriously contradicted what the Miami officers had told the court.

Nancy's testimony tipped the scales. On November 12, after two hours' deliberation, the jury found Freddie not guilty. The mob that had been howling for his blood a few months earlier now danced in the streets. How could they ever have thought that poor fellow could have killed Sir Harry? But if Freddie didn't do it, who did? Strangely, though he had been acquitted of the crime, Freddie was told to get out of the Bahamas. He and Nancy went to Cuba. They were eventually divorced.

Erle Stanley Gardner, the novelist who created Perry Mason, said the Oakes murder was the greatest mystery of all time. As Sir Harry was laid to rest in Bar Harbor, Maine, and after Freddie de Marigny was released, theories cropped up by the score. Some claimed Nazi agents were responsible. They had been afraid Sir Harry might expose the Duke's alleged connections with Hitler.

Others pointed to American organized crime. Lansky and Luciano had knocked Oakes off, according to some people, because he stood in the way of their casino scheme. There was even speculation that Christie had witnessed Sir Harry's murder at the hands of Luciano's thugs, and was then told to keep his mouth shut if he knew what was good for him. Furthermore, he was instructed to pass that warning on to the Duke of Windsor.

None of this, however, could be proven. All attempts to reopen the investigation were stonewalled. Years later an American journalist named Betty Renner went to Nassau to look into the Oakes murder. Her body was found in a well. That murder, too, went unsolved.

Sir Harry Oakes' former home in Kirkland Lake is now a museum to his memory. His name is in the Canadian Mining Hall of Fame. He is, however, remembered as much for his brutal, unsolved murder, as for his spectacular discovery of gold.

THE WAKAW MYSTERY

Prairie Massacre

In April 1916, Canada and her allies were mired down in a bloody stalemate in the most horrific war the world had ever known. In the muddy, rat-infested trenches of France and Belgium, soldiers of the Canadian Expeditionary Force were dying from artillery barrages, machine-gun fire, poison gas and the ravages of disease. The word *massacre* had appeared in the newspapers so often, it had lost its potential for shock. Yet, one massacre—miniscule though it was compared to the appalling carnage in Europe—would stun Canadians with its sheer, cold-hearted ruthlessness. For this was a massacre not of armed troops in No Man's Land, but of a defenseless family in rural Saskatchewan.

In the early morning of April 6, 1916, a farmer living in the vicinity of Wakaw, a small community ninety km (fifty-five miles) northeast of Saskatoon, stepped out of his house and was startled to see smoke rising over the property of his neighbour, Prokop Manchur. He hurried over to investigate. What he found was horrifying. The house and barn had both been burned to the ground. A man lay dead in the snow between the remains of the two buildings. He had been shot in the head. There was no sign that anyone else had escaped the burning house. The stench of burned flesh told the neighbour that the cattle and horses had been cremated in the barn. There was nothing to do but send for the police.

A Royal Canadian Mounted Police constable named Dey was the first officer on the scene. He was soon joined by an inspector named Duffus, a Staff Sergeant Prime, and two more constables. Their report described the scene of one of the worst incidents of mass murder in Canadian history.

"Amongst the ruins of the fire were found the charred remains of Prokop Manchur, age forty-six, and his daughters, Antone and Paulina, aged fifteen and twenty years respectively. In the cellar, which was under an adjoining room, were found the remains of Mary Manchur (wife of Prokop) and her baby, aged two years. They were both dead, but the bodies were not burned. Entrance to the cellar was gained by means of a ladder from the room above. Mary Manchur's legs were caught in the rungs of the ladder, and her forehead was against a large stone on the floor. The front of her head was smashed in and part of the brains were deposited on the ground. Her baby was lying by her side, in a position which suggested it had fallen out of her arms. Upon examining these two bodies it was found that Mary Manchur had two bullet wounds in her arm and two bullets were also found lodged in the baby's body.

"Upon examining the charred remains of the three victims found in the kitchen, evidence of bullet wounds was found in each. Lying on the snow a short distance from the house was yet another body, the remains of John Mychaluk, brother-in-law of Prokop Manchur. These remains were begrimed with smoke, but not burned. In the centre of the forehead was a bullet hole which went right through the head."

An entire family of six had been wiped out, and the flames had left little in the way of evidence. Examination of the remains of the horses and cattle showed that they had all been shot before the barn burned down around them.

From interviews with neighbours the police learned that Paulina Manchur had been briefly married to Mike Syroshka, an Austrian immigrant. The marriage had not worked out well, and Paulina left her husband and returned to her father's home. Syroshka had allegedly threatened to kill the entire Manchur family if Paulina did not return to him. Syroshka and a friend named Stefinuk were arrested on suspicion. Both men had solid alibis for their whereabouts at the time of the fire and were released. The police turned their attention to the scanty evidence found at the murder scene.

A .32 calibre Winchester rifle had been at John Mychaluk's feet. There were eight cartridges in its magazine, and one used shell in the chamber. Part of a plastered wall in the house had not burned down, and in it the police found two .32 bullets. The police painstakingly sifted through the ashes of the house and found a large number of cartridge casings. These had been ejected from the Winchester each time the killer pumped a new bullet into the chamber. Some of the bullets removed from the bodies were intact, and fitted the cartridge casings perfectly. There was no doubt that the gun at Mychaluk's feet was the murder weapon. Moreover, powder burns around the bullet hole in Mychaluk's forehead indicated he had shot himself.

A sheepskin coat had somehow survived the fire. It was positively identified as Mychaluk's. He had been seen wearing it earlier on the night of the fire. In one pocket was a cartridge box for fifty Winchester .32s, with only three bullets left in it.

Police were puzzled when nobody who had known Mychaluk had ever seen the Winchester in his possession. At that time most men in rural communities owned rifles or shotguns. When a man had a new gun he proudly showed it to friends and neighbours. Further investigation revealed that Mychaluk had bought the rifle in Wakaw, along with a box of .32 cartridges. The storekeeper who'd sold him the gun still had his counter cheque, dated six weeks before the date of the murders. Mychaluk had kept his new rifle a secret.

As the Mounties dug into the affairs of the Manchur family, they learned that all had not been well down on the farm. Mychaluk, who lived with the Manchurs, had quarrelled with his sister and her husband over money. There had also been questionable relations between Mychaluk and Paulina. Most shocking of all, Mychaluk had insinuated that Prokop and Paulina were guilty of incest.

A neighbour said that two weeks before the murders, Mychaluk told him he'd had a violent quarrel with Prokop and Mary. They wanted to put him out, Mychaluk had said, and refused to pay him $700 he claimed they owed him. Mychaluk told the neighbour, "if he ever got the Manchur family into one corner something would happen to them like the world had never seen before."

Mychaluk had been out on the evening of the murder, and was seen returning to the house at 11:30 p.m. He was wearing the sheepskin coat in which the cartridge box was later found. Neighbours said it was about 1:15 a.m. when they saw a glow in the night. Evidently no one thought it was a due to a burning house.

The Mounted Police concluded that Mychaluk had shot the animals and set fire to the barn. Then he stood in the doorway of the house and gunned down the whole family. The house had only two rooms and one door, so there would have been no escape for the victims. Mary Manchur was probably trying to hide herself and her baby, a girl named Olga, in the cellar. After killing his sister, his brother-in-law and his nieces, Mychaluk had turned the gun on himself. Sparks from the blazing barn had set the house on fire. The coroner's jury agreed with the Mounties' conclusions, and the case was closed.

Not everyone, however, agreed with the Mounties' findings. Charles Augustus Mahoney was the head of the Secret Service for the Saskatchewan Attorney General's department. He was an experienced detective who was in Wakaw at the time to investigate bootlegging activities. He thought the Mounties' murder-suicide scenario was too neat. For one thing, there was no proof that the bullet that killed Mychaluk—which was never recovered—was fired from his Winchester. There was no explanation for the barn being set ablaze, and no proof that the fire had *accidentally* spread to the house. Not long before the Manchur fire, an arsonist had set fire to granaries belonging to a farmer named Steve Makahon. Could there be a connection?

Mahoney had his own scenario for the crime. An unknown person with a grudge against the Manchurs had shot the animals and started the barn fire. John Mychaluk, armed with his rifle, had gone out to investigate. Caught in the act, the arsonist shot

Mychaluk in the head. Now the arsonist had a murder to cover up. He picked up Mychaluk's rifle, went to the house, threw open the door and blasted the entire family. The killer then set the house on fire. He left Mychaluk's rifle at the dead man's feet so it would appear that he had taken his own life. Mahoney felt the case required further investigation, but he had no authority to proceed. However, he was soon to be promoted from a provincial government employee to Saskatchewan's top policeman.

The war had left the Mounties with a serious manpower shortage. Many constables whose period of enlistment had expired joined the army. The war had also added to the force's workload. The Mounted Police had to keep an eye on enemy nationals, patrol the border with the still-neutral United States and conduct counter-espionage operations. The Mounties were therefore withdrawing from Saskatchewan and Alberta. Those provinces were obliged to form their own provincial police departments. In December 1916 Charles Mahoney was given the job of organizing and heading the Saskatchewan Provincial Police.

Mahoney was short of just about everything: money, cars, uniforms and equipment. But he managed to forge a forty-man department sprinkled with veteran officers he brought in from police departments across the country. For the investigation of major crimes he assembled a "flying squad" of detectives. These men were based in Regina, but could be dispatched to any place in the province as the need arose.

As soon as he was able, Mahoney reopened the Manchur case. He gave the assignment to Detective Sergeant George Harreck. Assisting Harreck was Constable William Sulaty. When the Mounties conducted their original investigation, they were hampered by a language barrier. Many of the people they interviewed were Russian or Polish immigrants who spoke little or no English. Working through interpreters was often difficult. Constable Sulaty was of both Russian and Polish background. He spoke both languages fluently. He was also a veteran police officer who had served with the departments in Winnipeg and Regina.

Harreck and Sulaty studied the evidence again. Over a period of many weeks they interviewed every witness the Mounties had spoken to. These interviews led them to new witnesses and fresh information. Among other things, they learned that Mike Syroshka's "solid" alibi was false. They were convinced that he had shot Mychaluk and the Manchur family. Oddly enough, though they believed they had enough circumstantial evidence to prove he set the fires, they could not prove he had done the shooting.

The investigation of the Manchur murders, which were now over two years old, had to be put on hold when another case demanded the immediate attention of the fledgling police department. In November 1918 a Prince Albert deputy sheriff named James McKay had gone missing after leaving town to serve a warrant on Dr. Joseph Gervais. Gervais had bought a team of horses and then refused to pay fifty dollars he still owed for them. McKay left for the doctor's farm on November 15 and did not return to town. His disappearance was reported to the provincial police. Their investigation would uncover a diabolical plot that involved robbery, bootlegging and murder.

Dr. Gervais had taken in two young draft dodgers, Victor Carmel and Jean Baptiste St. Germain. The three had gone on a crime spree of bootlegging (they had their own still), cattle rustling and robbery. Because they got away with these crimes for a while, Gervais came up with an absurd plan to bring in draft evaders from across Canada and set up a bandit empire with himself as the leader. To do this he needed more land. He and his two henchmen went to the home of a neighbour, Adolph Lajoie, with an offer to buy his farm. They drew up an agreement of sale, which Lajoie signed. Then Gervais pulled a gun and shot Lajoie through the heart. For good measure he put a second bullet into the man's head. The killers laid Lajoie's body on his bed with his clay pipe beside him. Then they soaked the cabin with coal oil and set it ablaze. Because Lajoie lived alone in an isolated location, a week passed before the "accident" was discovered. The investigating constable concluded that Lajoie had fallen asleep while smoking his pipe in bed. There was no autopsy.

Dr. Gervais was not at home when Deputy McKay arrived at his farm. When Carmel and St. Germain saw the officer pull up in his car, they immediately thought he had come to arrest them as draft evaders. They gunned him down, dumped the body in the North Saskatchewan River, and buried his car.

The police arrested Dr. Gervais at his farm without any trouble. But their first encounter with Carmel and St. Germain resulted in yet another killing. The pair had fortified themselves in a dugout at the riverbank. When the police approached, they opened fire without warning. Their volley killed Corporal Charles Horsley, a soldier who had accompanied the police officers.

A few days later a posse of police and soldiers led by Commissioner Charles Mahoney himself found the two fugitives hiding in a haystack on a farm near Prince Albert. The pair had revolvers, but this time they did not attempt to shoot it out. They surrendered and were taken to the Prince Albert jail. Only then did the police learn the truth about Adolph Lajoie's death and of Dr. Gervais' ambition to become Saskatchewan's outlaw king. Gervais, Carmel and St. Germain were eventually hanged for the murder of James McKay.

With the Gervais gang rounded up, Sergeant Harreck and Constable Sulaty could return to the Manchur case. They learned that Mike Syroshka was the arsonist who had set fire to Steve Makahon's granaries. They now had more than enough evidence to link him to the Manchur fire, if not the murders. Mahoney told the two officers to arrest Syroshka for arson. Perhaps more witnesses would feel free to come forward with Syroshka behind bars. On December 7, 1918, Syroshka was arrested for the second time. This time there was no alibi.

The trial was delayed due to the Spanish flu epidemic that was ravaging Canada—and the rest of the world—at that time. No new witnesses came forward. The trial finally began on June 17, 1919, and lasted until July 1. Syroshka was tried on two charges of arson. But everyone knew the law really wanted him for murder. He was found guilty and sentenced to six years in prison on each charge. The jury also recommended that when Syroshka had served his time he be deported to his native Austria—a recommendation with which the judge agreed.

No one was ever officially tried for the Manchur murders. Charles Mahoney was satisfied that the man he considered responsible would spend a long time in prison, even if it were for another crime. But the nagging question would never be answered once and for all. Did Syroshka murder John Mychaluk and the Manchur family? Or did Mychaluk actually go on a rampage of murder before ending his own life?

THE SMALL MYSTERY

Did Somebody Get Amby?

Not many people liked Ambrose J. Small. He had a few cronies who hung around to drink, gamble and carouse with him. But friends? On one occasion an American visitor to Toronto who'd had the misfortune to do business with Small encountered a *former* friend of the man and mistook him for Ambrose. The American said, "Mr. Ambrose J. Small, I have never met you before, but you will know who I am when I tell you that I am John C. Fisher of the New York Casino. And let me tell you, Mr. Ambrose J. Small, that I have come all the way from New York to give myself the pleasure of saying to you that you are a damned liar and a damned thief."

The man to whom he spoke, a Toronto theatre manager named O.B. Sheppard, who had also been badly used by Small, extended his hand and replied, "Mr. Fisher, I have heard of you and I am glad to meet you. I may be a damned liar and a damned thief, but you insult me, sir, when you call me Ambrose J. Small."

It bothered Small not a whit that people hated him. He was rich, and he had not achieved that by being nice. The little man with the huge, drooping moustache had been born into poverty in 1867, on a farm north of Toronto. As a youth he had taken a part-time job as an usher in Toronto's prestigious Grand Opera House. From that humble beginning Small had lied, cheated and double-crossed his way to the top of the theatre business in Ontario. He had emerged as the owner of a string of theatres all across the province, with a few in Quebec as well, a small empire with its headquarters at the Grand in Toronto. His crown jewel was the new, elegant Grand Opera House in London.

People did not begrudge Small his success. It was the underhanded means Small employed that made colleagues want to spit when they uttered his name. If Small could not get what he wanted with legitimate business practices, he resorted to blackmail and character assassination. Any naïve souls who put their trust in Small soon regretted it. He would charm reputable businessmen into deals that looked good, and then spring the trap. When Small wrote up contracts for the managers of touring theatrical groups, he planted tricky little clauses he called "jokers" in them. If the manager did not catch these cleverly disguised snares, he would find out too late that he and his company had been robbed of their fair share of the box office receipts.

All this was beyond what was considered "hard business." Small actually took a perverse joy in conning people and stabbing associates in the back. Nothing mattered to him but the money that piled up in his bank account. His meanness ranged from bilking producers out of thousands of dollars, to stiffing the manager of his Guelph, Ontario, theatre for twenty-five cents worth of sawdust.

Small was just as crooked in his favourite pastime, betting on horse races, as he was in business. He had connections, and more than once "fixed" a horse race. One such deal netted him an easy $10,000, and earned him the hatred of Toronto's sporting society. Toronto journalist Hector Charlesworth knew Ambrose Small well. He wrote in his book, *More Candid Chronicles,* "If I heard once, I heard a score of times the ominous words, 'Somebody will get Amby some day.'"

Aside from two spinster sisters, Gertrude and Florence, whom he supported, there were two important people in Ambrose Small's life. One was his secretary, Jack Doughty. Doughty had two children from a failed marriage who were cared for by his unmarried sister, Jeannie. Doughty did not like Small, though he worked for him for fifteen years. His salary of forty-five dollars a week was actually fair for that time, but Jack felt that Small did not adequately reward him for his work in building the theatrical empire. In conversations with his sister, Doughty often referred to Small as a skinflint. Whenever Doughty asked for a raise, Small contemptuously replied, "Don't bother me, Jack. You never had it so good." Boss and secretary frequently quarrelled over money.

The other major figure in Small's life was his wife Theresa, whom he had married in 1902. It was an unusual match: the moralistic, devoutly Catholic Theresa with Ambrose, a Catholic Church-hating Protestant who routinely took unfair advantage of chorus girls. Moreover, Theresa was the younger sister of Ambrose's stepmother, his father's second wife. Theresa was well-educated and loved the trappings of high society. Ambrose had received little formal education and was a boor.

The marriage was, in fact, centred on money. Both had lots of it and wanted more. Theresa had inherited a sizable fortune from her parents. Ambrose, for all his faults, had a gift for making money, even if he did do it the dirty way. Their union was a potentially profitable business investment.

Outwardly the "rich, rich Smalls," as envious people called them, seemed to have it all. They lived in a sixteen-room mansion in Toronto's exclusive Rosedale district. Theresa was a leading figure in high society and her every movement was reported in the social pages. Ambrose's theatres were making money as fast as he could rake it in.

Privately, things were not very harmonious in the Small household. Ambrose and Theresa slept in separate bedrooms. There were no children, because Ambrose didn't like kids. Husband and wife usually went on separate vacations. Theresa took shopping trips to Paris and Rome. Ambrose went to racetracks in American cities. Jack Doughty resented Theresa because she spent money lavishly while he struggled along on forty-five dollars a week. Ambrose's sisters hated Theresa because she was Catholic and because they thought she discouraged Ambrose from increasing the allowance he provided for them.

Then there were those chorus girls! Theresa, who was an equal business partner with Ambrose, would show up at the Grand to check on the day's receipts. This interfered with her husband's dalliances. While Theresa was on one of her trips to Italy, Ambrose had a secret room built at the back of his office. No one else knew of it except Doughty, general manager James Cowan, and the women Small entertained there.

Even with the pick of showgirls at his beck and call, Small was not satisfied. During the latter part of the First World War he took a mistress named Clara Smith. Clara was pretty and much younger than Small. Their trysts took place at her apartment, rather than his secret room at the theatre—where he still partied with chorus girls. Clara told "Amby" she knew him better than his own wife did. She wrote him love letters, which Small foolishly kept.

One April day in 1918, Theresa found some of the letters, which she later described as "smutty." Before going out to a concert, she left several of them in a place where Ambrose would be sure to find them. Small found the letters and destroyed them. He left Theresa a note that said, in part:

"Theresa, Dear Theresa

"Don't bother your dear little head about this rotten stuff any more (sic). It's all over and no earthly use digging it up any more (sic)... Amby. God Bless You."

But the affair wasn't over. Small continued to see Clara. Theresa had kept one of the letters as proof of Small's infidelity.

By the end of the Great War, Ambrose Small saw a new threat rising on the horizon: moving pictures! At one time they had been little more than a sideshow gimmick. Now the movies were developing into a major industry. For a few cents a person could sit in a dark room and watch incredible scenes of action, adventure, romance and comedy played out on a screen by "stars." It was something wonderful and new with which the old-fashioned stage could not compete. The theatre had given Small everything he had, but he was no sentimentalist. He decided to sell out—for every nickel he could get.

Small found a taker—a *sucker,* in his opinion—in Trans Canada Theatres Limited, based in Montreal. That company was willing to pay the Smalls a cool $1.7 million for their chain of theatres. One million dollars was payable upon the signing of the document. The rest would be paid in instalments. Small could not have been happier. Already a millionaire, he had now more than doubled his fortune.

On December 1, 1919, W.J. Shaughnessy, a leading Canadian financier and representative for Trans Canada Theatres, boarded his private railway car in Montreal. He was on his way to Toronto to close the deal with Ambrose and Theresa Small. He carried with him a certified cheque for one million dollars. Due to a blizzard, the train rolled into Toronto an hour and a half late the following morning.

Shaughnessy hurried to the Trader's Bank Building at 65 Yonge Street, and went up to the tenth floor legal office of Sir Allan Aylesworth, K.C. Theresa Small and her attorney, E.W.M. Flock of London, Ontario, were already waiting. The meeting had been set for 10:00 a.m., and Shaugnessy was ten minutes late. That didn't matter, because Ambrose wasn't there. Small liked to keep people waiting, especially if they were big shots like W. J. Shaugnessy.

Small walked in forty-five minutes late, a Havana cigar clenched in his jaw. He and Flock went over the contract Shaughnessy laid out on the table. Satisfied that no one was trying to slip a "joker" past him, Small said, "Agreed!" Everybody signed the document, and Shaughnessy handed Small the cheque. Ambrose passed it to Theresa. "Here, take it and put it in the bank," he said cheerfully, "and don't spend it on the way over. That's a million in cash."

Theresa smiled and said her goodbyes. At 11:45 she made the deposit at the Dominion Bank. The amount sent a buzz through the bank's staff. Those rich, rich Smalls!

At 12:30, Theresa met Ambrose for lunch at the Victoria Room of the King Edward Hotel. Small's euphoric mood after the sale was somewhat spoiled when Theresa reminded him that he had promised to accompany her to the St. Vincent de Paul Children's Orphanage, where she was making a donation. The combination of children and Catholics was more than Ambrose could stomach. He tried to back out of the engagement, but Theresa held him to his promise.

With that distasteful bit of philanthropism out of the way, Ambrose parted company from Theresa. He had a four o'clock meeting with lawyer Flock at the Grand to tie up some loose ends after the sale. He told Theresa he would be home by six to have a celebratory dinner with her. Theresa did a little shopping with her sister, whom she told of their plans to travel the world. Then she went home. She did not know that she would never see her husband again. Or did she?

After he left Theresa, Small went on an uncharacteristic shopping spree of his own. First he ordered a $9,000 Cadillac for his wife. Then he put in another order for a ten thousand dollar pearl and diamond necklace. He met Flock, and the lawyer was startled to learn that Small's generosity knew no bounds on that momentous day. He told Flock that any of his employees who lost their jobs as a result of the sale were to be paid a week's salary. He wanted Flock to find those people new jobs.

He had not forgotten Jack Doughty, his long-suffering secretary. Jack would have a new job with Trans Canada Theatres, and would get a raise in pay. However, Jack would have to move to Montreal. Small told Flock he'd give Jack the good news that very day.

Small invited Flock to join him and Theresa for supper, but the lawyer had to catch the six o'clock train to London. The two men walked to the theatre entrance where they said goodbye. The time was 5:30 p.m., December 2. Flock looked back from the sidewalk and saw Ambrose standing in the doorway. Then he hurried off to catch his train. He would be the last person known to have seen Ambrose J. Small alive.

Theresa was not surprised when Amby didn't show up for dinner as he had promised. But when he wasn't home by eleven o'clock she called the theatre and spoke to manager Cowan. He hadn't seen Small either. One of Small's drinking and gambling buddies, Thomas Flynn, was at the theatre looking for him. He took the phone from Cowan and told Theresa to leave Amby alone and let him have some fun. Then he hung up on her.

A question that hung over the case from the beginning was, why didn't Theresa tell the police earlier that her husband was missing? She would explain that she thought he was with another woman, and she was afraid that the scandal would become public. But Small had not packed any suitcases. He had not withdrawn money from any of his accounts. There was no evidence of him paying for travel, food or accommodation by cheque.

On December 16, a full two weeks after Flock left Small at the theatre, either James Cowan or Thomas Flynn informed the Toronto police that he was missing. Detective Austin Mitchell went to speak to Theresa. She told him Ambrose was no doubt with another woman, and she begged him to keep the story out of the newspapers. Mitchell obliged. He did not even make an official report of his interview with her. This would come back to haunt the detective.

Thomas Flynn pestered Mitchell, wanting to know what the police were doing to find Small. Mitchell said Small was out of town and would likely be home in time for Christmas. But Christmas and New Year's came and went with no news of Small.

On January 2, 1920, Flynn called the Toronto *Daily Star* and gave the newspaper the scoop of the year. The next day all of Canada knew about the missing millionaire. Toronto Police Chief Inspector George Guthrie's phone was ringing off the hook, and he didn't even have a report on the case. He summoned Mitchell, who told him Small was off somewhere celebrating his big sale. There was no reason, he said, to suspect foul play.

The newspapers and the general public did not agree. Rumours flew thick and fast. Small had amnesia. Small had been kidnapped. Small had run away. Small had been *murdered!*

Then, as police and reporters questioned people about Small, there was another shocking development: Jack Doughty was missing! So was $100,000 in bonds from Small's safety deposit box in the Dominion Bank.

Police learned that on the morning of the day Small disappeared, Doughty had taken the bonds from the bank. At some unspecified time that same day, he had been at the theatre. Then he had boarded a train for Montreal to report to his new employers. He'd returned to Toronto to spend Christmas with Jeannie and his children. He'd left again for Montreal, but had not shown up at the offices of Trans Canada Theatres. Jeannie told police that if Jack wasn't in Montreal, she didn't know where he was. She did not tell them that her brother had given her a package to hold for him.

Small's description was sent all over Canada and the United States. Reports of sightings were soon pouring in. One came from as far away as Juarez, Mexico. Some people in Toronto claimed to have seen the tycoon on December 2 *after* the time Flock had left him, but these reports were either false, or were errors made by witnesses who had their dates confused. Not all who wondered over Small's whereabouts were concerned about his well-being. Some people in the theatrical community could not help but smile at the thought that something bad might have happened to Ambrose J. Small.

Police received a tip that there had been mysterious goings-on in a ravine near the Smalls' Rosedale home the night he vanished. They searched the ravine, but found nothing. In the coming months that ravine would be dug up more than once. Searchers would find nothing but some very old bones.

Detective Austin Mitchell had no one but himself to blame for the cold trail he now faced as he looked for clues that might lead him to Small. Edward L. Hammond of the Criminal Investigation Branch of the Ontario Provincial Police was assigned to the case as Mitchell's partner. The two officers did not work well together. Hammond suspected Theresa knew more than she was telling, and wanted to pressure her. Mitchell and Chief Inspector Guthrie told him to leave her alone. Mitchell, who believed in the occult, consulted with self-styled mediums and clairvoyants. Hammond considered them "a bunch of nuts."

The so-called psychics weren't the only people contributing to the sensationalism surrounding the mystery. Private detectives, anticipating a big reward, were snooping all over Toronto. Stories circulated about a letter (that turned out to be a hoax) which said Small had been abducted by gangsters and was being held for ransom. When Sir Arthur Conan Doyle, creator of Sherlock Holmes, arrived in New York City for a visit, the press asked him if he was going to help the Canadian police find Ambrose Small. The famous author said he might, if he were asked. Newspaper headlines announced that Sherlock Holmes was on the case. But no one asked for Doyle's assistance.

By June 1920 the Toronto police were desperate for a solid lead. They posted a $50,000 reward for information leading to the discovery of Small alive; $15,000 for information leading to the discovery of his body. Meanwhile, another $15,000 reward was offered for information leading to the arrest of Jack Doughty.

All across Canada and the United States police exhumed unidentified bodies to see if one of them might be Ambrose Small. Every drowning victim that washed up on the shores of Lake Ontario was closely examined. Police in European cities looked again at unclaimed bodies in morgues.

Toronto police ran up one blind alley after another. But one witness they spoke to just might have caught a final glimpse of Ambrose Small. George Soucy, an engineer employed by the Maclean's Publishing Company of Toronto, told Mitchell that late on the night of December 2, he was in a streetcar travelling north on Yonge Street. He looked out a window and into the windows of a black car, also going north. Two men were in the front seat. In the back seat was a man whom Soucy swore was Ambrose Small. The man in the back was either asleep, or dead! Was Soucy mistaken, as were so many other "eyewitnesses"? Or had he actually seen Ambrose Small and the men who "got" him?

It didn't take Austin Mitchell and Edward Hammond long to learn how much Jack Doughty hated his boss. Fred Lennon, sales manager for Canadian Universal Films, said that Doughty had told him of plans to kidnap Small. Fred Osborne, a former janitor at the Grand, said Doughty had tried to draw him into "hare-brained" plots to murder Small and grab a lot of money.

Thomas Shields, the furnaceman at the Grand, told what seemed to be the most incriminating story of them all.

Shields said he had heard Small and Doughty fighting in the furnace room. When he crept in to look, he saw Doughty holding a shovel over Small's head. Shields said he hurried away in fear. He was certain that was the night of December 2.

Shields' story didn't fit other information the police had on Doughty. It would not have been possible for the secretary to have killed Small, disposed of the body, and then caught the Montreal train. Nonetheless, they examined the furnace of the Grand for bone fragments. They also sent a team of men to sift through the mountains of furnace ashes at a Toronto dumpsite. Another team dredged a place in Toronto Bay where ashes were regularly dumped. No bits of Ambrose Small turned up.

Mitchell and Hammond's questioning of people connected with Small and Doughty only seemed to compound the mystery. They learned from James Cowan that on December 3 Theresa had been in Small's office. She was looking for something, but Cowan didn't know what. The detectives asked Theresa about it, but she would not give them a straight answer.

Jeannie Doughty told them Jack had not been happy about the sale of the theatre chain. Nor had he wanted to move to Montreal. She surprised the investigators when she said that during his Christmas visit to Toronto, Jack had gone to see Theresa twice. This was unusual, because it was no secret that Jack and Theresa were not friends. Moreover, since her husband's disappearance, Theresa had become reclusive. She was not accepting visitors, except for priests and nuns and a few close relatives. She wasn't even answering her phone.

When the detectives asked her about Doughty's visits she admitted he had been there. But she would not tell them what she and Jack had talked about. It was private, she said, and had nothing to do with Amby. She had not known at the time about the stolen bonds. She said she did not think the theft and her husband's disappearance were connected. Theresa showed them the letter written by Clara Smith she had kept. Perhaps *that* woman knew something. But the officers had already spoken to Clara, and were convinced she knew nothing. Seven months after Ambrose had vanished, Theresa still insisted he was with another woman somewhere, and would turn up sooner or later.

In September the Toronto police finally got a break. A man who worked for a lumber camp in Oregon saw Jack Doughty's picture on a wanted poster in the Portland Post Office. He recognized him as a man who called himself Charlie Cooper, a clerk in the lumber camp's office. He informed the Portland police. A little over a week later, Detective Austin Mitchell walked up to "Charlie Cooper" and said, "Hello Jack. How are you?"

Doughty's return to Toronto caused a sensation. At last there would be some answers. But Doughty denied knowing anything about Small's disappearance. He even denied stealing the bonds. He claimed Small had given them to him as a reward for his long years of service. Theresa scoffed at that. "Amby wouldn't have given away ten cents unless he was getting twenty cents back."

Without a body, the police could not charge Doughty with Small's murder. However, the former secretary was prosecuted for stealing the bonds. At the trial, which began on March 21, 1921, Jeannie Doughty testified that she had told Jack to give the bonds back to Mr. Small. Jack had replied that he couldn't return them to

Mr. Small. The word *couldn't* got the attention of the prosecution and the press. It implied that Doughty knew Small was dead. But the law could not lay a charge based on an implication. Doughty was convicted of robbery and sentenced to five years in prison.

As the months passed, public opinion turned against Theresa. Gossipmongers said she had refused to pay a million-dollar ransom to save Small's life. Theresa stirred up a hornet's nest when she announced that in her will she was leaving all of her money—except for the provision Ambrose had made for his sisters—to the Catholic Church. Protestant Toronto was appalled. The Orange Lodge, a powerful force at the time, railed that Theresa and the Catholic Church had conspired to kill Ambrose so they could get their hands on his money. Gertrude and Florence Small tired to contest their brother's will, which left his estate to Theresa. They said the will was a forgery, that Theresa had destroyed the *real* will. In their corner was a confidence man named Patrick Sullivan who was posing as a "criminologist." He had the ear of the press, and he launched a vicious attack on Theresa and the Toronto police, claiming they were all part of a "papist" conspiracy.

Reeling under the pressure brought about by public outrage, the police were desperate to find *anything* in the way of a clue to Small's disappearance. They dug up the basement of the Grand. They searched Theresa's house from attic to basement, which they also dug up. They found nothing.

While Theresa endured this humiliation, Sullivan began circulating an underground tabloid called the *Statesman.* Its pages were full of anti-Catholic propaganda and personal attacks on Theresa. It even carried doctored photographs that depicted Theresa engaged in sexual acts with Catholic priests. The police shut down the publication, but the damage to Theresa's reputation was done. The one-time darling of society was now a prisoner in her opulent home.

Then came the stories that in convents Theresa often visited, notices appeared on bulletin boards *before* Small's disappearance became public knowledge, requesting prayers for his soul. Who else but Theresa could have put them there? The nuns in these convents denied any such notices had been posted, but the rumours continued.

In 1924 the Supreme Court of Ontario declared Ambrose Small officially dead, and it upheld the will. Sullivan and the Small sisters would continue for some years to challenge the will, but without success. The money was Theresa's to do with as she pleased.

Theresa Small died in her home in 1935, with just a few friends from her church at her side. All others had abandoned her. In her will she mentioned a few close relatives and provided for Gertrude and Florence. The bulk of the money went to Catholic charities.

In 1946 Toronto's Grand Opera House was torn down. Any secrets it might have housed were lost forever. In 1960 the police officially closed the case on Ambrose Small. But the question still nags at historians, writers, and sleuths—both professional and amateur. What happened to Ambrose J. Small?

Small was almost certainly murdered. But by whom? Jack Doughty and Theresa Small are prime suspects. If Doughty was indeed responsible, how was he able to kill Small, get rid of the body so effectively, and still catch that train to Montreal? Accomplices? Possibly. But the kind of people who engage in such nefarious work as murder don't have a very good record for keeping their mouths shut about it. In the decades following Small's disappearance, not a whisper reached the ears of police or the press. As for Theresa, would her Catholic conscience have allowed her to be part of such an enormous mortal sin? Or was the legacy she bequeathed to the Church a way of seeking absolution? Just what would Theresa and Jack have talked about during those Christmas visits in 1919, if not Ambrose?

Of course, Doughty and Theresa were not the only people with motivations for killing Small. He was a nasty, selfish individual who had hurt almost everyone who came in contact with him. Anybody from the shadows of Small's past could have been stalking him that December night.

If Small was murdered by person or persons unknown, what was done with the body? Was it weighted and dumped in Lake Ontario? Canadian author Orlo Miller, in his book *Twenty Mortal Murders,* makes a case for it being incinerated in the furnace of the Grand Opera House in London—a theatre that is said to this day to be haunted by Small's ghost. Or, if George Soucy was correct in his statement that he saw Small in the back of a black car heading north on Yonge Street, could it be that the killers buried him in an unmarked grave north of Toronto, in the very countryside in which he had been born and raised? The questions will probably never be answered. The one thing that seems certain is that within hours of his greatest financial triumph, *somebody* got Amby.

THE DELORME MYSTERY

My Brother's Keeper

The brutal slaying of a twenty-four-year-old Montreal man was shocking enough. But due to the involvement of one individual, the aftermath of this murder was unlike anything Canadians had ever seen. Sensationalism soared to unprecedented heights. Reactions to the murder investigation shook the very social foundations of the province of Quebec and sent shockwaves across the country. When at last a suspect was officially charged with homicide, the nation anxiously awaited what the newspapers predicted would be "the trial of the century."

In the early morning of January 7, 1922, Euzebe Larin left his home in the Montreal suburb of Notre Dame de Grace to go to work. As he passed a tool shed at the corner of Coolbrook and Snowden Avenue, he saw a dark form on the snow-covered ground. Larin took a closer look, and saw it was the body of a well-dressed young man. His hands were tied and the tails of his coat were pulled up over his head and fastened with safety pins. Larin did not touch the corpse, but hurried to the nearest telephone to call the police.

The first officer on the scene was Detective Dominique Pusie. He loosened the pinned-up coat and saw two frozen, blood-soaked quilts wrapped around the victim's head. The detective found no clues on the ground around the body, so he waited for the hearse that would take it to the morgue.

At the Craig Street morgue the clothing and quilt were removed from the corpse. Police examined the contents of the dead man's pockets: a rosary, the stub of a ticket from the Princess Theatre, a partly torn picture of a young woman, an undated letter from someone named Adelard, and an identity card with the name Raoul Delorme. A piece of watch chain attached to the waistcoat showed that a pocket watch had been torn away. That and the fact that there was no money on the body pointed to robbery.

The autopsy revealed the man had been shot six times in the face and the back of the neck with a small-calibre gun. There were scratches and some bruising on the right hand and wrist. Both wrists bore the marks of the rope that had bound them.

A detective and a constable went to the address shown on the identity card: 190 St. Hubert Street, in the heart of Montreal. They were surprised when a man wearing a priest's cassock answered the door. They asked if this was the residence of Raoul Delorme. The priest answered nervously: "Yes. Raoul is my brother. Has anything happened to him? Is he in trouble? He didn't come home last night."

The officers told the priest, who identified himself as Father Adelard Delorme, that they'd found a body with Raoul's identity card on it. They asked him to accompany them to the morgue to see if it was, indeed, his brother. Father Delorme replied, "Give me a minute, and don't say anything to my sisters."

At the morgue Father Delorme looked at the bullet-punctured face. "It's him alright," he said unemotionally. He uttered a quick blessing and made the sign of the cross. Then he left the room.

Montreal Chief of Police Adrien Lepage assigned the Delorme case to Detective Georges Farah-Lajoie. He told him to drop everything else and put all of his time and energy into solving this murder. The brother of a Roman Catholic priest had been slain and then dumped in the street like a dog. In staunchly Roman Catholic Quebec, where the Church was a force to be reckoned with and priests were held almost in awe, there would be a cry for the killer or killers to be brought to justice as quickly as possible.

Chief Lepage chose Farah-Lajoie for this important case because he was one of the most highly qualified detectives in Canada. Born in Syria, Farah-Lajoie had been in Montreal since 1900. He had travelled the world and spoke seven languages. He'd made himself the bane of organized crime in the city, and had once single-handedly prevented an assassination attempt on a visiting papal delegate. Significantly, though his French Canadian wife and his children were Roman Catholic, Farah-Lajoie was not. He was a member of the Greek Catholic Church. Farah-Lajoie could question a priest with no built-in feelings of intimidation.

From discussions other officers already had with Father Delorme, Farah-Lajoie knew something of the Delorme family background. Raoul was actually Adelard's half-brother. The priest also had a sister named Rosa, and two half-sisters, Lilly and Florence—all younger than he. The Delormes all lived in the St. Hubert Street house.

Their father, Albert Delorme, was a contractor who'd died in 1916. He had left a considerable estate, valued at about $200,000 (almost two million dollars in today's terms). The estate included numerous houses throughout Montreal, which the Delormes rented out.

Though Adelard Delorme, now thirty-seven, was the eldest son, because he had gone into the priesthood Albert had willed the bulk of the estate to Raoul. He'd expected that one day Raoul would marry and carry on the family name. However, Father Delorme was made sole executor. He was to manage the money and properties until Raoul reached the age of twenty-five, which he would have done in 1922. Father Delorme had obtained a special exemption from parish work so he could live at home and care for his siblings as well as the family business. The archbishop of Montreal had appointed him chaplain of the Public Welfare Service, whose headquarters were just a few minutes' walk from the Delorme home. Father Delorme said mass there everyday.

At the time of his death Raoul was enrolled as a student at the University of Ottawa. He had come home on December 22 for the Christmas and New Year's holidays, and was scheduled to take the train back to Ottawa the day his body was found. His bags were already packed.

Detective Farah-Lajoie examined the spot where the body had been found, and interviewed Euzebe Larin. He quickly concluded that the killing had not happened in front of the shed. There was no evidence of a struggle there. The ice on which Raoul had lain showed no sign of melting from the warmth of the body. Raoul was already stone cold dead when he was put there.

The detective then went to the morgue to examine the body and the clothing. The angle of the bullet holes in the neck, face and head, and powder burns on the skin showed that the gun had been fired from close range and that Raoul had been in a sitting, kneeling or bent-over position. The doctors found no evidence of alcohol, narcotics or poison in the body. They recovered two small-calibre bullets from the chin and jaw. The other bullets had passed right through.

One bullet had pierced the collar of Raoul's jacket, but there was no bullet hole in his overcoat. That told the detective that Raoul's overcoat had been put on him after the murder. Quite likely the shooting had happened indoors. Raoul had not been wearing overshoes or a hat. The shoes on his feet were freshly polished, and the soles were smooth and clean. This evidence also suggested an indoor killing.

The quilts wrapped around the head and the coattails pinned over them were obviously intended to prevent the leakage of blood. Undoubtedly this was to keep bloodstains out of the vehicle used to transport the body from the crime scene to the place of disposal. They were homemade quilts, stained with what appeared to be grease and soap. The doctors had found a feather stuck to one of them. Farah-Lajoie also examined the ropes that had bound the wrists and quilts. He believed Raoul's hands had not been tied until after death.

Father Delorme had told police that the day before the discovery of the body, Raoul had gone out after lunch. He said he was going to a movie—a pastime of which the priest disapproved—and borrowed twenty dollars from his brother. He'd also borrowed Father Delorme's gold watch. According to the priest, Raoul said he would not be home for supper. He was dining with friends (whom he did not name) and later might go with them for a motorcar ride. If he was not home by eleven-thirty, he'd be staying the night with one of those friends.

Farah-Lajoie took a photograph of Raoul to the neighbourhood of the Princess Theatre and showed it to restaurant owners and cab drivers. No one recalled seeing him. The detective's next step was to personally talk to Father Delorme. He went to the house accompanied by two other policemen.

Father Delorme received the investigators hospitably, offering them all cigars. Farah-Lajoie declined the offer, preferring to smoke his own Pall Mall cigarettes. He noticed immediately that the priest was favouring his right arm, apparently trying to keep his wrist hidden in the sleeve of his cassock. Nonetheless, the detective saw a badly discoloured welt encircling the wrist. He asked Father Delorme if he'd injured his hand. The priest replied that he had, in fact, fallen on the ice and hurt himself.

Father Delorme gave the officers a long, rambling account of family affairs and of his relationship with his brother and sisters. He was proud to point out that nothing happened in the house without his permission. It was soon clear to Farah-Lajoie that since Alfred Delorme's death, Adelard dominated every aspect of Raoul's life. He scrutinized Raoul's spending, kept in touch with officials at the university, and even tried to introduce Raoul to "honest and pretty Catholic girls." At first glance such devotion to the welfare of a younger brother seemed admirable. But Raoul was almost twenty-five years old! Surely he didn't need to be looked after as though he were just a boy.

Farah-Lajoie asked to see Raoul's room. Father Delorme gave the officers a tour of the entire twenty-room house, from the third floor to the basement. In the basement, where there was a coal-fired furnace, Farah-Lajoie asked about a particular door. Father Delorme explained that the house was part of a triplex, and the door led to the basement of an adjoining house. Then he made the odd statement that no foul play could possibly have occurred in the basement, because the neighbours would have heard it.

After the tour, Farah-Lajoie asked Father Delorme if he owned a gun. The priest said he did. He'd inherited it from his father, and kept it in his car for protection. He took the officers to the garage where he proudly showed them his car, a four passenger Franklin. The gun was in a pocket on the driver's door, along with a box of bullets.

The firearm was a .25 calibre Bayard automatic. The priest said he had fired it only once, to scare off a dog that was threatening Raoul. That many people would consider it unusual for a priest to be driving around in a luxury car with a gun within reach did not seem to occur to him. He did not object when the detective said he was taking the gun and bullets with him.

In their earlier conversation Father Delorme had mentioned Raoul buying a new pair of overshoes. Farah-Lajoie asked to see them. The priest took him to a hall closet in which the detective saw two pairs of overshoes, one old and one new. Both were Raoul's. When Farah-Lajoie said he was taking the old pair with him, Father Delorme suddenly became nervous.

Back in the priest's study Farah-Lajoie asked Father Delorme for a complete account of his activities on the day Raoul was last seen alive. The priest recounted the entire day, beginning with his early morning mass at the Public Welfare Service. He said, among other things, that Ernest Leclerc, his furnace stoker, was in the basement working on the furnace from about 6:15 p.m.

until just after 9:00 p.m. Raoul, he recalled, left at about 2:30 that afternoon, but phoned later.

"At seven Raoul telephoned to tell me he had met with some friends who had a car. He said he would be having dinner with them 'in some style' at a downtown restaurant and afterwards they were going to the Allan Theatre and for a drive. He added that if he didn't return that night, he would be back the next morning. When I asked him if he wouldn't rather invite his friends home for the evening, Raoul answered, 'It's my business. If I'm not home tonight, I'll be there tomorrow.' And hung up. I told my sisters about Raoul's call, and they both seemed concerned."

Father Delorme said his sisters went to bed while he was in the garage working on his car. When he came in after ten, he found the house cold, so he went downstairs to check on the furnace. The fire had gone out, and he spent the next three hours cleaning it out, refuelling it, and starting a fire. He said the noise he was making kept Lilly awake. She finally went to the basement door and called to him to go to bed.

Father Delorme said he finally retired for the night after 1:00 a.m. Then, after two o'clock, his telephone rang. "All I could hear at the other end of the line was a plaintive voice calling my name. I tried to find out who was there but couldn't get any answer. I finally hung up. Around three o'clock the phone rang again. I didn't answer until one of my sisters said it might be Raoul. When I did answer, all I heard was the same kind of wailing sound. I hung up. When the same call came through an hour or so later, I asked the operator where the calls were coming from. 'A phone booth,' she said. I asked her for the number, but she said it was against regulations to reveal it. I insisted, telling her I was a priest and didn't want to be bothered anymore. She promised not to put any more calls through to my number until morning."

When Father Delorme was finished, Farah-Lajoie asked if he thought Raoul might have committed suicide. The priest scoffed that with six bullets in the head that wasn't very likely. The detective advised him not to discuss the case with anyone. Father Delorme wanted to offer a large reward for the capture of his brother's killers, but Farah-Lajoie said it was too early in the investigation for that.

When Farah-Lajoie returned to the police station he learned that a bloodstained hat had been found in Cote St. Michel, a north end suburb sixteen km (ten miles) from downtown Montreal. He picked up the hat, which had only a couple of drops of blood on the visor, and some grease stains, and took it to 190 St. Hubert Street. Father Delorme and his sister Florence identified it as Raoul's. Florence had sewn a tear in the lining for him the very morning of his disappearance. When Farah-Lajoie told Father Delorme where the hat had been found, the priest said, "That's where the murder must have taken place. You have a very good lead there."

The following day Farah-Lajoie learned that only a week before the murder, Raoul had taken out a $25,000 life insurance policy. His brother Adelard was the sole beneficiary. The detective went back to talk to the priest.

Father Delorme admitted to encouraging Raoul to take out the policy. Adelard himself had paid the first premium. There was nothing suspicious about that, he said. He had done it so Raoul could learn something about saving money. The priest added that he himself was financially secure, receiving $6,000 a year from his father's estate.

Farah-Lajoie asked if Raoul had left a will. Father Delorme said his brother *might* have written one before an appendectomy he'd had the previous year. If there was a will, the priest added, he hadn't seen it, and it was probably with Raoul's notary.

By now Raoul's murder was making banner headlines in Quebec. Father Delorme had been interviewed by reporters who wrote of his "great state of anguish." But there was also talk around Montreal that Father Delorme was not a man of good reputation. People wondered what kind of priest smoked expensive cigars, drove a fancy car and lived in a house that was almost a mansion? Farah-Lajoie heard the gossip and dismissed it as the innuendo of a few anti-Catholic bigots who would say anything to smear the Church.

The newspapers said hoodlums murdered Raoul. Farah-Lajoie disagreed, even though Raoul's empty pockets and the missing gold watch certainly made it *look* as though bandits had killed him. Raoul was a quiet young man who did not run with a fast crowd or flash a lot of money. His brother wouldn't let him. He went out with twenty dollars in his pocket. For a working man in 1922 Montreal that was a lot of money. But did it warrant killing the victim and then hauling the body halfway across town? And how many professional criminals used small-calibre pistols of the type that were generally thought of as ladies' guns?

While Farah-Lajoie pondered these questions, Father Delorme complained of receiving threatening letters. Farah-Lajoie read them, and considered them the work of cranks. It concerned him more that he hadn't found a single friend of Raoul's who had been with him for a night on the town.

Farah-Lajoie attended Raoul's wake in the Delorme house. Father Delorme took him aside and invited him to also attend the funeral the next day, "in case the murderers decide to show up." The detective again asked about Raoul's will. Father Delorme said, "I think he left his will in Ottawa." Then he added, strangely, for a priest burying his only brother, that he hoped Raoul hadn't forgotten him in his will. The next morning Father Delorme tearfully said the funeral mass. The body was placed in a vault to await spring thaw and actual burial.

While Raoul Delorme's body lay frozen in a crypt, Detective Farah-Lajoie followed up every clue he had and every tip the Montreal police received. Most of the latter were useless, including one that took him to Ottawa on a wild goose chase. When Farah-Lajoie returned to Montreal an officer on his investigating team, Detective Theodule Pigeon, had information that led to the first break in the case. After conferring with Pigeon, Farah-Lajoie visited the gunsmith shop of Oscar Haynes. He took along Father Delorme's Bayard automatic and the box of bullets.

Haynes said he knew Father Delorme well. The priest often brought his gun in for servicing and cleaning. On December 27, Haynes recalled, Father Delorme traded in his old .32 calibre Iver Johnson revolver for the Bayard. He also bought two boxes of .25 calibre steel bullets.

The gunsmith identified the Bayard and the box of ammunition Farah-Lajoie showed him as the ones he'd sold to Father Delorme. He also said that someone had recently done a poor job of cleaning the gun; the person had used too much oil.

An idea came into Fara-Lajoie's mind that he would previously have considered unthinkable. Even with the information he had from the gunsmith, Farah-Lajoie didn't want to believe what his detective's logic was telling him. But he had to follow this hunch through.

Farah-Lajoie used Hayne's firing range to test-fire Father Delorme's bullets with four different guns, including the priest's Bayard. He took the bullets to the crime lab. A ballistics expert said that in his opinion, the bullets that had been recovered from Raoul's body had the same marks on them as one of the bullets Farah-Lajoie had given him—the bullet the detective had fired from Father Delorme's Bayard.

The evidence pointed to the inconceivable: that Father Adelard Delorme had slain his own brother! Why had the priest said he'd inherited the Bayard from his father, when he'd owned it less than two weeks? Ballistics indicated the gun was the murder weapon. Father Delorme would benefit financially from Raoul's death. But could a Roman Catholic priest commit *murder*?

Farah-Lajoie asked Coroner Edmund McMahon to draw up a warrant for Father Delorme's arrest. McMahon was stunned. Even after Farah-Lajoie explained the evidence, McMahon could not believe it. *Priests were not murderers!* Moreover, as a practicing Catholic who'd been born and raised in Quebec, McMahon knew what would happen if the police charged a priest with murder. "Every priest and nun in the province would want our heads." Before he could draw up a warrant, he said, he would need more evidence.

Even as Farah-Lajoie presented his case to McMahon, Father Delorme was holding a press conference. Ignoring Farah-Lajoie's advice, he announced he was offering a $10,000 reward for information leading to the arrest and conviction of the killers. He described the gold watch that had been torn from Raoul's waistcoat. The initials "A.D." were engraved on the back. "If you can find that watch, it will lead you to the killer."

This was the first of several press conferences Father Delorme would hold. He was aware of the rumours about him that had been circulating. This gossip had been enhanced by leaks about evidence the police had, and Detective Farah-Lajoie's suspicions. Father Delorme used the press conferences to defend his name publicly. He also seemed to revel in the publicity. *L'Affaire Delorme* was front-page news not only in Quebec, but across Canada and internationally.

"It hurts my feelings to see my name dragged in the mud. How could anyone suppose that I would kill my brother for $25,000 when I have assets of my own? We must find the murderers! When that happens I will demand that, to set an example, punishment be carried out in the Mount Royal Arena, whatever the price! I want revenge for my brother's blood. The diabolical rumours must be stopped. We must silence those detractors who are spewing insults and abuse on everyone. They can be found even in high society. But who are they? Free thinkers, atheists, anticlerical people, policemen, vain men—in a word bad citizens. We must see their names are revealed."

At a meeting held on January 17, Coroner McMahon asked Father Delorme if he could explain about the "inherited" gun. The priest said he had inherited the Iver Johnson from his father. He'd simply forgotten to tell the officers he had traded it in for the Bayard. That satisfied McMahon, who knew he had to tread carefully. His office was being assailed, on one side by people who were appalled that police would even *suspect* a priest of such a crime, and on the other by anti-Catholics like the Freemasons who charged that Father Delorme was hiding behind his cassock and collar.

The Catholic Church would not take a stand on the issue, but from their pulpits priests defended Father Delorme. The $10,000 reward drew private investigators who scoured the city in search of information that might lead them to the killer—and the big money. It also attracted self-styled psychics who claimed they could locate the guilty parties, for a substantial fee.

Though Farah-Lajoie's evidence pointed directly at Father Delorme, the police still looked for any lead that might direct them to other possible suspects: bandits, a madman, *anyone* but a priest! They found nothing. On January 24 a coroner's inquest was held.

Ernest Leclerc, the furnace stoker, testified he had been in the basement of the Delorme house only an hour, not three hours as Father Delorme had stated. The neighbour who lived in the adjacent house said he heard the engine of Father Delorme's car at about eleven o'clock on the night in question, but didn't know if the car was entering or leaving the garage. Tire tracks in the snow the next morning showed that someone had taken the car out. He also said he'd been awakened at about one in the morning by the sound of coal being shaken in the Delorme's furnace. He heard a woman's voice call, "Aren't you going to bed, Adelard?"

Flora, Lilly and Rosa all gave conflicting testimony as to the exact times Adelard had been home. Florence and Lilly were both described as women of low intelligence. Florence insisted that Raoul had worn his new overshoes that day, even after being told that Detective Farah-Lajoie had found them in the closet. She wept when the coroner asked her how the overshoes could have come home on their own. Lilly broke into tears even before the coroner could ask her a question. By the end of the day, the inquest had solved nothing.

While Farah-Lajoie searched for more evidence, speculation over who killed Raoul ran wild. One story had the shy young man bumped off by bootleggers. Another had him running around with a sleazy crowd from the burlesque theatre, and then being murdered by a vengeful woman.

Father Delorme threatened reporters who wrote articles suggesting he might be the murderer. He summoned one, Narcisse Arcand, to his house. "So now you're starting to make trouble for me," the priest told the newspaperman. "Your stories are starting to harm me. I have friends at *La Presse* and if you and I don't get along, you're going to be in big trouble."

On January 26 Farah-Lajoie and Chief Lepage showed up at the house to examine Father Delorme's car. In it they found two bloodstained cushions, four cardboard boxes covered with chicken feathers, and two oil-stained blankets. The priest had explanations for everything. Nonetheless, the policemen took it all to the crime lab. The blood on the cushions proved to be human.

Back to the house went Farah-Lajoie. With him was Dr. Wilfrid Derome, a professor of forensic medicine and toxicology at the University of Montreal and founder of the Montreal Laboratory of Forensic Medicine. While Father Delorme fumed, Dr. Derome had the seats removed from the car and taken to his crime lab. Farah-Lajoie searched the basement and found a piece of rope similar to the one that had bound the quilts to Raoul's head. As the detective and the scientist were leaving, they said they would be taking the car for a thorough examination. Father Delorme replied, "Every day you take something out of here. At the end I suppose it will be my turn to go."

The inspection showed there had been an attempt to scrub human blood from the car's back seat. The soap was identical to the soap found on the quilts. The oil stains on the blankets taken from the car matched the stains on the quilts. Once again Farah-Lajoie asked McMahon for an arrest warrant. Again McMahon insisted on more evidence.

The police put a twenty-four-hour watch on the Delorme house. The priest called another press conference and proceeded to rage incoherently against the police, the press and the rumours that were sweeping through Montreal and beyond. Then he told the reporters he'd have them arrested if they repeated a word he'd said.

On February 1 Father Delorme phoned Quebec Premier Louis-Alexandre Taschereau, who was also the province's attorney-general. Father Delorme said he was making a "petition for justice." He asked, "Does justice have the right to throw me as fodder to the press and the public, who seem to love sensationalism?... I insist, Mr. Attorney General, that this investigation be terminated without further delay, one way or the other, but in accordance with your righteousness, your judgment, and your wisdom. I am satisfied with the conscientious work which your officers are doing in this mysterious case. But for heaven's sake please finish hounding me from every angle."

After receiving the premier's promise to give his request every consideration, Father Delorme called the newspapers and asked them to publish a statement.

"I request permission from the newspapers to categorically deny the slander that the public seems to enjoy spreading about me.

I deny having gone to the Bishop of Montreal to obtain the help of the diocesan authorities.

I also deny having gone to see Chiefs Lepage and Belanger with the diocesan authorities.

I deny having used money to buy silence anywhere.

I deny having had an interview with any judge, lawyer or magistrate.

Finally, I declare that I have carried out meticulously all of the duties of my ministry."

Taschereau summoned Coroner McMahon and Chief Lepage to Quebec City. He reviewed the evidence with them, then ordered the inquest to be reopened on February 14. He also appointed Joseph Charles Walsh, K.C., as Crown prosecutor. Then the premier issued his own press release, admonishing the newspapers for interfering with the police investigation and indulging in sensationalism.

On the evening of February 13 a special session of the Provincial Cabinet issued an order for Father Delorme's arrest. Narcisse Arcand warned him about it the next morning. The priest was furious.

"You're crazy!" he roared. "Don't you know this is a cassock?...Let them try and arrest me! I had a revolver in my car, but I have another one and I won't hesitate, you can be sure."

The reporter left immediately and informed Chief Lepage. Rather than risk a violent confrontation between the police and the priest, Lepage phoned Father Delorme and asked him to come to the station to review some information—something the priest had done before. Father Delorme complied, and was kept at the police station until the two o'clock inquest.

The courtroom was packed. Father Delorme appeared confident, even arrogant, as he entered. Not until he was informed that Walsh was a Crown prosecutor did he seem to realize the true seriousness of his situation. Father Delorme described again his activities of the last day Raoul was home and of the subsequent evening. He was once more evasive about Raoul's will. This time, however, the document was produced in court. Aside from a few provisions made for the Delorme sisters, the entire estate Raoul would have inherited on his twenty-fifth birthday was bequeathed to his brother Adelard! The court also learned that Father Delorme had been "borrowing" large sums of money from the inheritance he'd been holding in trust for Raoul.

The coroner's jury retired for a little over an hour. It returned with the decision that Father Adelard Delorme stand trial for the murder of his brother. While he awaited that trial, Father Delorme's residence would be Montreal's grim Bordeaux Prison.

The news electrified Montreal and the province of Quebec, stunned Canadians from Halifax to Victoria, and made front-page headlines in New York. To Father Delorme's sympathizers he was a martyr, unjustly persecuted by police. Anti-Catholic bigots gloated over his arrest.

Detective Farah-Lajoie, who only wanted to get on with his investigation, was branded anti-clerical and a pagan. A newspaper claimed the Freemasons had offered him up to $50,000 if he could find enough evidence to hang the priest. Farah-Lajoie's children were abused at school. His wife's parish priest urged her to use her influence to discourage her husband from investigating

Father Delorme. A bishop personally pleaded with the detective not to be so zealous in his pursuit of a man of God. The Delorme sisters went so far as to accuse him of stealing Father Delorme's raccoon coat from their house.

With the priest in jail, Farah-Lajoie was free to search the house unimpeded. The sisters protested, but there was nothing they could do. In Florence's room the detective found homemade quilts that matched the ones found on the body.

Father Delorme's preliminary hearing began February 21. Defending him were cousins Gustave and Philippe Monette, both highly respected lawyers. They requested, and were granted, a postponement. Because of the crowds and threats that had been made against both the defendant and the police, Father Delorme was smuggled in and out a back door of the court building while a policeman dressed in a long black coat and a black hat was used as a decoy. Father Delorme was thrilled to be part of such a ploy.

When the hearing resumed March 14, the Monettes tried for another postponement on the grounds that their client was mentally unfit. This time the request was denied. In addition to the other circumstantial evidence, the Crown now had the matching quilts, as well as the crime lab's report that the feather found with the body matched the ones in Father Delorme's car.

Then Dr. Wilfred Derome startled the court by bringing in a headless mannequin dressed in Raoul's bloodstained clothing. Pointing out the bullet holes in the shirt and coat collars, and the way the bloodstains had spread, Dr. Derome demonstrated how he believed Raoul had been shot by an assailant standing above him.

Derome's evidence was dramatic, but what followed was even more startling. Father Louis Rheaume of the University of

Ottawa testified that he had seen Father Delorme help Raoul write his will just before the young man's surgery—the will the defendant stated he had never seen. Father Delorme was returned to his cell in Bordeaux to await the next trial, scheduled for June.

Meanwhile, a Pall Mall cigarette package containing Father Delorme's missing gold watch was delivered to the Chief of the *Sûreté Provincial,* Quebec's provincial police. On the wrapper were the chief's home address and "A. Delorme watch." The handwriting was identified as Father Delorme's. Everyone knew Farah-Lajoie smoked Pall Mall cigarettes. Was this an amateurish attempt to imply he had stolen the watch?

Between June 1, 1922, and October 31, 1924, Father Delorme was tried four times. During that period the Church suspended his right to say mass. In court he was not to be referred to as "Father," though he still wore his cassock and collar. His behaviour in the courtroom was sometimes dignified, but often bizarre. There were instances when he disrupted the proceedings with angry outbursts, and times when he seemed to doze off. When the court was moved to the garage where his Franklin was parked so the jury could inspect it, Father Delorme got into the car and began explaining all its special features.

The series of trials saw changes in judges, prosecutors and defence counsels. The hearings were conducted in French, French and English, then French again. Jurors toured the Delorme house, handled the bullets that killed Raoul (the body had been exhumed and a third bullet found in the neck), and gazed upon the victim's skull, which was presented by the Crown as an exhibit.

Exchanges between the prosecution and the defence were frequently heated. One day the jurors would hear the defendant described as a scholar devoted to his family. The next day he'd be demonized as a vain megalomaniac with visions of grandeur. When Pope Benedict XV died in January 1922, Father Delorme was alleged to have said the pope had suffered a heart attack upon hearing of the vile accusations brought against the Canadian priest. The pontiff actually died of pneumonia.

The defence managed to have the first trial changed to a hearing to determine the accused's sanity. It showed there had been a long history of mental illness in both his mother and father's families. Florence and Lilly, when placed on the witness stand, proved unable to answer simple questions. Their intellect, to use the terminology of the time, was not much above that of an imbecile. All this seemed to provide the jury with an easy way out of a dilemma. If Father Delorme were declared mentally unfit, he could not be tried and convicted. The jury ruled him insane, and the priest was packed off to an institution.

But many newspapers and a large percentage of the public cried foul. They said the court, under pressure from the Church, was dodging the issue. Had Adelard Delorme not passed the courses necessary for him to be ordained a priest? Had he not once taught at the college level himself? Had he not managed the Delorme estate since his father's death? How could such a man be judged insane? In May 1923 the lieutenant governor of Quebec declared Father Delorme mentally fit and had him moved back to Bordeaux Prison.

The next three trials were to decide if Adelard Delorme should go free or hang. In addition to the evidence that had been presented in the previous hearings, the jurors learned that the telephone company had no record of the late-night phone calls

Father Delorme had spoken of. They heard vague tales of Raoul being seen in a big McLaughlin car with four strangers, and others of Father Delorme trying to dump the body in the St. Lawrence. There was conflicting evidence concerning the times Adelard and the sisters had been home. The prosecution demonstrated that Lilly had difficulty telling time.

The defence argued that no murder could have been committed in the basement because neighbours would have heard shots, and the clothing of the deceased would have been covered with dust from the furnace. The defence also accused Farah-Lajoie of fabricating evidence.

The prosecution's response was that the murder did not take place in the basement, but more likely in Raoul's room, which would have been easy to clean up afterward. The thick walls of the house would have contained the sounds of struggle and gunfire. Nor had the murder necessarily happened at night. Raoul might have returned home late in the afternoon. The prosecution even had a possible scenario.

The Crown believed that Adelard had long since planned to kill Raoul so he could claim the estate. That's why he traded in his clumsy old revolver for the easy to handle Bayard automatic. His last chance to kill Raoul was on that final night of the Christmas holiday. One more day and Raoul would be gone back to Ottawa.

Quite likely he intended to make the murder look like a suicide. He stealthily approached Raoul, who was probably sitting in his room, and attempted to shoot him in the side of the head. But Father Delorme botched that first shot, and the bullet struck Raoul in the jaw. Now a death struggle ensued between the brothers. Raoul, the smaller of the two, in shock and pain, grasped

Adelard's right wrist, trying to force the muzzle of the gun away from his head. That would account for the welt Farah-Lajoie had seen on the priest's wrist.

Adelard had a vise-like grip on Raoul's right hand, probably digging his fingernails in as he struggled to subdue the young man, which would explain the scratches and bruising on Raoul's hand. The priest squeezed the trigger five more times, emptying the full clip of steel bullets into Raoul's head and neck.

Finally the victim was dead. But Adelard could no longer stage the killing as a suicide. So he wrapped the head in quilts to contain the blood, dressed the dead man in his coat (but forgot about the overshoes) and carried him down to the car. He dumped the body in one part of town, after rifling the pockets to make it look like the work of robbers. Then he smeared the hat with some blood and dropped it in another part of town to confound the police.

Such was the Crown's theory. But it was based on circumstantial evidence. The defence had explanations for every point of evidence the Crown presented. For example, a child with a nosebleed had supposedly caused the bloodstains on the back seat of the Franklin.

The accumulated evidence, however, and the lies in which Father Delorme had been caught, weighed heavily against him. Each presiding judge, in delivering instructions to the jury, strongly indicated that he expected a guilty verdict. The Quebec judicial system had been roasted in the Canadian and international press for having a double standard when it came to the clergy, and the judges wanted the world to know that Quebec courts were impartial no matter who was in the prisoner's box.

But in each trial there were jurymen who could not bring themselves to convict a priest and send him to the gallows. The jury for the second trial voted ten to two for conviction. The third jury was locked at ten to two for acquittal. By the fourth trial, public interest in the case had waned considerably. The jurors knew that if they failed to come to a unanimous decision to convict, Father Delorme would be automatically acquitted. They found the priest not guilty.

After 989 days in custody Father Delorme was free to go. The Church restored all the privileges of a fully ordained priest. But he did not return to 190 St. Hubert Street. The Church posted him under a different name at Montreal's Institute For the Deaf and Dumb, where he remained until his death in 1942.

Officially the murder of Raoul Delorme remains unsolved, so in that sense it is a "mystery." But many people had no doubt of Father Delorme's guilt. In a present-day court of law he quite likely would be convicted.

The true mystery lies in just what happened in the Delorme house that January 5. If Father Delorme did in fact murder his brother, just how much did the sisters know about it? Could Rosa—somewhat more mentally adept than the others—have been involved? Was the furnace stoker, Leclerc, an accomplice? He disappeared after the first trial and was not seen in Montreal again until just before the third trial. He had evidently been jailed in Vermont for horse theft. Or could it be that someone else killed Raoul, and Father Delorme was protecting that person? Not likely perhaps, but also not impossible in a case so riddled with the extraordinary.

MYSTERY MAN

Brother Twelve

The great American showman P.T. Barnum is credited with coining the phrase: "There's a sucker born every minute." A character played by another American, comedy film star W.C. Fields, took this credo a step further when he said: "Never give a sucker an even break."

Barnum and Fields were both in the entertainment business, and the cynicism and opportunism suggested in their statements have to be taken within that context. Con men and charlatans of various stripes had been relieving the gullible of their money by every sort of pose, sleight of hand and deceit imaginable for centuries before either of those men ever drew breath. Sometimes the tricks were seen as entertaining carnival games, other times as outright fraud. In either case, the victim lost money, and perhaps a degree of self-esteem.

But what of those imposters who prey upon the minds and souls of the "suckers"—the self-proclaimed messiahs, prophets and evangelists who draw admiring believers into their snares with promises of salvation? When we consider a sinister character like the Reverend Jim Jones and the horrific events at his

Jonestown settlement in Guyana, we find ourselves in a realm far removed from that of the common flim-flam man. Shaking a mark down for a few dollars is not at all the same as threatening a person's very existence in this world and the next as a means of acquiring that person's money and property. Many nations have had pretenders who claimed to have divine or supernatural connections, and who tricked people into believing their "teachings" to be true. Canada is no exception.

Edward Arthur Wilson, who would earn fame and notoriety as Brother Twelve (also The Brother, XII) was born in Birmingham, England in 1878. His father was an Anglican missionary and his mother a native of India. Nothing is known of his early life. In adult years he claimed to be everything from the son of an Indian princess to a former African slave trader. He also said he had been a cadet on a sailing ship in the Royal Navy. The latter may have been true, as Wilson was certainly a skilled sailor.

In 1905 Wilson was in Victoria, British Columbia, working for the Dominion Express Company. Because of his love of sailing, he became very familiar with the Strait of Juan de Fuca and the Gulf of Georgia. By 1912 he was in California, where he joined the Theosophical Society, an organization founded in 1875 for the study of "mediumistic phenomena" and Eastern religions.

Wilson said that even as a child he had been in touch with super-physical beings and had even received visitations from them. He evidently spent much of his youth studying the world's religions and the occult. He corresponded with mystics and students of the occult all over the world, and expressed a firm belief in reincarnation. He began to call himself a *chela,* a word that originally meant a disciple of a Hindu teacher.

Wilson's wanderings took him from the United States to Tahiti, Italy and France. He probably served with the British Merchant Marine during the First World War. Everything he did, he said later, was in preparation for the spiritual work for which he was destined.

On October 22, 1924, while he was in the south of France, Wilson had the "vision" that would change his life—as well as the lives of all those who came under his spell. He was lying on his bed not feeling very well, he wrote, when all suddenly became very still and quiet. His window was open, but he heard none of the usual night noises. He realized he was about to hear a voice!

"Immediately I had the sensation of looking down an immense vista of Time, a roofless corridor flanked with thousands and thousands of pillars. I seemed to be looking into both Time and Space at once.

"Then, from an immeasurable distance, came the Voice, faint but very clear and wonderfully sweet; it conveyed a sense of unutterable majesty and power. The bed shook, the room wherein I lay was shaken, and the very air throbbed and vibrated. I listened to the Voice, filled with a sense of its immense and awful distance. It said:

'THOU WHO HAST WORN THE DOUBLE CROWN OF UPPER AND LOWER EGYPT, OF THE HIGH KNOWLEDGE AND THE LOW, HUMBLE THYSELF. PREPARE THY HEART, FOR THE MIGHTY ONES HAVE NEED OF THEE. THOU SHALT REBUILD, THOU SHALT RESTORE. THEREFORE, PREPARE THY MIND FOR THAT WHICH SHALL ILLUMINE THEE.'

"A cold wind blew down that enormous aisle of pillars; somewhere in the endless distance, lights seemed to move; then from above my head, the light flooded me so that the distance and the vistas were dissolved. Then the light faded and I lay still, filled with a sense of wonder and a great reverence."

All this and more Wilson revealed in his book *Foundation Letters and Teachings,* which he had published in 1924. He wrote another book called *The Three Truths,* which was published in 1927. Wilson also wrote scores of articles that appeared in magazines that catered to believers in the occult, as well as in his own publication, *The Chalice.*

Wilson said the physical world and the spiritual world were populated by old souls and new souls. Some of the former had been reincarnating for forty centuries. He himself, in past incarnations, had been Moses, Samuel, Daniel, John the Baptist, St. Paul and the pharaoh Akhenaten. The spirit world was ruled by a council of eleven of the great minds of history. When Wilson met these Masters of Wisdom during a seance, they immediately knew him as one of the greatest minds of all time, and made him the Twelfth Brother. Hence, his new name, Brother Twelve.

Brother Twelve taught that the current Theosophical leadership was corrupt and had betrayed the ideals of the Society's founders. He had been instructed, he said, to found a new Aquarian Foundation, based on the truths that lay at the heart of Ancient Egyptian Mysteries. Those who joined his new religion and who proved worthy through obedience and harsh discipline would be the only people with a chance of surviving the coming cataclysm and living on into a New Age.

The great disaster of which Brother Twelve warned involved not only the physical destruction of human civilization, but also an unleashing of demonic supernatural powers.

"All the evil forces and powers of the lower astral worlds will burst the barriers which have hitherto restrained them. They will shortly flood this physical world in such a tidal wave of horror as no living generation has seen. To find its parallel one must go back to the closing periods of the great Atlantean epoch."

One might wonder that otherwise rational, intelligent people would be taken in by any of this. However, it must be remembered that in the aftermath of the Great War and all its horrors, a great many bitter, disillusioned people were turning away from conventional religions and philosophies and seeking answers to profound questions elsewhere. Moreover, Brother Twelve, a small, swarthy man with white hair and a Vandyke beard that gave him the look of a magician, was a very charismatic individual. His eyes, people said, were hypnotic.

In June 1926 Brother Twelve, who by now was married to a woman named Alma, went to Southampton, England. He rented a little hall and invited English Theosophists to come and listen to him. Some local members of the Society did, and soon word was out about the compelling speaker, his miraculous visions and his brilliant writings. More Society members from London and southern England made the trip to Southampton to listen to predictions of the coming catastrophe followed by the promise of a glorious New Age. During this period Brother Twelve was alleged to have met some of Britain's most prominent men, including future prime minister Neville Chamberlain.

Among those who made the fateful decision to join the Aquarian Foundation were a retired chemist named Alfred H. Barley and his wife, Annie, a former schoolteacher. As required by the Foundation, the couple sold all their worldly possessions and turned the money—about $14,000—over to Brother Twelve. They were not the only ones.

After one of his visits to the other eleven Masters of Wisdom, Brother Twelve told his new followers of a revelation that had been made to him. The centre of spiritual energy and knowledge for the whole world in the New Age was to be a place on the east coast of Canada's Vancouver Island. He had never been there before, he lied, but he showed them on a map the place where he would build his "fortress of the future." There, he said, he and his disciples would be safe from the destruction toward which the rest of the corrupt, sinful world was hurtling.

In February 1927, Brother Twelve sailed for Montreal. His wife Alma, the Barleys and a few other converts were to meet him in British Columbia. After disembarking in Quebec, before getting on the train to the West Coast, Brother Twelve spoke in a few Theosophical Lodges in Eastern Canada and roped in a few more believers.

Brother Twelve established the Aquarian headquarters on 126 acres (50.9 hectares) of beautiful coastal property at Cedar-by-the-Sea, seven miles (11.2 km) south of Nanaimo. In May 1927 the Aquarian Foundation was incorporated under the Societies Act of British Columbia. Its Board of Governors included, besides Brother Twelve: Will Bevington Comfort, a popular American novelist; Joseph Benner, owner of the Sun Publishing Company of Akron, Ohio; Edward Lucas, a prominent Vancouver lawyer;

Maurice Von Platen, a retired Chicago manufacturer; Phillip Fisher, son of a wealthy family in Birmingham, England; and an American astrologer named Coulson Turnbull. Brother Twelve said the consciousness of these Governors would be expanded so they could become the instruments of the Masters of Wisdom.

The rank and file of the Aquarian Foundation's membership were people from all levels of society and all walks of life: tradesmen, doctors, lawyers, men of business. Among them: Sir Kenneth McKenzie of Tunbridge Wells, England; James Lippincott, of the famous American book publishing company; A. Laker, editor of a British magazine; Robert England, former United States Treasury agent; Roger Painter, a Florida businessman who'd made a fortune in poultry. Brother Twelve told Painter they had met before. When Brother Twelve walked the earth in the incarnation of St. Paul, Painter had been Christ's apostle Simon Peter.

Some of those people went to live in the commune on Vancouver Island. About eight thousand other members in North America and Europe subscribed to the Foundation's magazine, *The Chalice,* in which Brother Twelve explained his messianic mission while denouncing Jews, Catholics and Bolsheviks. These subscribers also donated money—lots of it! Cedar-by-the-Sea, which began as a tent city, was soon a thriving community of well-built houses. There was even a school, though there were no children. The majority of the Foundations members were older adults whose children (those who had any) were grown up.

One person who was drawn in by the articles in *The Chalice* was Mary Connally, a widow in North Carolina whose husband had left her a million-dollar estate. She sent Brother Twelve a letter that included a cheque for $2,000. Brother Twelve replied with thanks, and a suggestion that they meet personally in Toronto at the Prince George Hotel. Mrs. Connally was thrilled at the very idea of meeting the great man, and arrangements were made.

The religion business was working out very well indeed for Edward Wilson/Brother Twelve. It was about to get even better. On the eastbound train from Seattle, he met another lady of substantial means, Mrs. Myrtle Baumgartner of Clifton Springs, New York. She was the wife of a well-respected physician. As the train rolled across the continent, Brother Twelve convinced Myrtle that she was the reincarnation of the Egyptian goddess Isis, and he the embodiment of her husband/brother Osiris. Their destiny—their *duty*—he told her, was to conceive a child that would be the reincarnation of the sun god Horus, the redeemer of the world. Myrtle went for it, hook, line and sinker! She agreed to leave her husband and family and run off to the wilds of Vancouver Island. Myrtle wrote to her husband that her "Beloved" was the man she had been dreaming about all her life and that, "When you have come into the presence of that one once, you will never again wonder—you will *know.*"

Brother Twelve parked Myrtle in Chicago for a few days while he went to Toronto to meet Mary Connally and pick up her cheque for $28,000. Then Mary headed back to North Carolina so she could sell off everything and go to Vancouver Island. Osiris returned to Chicago, put Isis on the train, and continued west. By the time the pair arrived back in Cedar-by-the-Sea, the reincarnation of Horus had probably been conceived.

Alma Wilson was not at all happy with the situation. She reminded Edward Wilson in no uncertain terms that he was a married man. Brother Twelve patiently explained that the marriage of Osiris and Isis was not like an earthly marriage. It was a necessary sacrifice to bring about the New Age. Any sexual pleasure involved was incidental to greater things. Brother Twelve even wrote an article on the matter for *The Chalice.* Alma didn't buy any of it. She left the Foundation and her husband, and vanished from history.

In the centre of the Aquarian settlement was a building called the House of Mystery, to which Brother Twelve would withdraw alone when he wished to communicate with the Masters of Wisdom. Only he was allowed to enter this inner sanctum. A wire across the path leading to it marked the limit beyond which no others could approach. When Brother Twelve took his Isis into this sacred place, he told his followers to stand on the far side of the wire and assist him in his spiritual duties with meditation.

The Aquarians had been appalled at their leader's infidelity toward his wife. Now they felt he was defiling a sanctuary with his mistress. Meditation turned to conspiratorial grumbling.

Later, Brother Twelve confronted them with their "treason." He knew everything that had been said, and who had said it! The Masters of Wisdom, he claimed, had told him everything!

In that age when few people knew anything about electronic eavesdropping, the Aquarians would not have imagined that the area around the House of Mystery was bugged. Unbeknownst to anyone else, Brother Twelve had hired an electrician to install hidden microphones in the trees and behind stones, with concealed wires running to his private sanctuary.

But even though Brother Twelve had awed his followers with his "powers," he decided the House of Mystery was no longer private enough. He used $13,000 of the money Mary Connally had given him and bought four hundred acres (161 hectares) of property on Valdes Island in the Strait of Georgia, across from Cedar-by-the-Sea. There he planned to build a new House of Mystery. Only a chosen few would be allowed to set foot on Valdez Island.

Now the Aquarians were shocked to learn that their leader had deposited a donation of $28,000 in his personal account instead of the Foundation's account. This was against the Foundation's constitution. There was trouble in paradise when Robert England, Edward Lucas and Maurice Von Platen expressed doubts about Brother Twelve's divinity. England had Edward Wilson charged with misappropriating funds.

Wilson retaliated by accusing England of embezzling Aquarian Foundation funds himself. Both men were arrested. In North Carolina Mary Connally heard of what was happening and boarded a train for the West Coast. She arrived in time for the preliminary hearing in Nanaimo in September 1928.

It was a hot day and the courtroom was stifling. In the midst of the proceedings, Robert England's lawyer, an elderly man, suddenly suffered a dizzy spell and was unable to continue. The Aquarians believed Brother Twelve had used his Ancient Egyptian magic on the man. Mary Connally testified that she had given the money to Brother Twelve as a personal gift. Before the case could be brought to actual trial, Robert England mysteriously vanished.

Myrtle Baumgartner did not give birth to the god Horus. She suffered a miscarriage, then went insane. Mary Connally—who would soon have troubles of her own—cared for her for a while. Finally Myrtle had to be placed in a mental institution.

Brother Twelve had suffered setbacks. That was always the case with saints and martyrs, he said. "Time and again your work will be torn down, and you must patiently and painfully rebuild it." Rebuild he did.

He purged his commune of "traitors." They were soon replaced by new converts who were always arriving at Cedar-by-the-Sea. With more money from the ever generous Mary Connally, Brother Twelve bought the three small De Courcey Islands that lay between Cedar-by-the-Sea and Valdes Island. On one of them he built his new City of Refuge.

Brother Twelve's followers had always lived under strict rules: surrender all worldly goods; work hard everyday in the commune's fields, greenhouses, orchards and sawmill; give absolute obedience to the leader. They were forbidden to read books—except the ones written by Brother Twelve. Each follower was given a secret "inner name," like *Ramathiel* or *Serathiel*, which they were never to utter aloud but by which they would be known to the Masters of Wisdom. Now there was a new rule: men and women were to live on separate islands. The followers obeyed.

The colony was making money. Donations were pouring in. New converts surrendered every cent they owned. Brother Twelve took the money to the bank and converted much of it into gold coins. The coins were placed in Mason jars that were sealed with wax. The jars of gold were stored in wooden boxes specially made by the commune's carpenters. One carpenter later said they made forty-three of those boxes and each one contained $10,000 in gold coins.

With his wife gone and the unfortunate Myrtle Baumgartner institutionalized, Brother Twelve needed a new paramour. He chose thirty-nine-year-old Mabel Skottowe, widow of a Canadian soldier who had died in the Great War. It is uncertain if Mabel was originally from Canada, the United States or England. The members of the cult would soon regard her as a fiend from hell.

Brother Twelve told his followers Mabel was his right hand. "She is my eyes, my ears, my mouth; whatever she says you can take as coming from me." Wilson had legally changed his name to Amiel de Valdes. Mabel changed hers to Zura de Valdes. To Brother Twelve's flock she became known as Madame Zee.

Brother Twelve made Madame Zee the overseer of all work projects. She was, in effect, his slave driver, and she relished the part. Red-haired and wild-eyed, she strode about with a long bullwhip which she did not hesitate to use on anyone who appeared to be slacking or who questioned her authority. Her language was as vile as her temper. She drove one seventy-six-year-old woman to suicide. Three other members went insane.

Georgina Crawford, who had joined the commune with her husband Bruce, was made to pull stumps with her bare hands, and to haul hundred-pound (45.3 kg) sacks of potatoes. When she injured her knee in a fall and could barely walk, Madame Zee showed her no mercy. Georgina, wracked with pain, was forced to work from two o'clock in the morning until ten at night. She did not see her husband for weeks at a time.

Madam Zee was harsh to one and all, but she saved the worst of her cruelty for Mary Connally. By now the widow's money had run out—much of it used by Brother Twelve to buy the properties that made up his little empire. Mary was no longer of interest to him, and he did nothing to restrain Madame Zee.

Madam Zee forced the sixty-two-year-old woman to carry heavy loads, and to cultivate fields with hand tools from dawn to dusk. Mary was evicted from the sturdy house she had originally occupied in Cedar-by-the-Sea, and moved around to a series of shacks and hovels on the various islands. They were unheated, and she had only straw to sleep on. Each time Mary was told to move, she had to carry her own furnishings and luggage. No one was permitted to lift a hand to help her.

At the beginning of each ordeal, Mary was told it was a test to determine her worthiness to be among the elect of the New Age. She would try her hardest to please Madame Zee, and through her, Brother Twelve. At the conclusion of each "test" she was told she had failed.

Why did these people endure such abuse when they could have left the commune at any time? They sincerely believed that Brother Twelve not only was the one man who could guarantee their future, but that he also held the fates of their very souls in his hands. He told them he could destroy their souls for eternity, or render them incapable of reincarnating for eons, and they believed him.

In January 1930 Brother Twelve and Madame Zee left for England. Roger Painter was put in charge of the commune in the Master's absence. Of course, the Masters of Wisdom would keep him informed of everything. For legal reasons, the title to Cedar-by-the-Sea was put in the name of Alfred Barley, one of the first converts.

For a time there was relative bliss at the commune, although Roger Painter's wife Leona was left with the task of overseeing Mary Connally's brutal work routine. Leona hated the assignment. But she did it out of fear of losing her soul.

In November, Brother Twelve and Madam Zee returned in a twenty-five ton sailing vessel called the *Lady Royal.* Brother

Twelve had acquired the boat in England, either by purchase or as a gift from an admirer. He hired a crew and sailed the *Lady Royal* across the Atlantic, through the Panama Canal and up the West Coast.

Brother Twelve brought something else to the commune besides a new boat—fourteen rifles and a thousand rounds of ammunition. He put his followers to work constructing fortifications on the islands: gun pits and a stone fort with loopholes in the walls. Women were told to patrol the shores and warn of any approaching boats. Men were given guns and put on guard duty, and told to fire warning shots at any boats that came too close.

Madame Zee resumed her reign of terror. The followers laboured in misery and fear. Brother Twelve's behaviour became increasingly erratic. He would fly into a rage at the most trivial things. In one incident, he had a minor misunderstanding with Roger Painter, one of his staunchest disciples. Painter later reported:

"And like a flash, he came at me, and cursed me for everything under the sun, and called me a dirty lowdown sneak, and said that I had undermined him. And he talked with me there for three solid hours, and called me every name under the sun."

Bruce Crawford would later observe that he had gone to Cedar-by-the-Sea in search of a brotherhood of love, but after a while realized it was "a brotherhood of hell."

Brother Twelve heard the rumblings of dissent and took action. He banished about a dozen "traitors" including Mary Connally, the Painters and the Barleys. He no doubt thought that fear for their souls would keep them quiet. Even if it didn't, they had no evidence they could take to the authorities.

But the all-knowing Master evidently forgot that the title to Cedar-by-the-Sea was now in Alfred Barley's name. The exiles held a meeting, and decided to take legal action against Brother Twelve to recover their money. They retained the services of a Nanaimo lawyer and filed a lawsuit against Amiel de Verdes. The case came to trial in April, 1933. The attention it drew gave the outside world its first look into the strange goings-on in the commune south of Nanaimo.

On the morning of the trial, Victor B. Harrison, the lawyer representing Roger Painter's little group of exiles, was stunned to learn that his clients were terrified of taking the stand to testify. They believed that if they stepped into the witness stand, the Master would use his power to kill them on the spot. The resourceful Harrison quickly got hold of an old Haida artifact. He told his clients it was a powerful Native talisman that would protect the holder from any power under heaven. This worked! One by one, with the "protection" firmly in hand, the plaintiffs took the stand and told their harrowing stories.

Now the public learned of the abuses, both physical and mental; of elderly people forced to work like horses with barely enough food or water to keep them alive; of the whippings by sadistic Madame Zee; and of the enormous sums of money taken under false pretenses.

Once all the horror stories had been told, the court quickly found in favour of the plaintiffs. Most noteworthy of the settlements were those that went to Mary Connally and Alfred Barley. Mary was awarded $26,000 against her losses, and an additional $10,000 for physical injuries—injuries, she said, for which no amount of money could compensate. She was also awarded ownership of the

DeCourcey Islands and the real estate on Valdes Island that had been purchased with her money. Barley was awarded $14,000 plus the legal title to the land at Cedar-by-the-Sea.

There quite likely would have been further legal action which no doubt would have included criminal charges against Brother Twelve and Madame Zee. But when the pair realized the game was up, they quickly vanished. Before making their hasty exit from British Columbia, they did as much damage to the commune as time would allow. They scuttled the *Lady Royal* with dynamite, set fire to some outbuildings, and smashed furniture with axes. Brother Twelve and Madame Zee left two mysteries in their wake: where did they go, and what happened to that hoard of gold coins?

According to one story, Brother Twelve and Madame Zee escaped to England where he adopted her late husband's name, Julian Skottowe. He was in poor health, and the pair went to Neuchatel, Switzerland, in search of special medical attention. There, Brother Twelve died on November 7, 1934, at the age of fifty-six. He was penniless. Madame Zee disappeared without a trace.

It is possible that Brother Twelve's death in Switzerland was a hoax. One account says that in 1936 Mary Connally received a secret message, and immediately sent a lawyer to San Francisco with a suitcase full of money. The cash was handed over to a man "with gleaming eyes." Was Brother Twelve still alive, and the widow he had so badly used still under his spell?

Over $400,000 in gold, in forty-three wooden boxes! Dead weight of about half a ton! Could Brother Twelve and Madame Zee have taken that with them in their speedy departure from

British Columbia? It wouldn't seem possible, with the *Lady Royal* lying at the bottom of the Strait. If they did somehow manage to abscond with the loot, why did Brother Twelve die a pauper in 1934? If, in fact, he did not die at that time, why did he have to contact Mary Connally for money in 1936? (If, again, that story is true.)

If Brother Twelve did *not* get away with the gold, what became of it? Mary Connally, who remained at the former commune until 1941, didn't find it. Nor has anyone since. In his book, *My Country: The Remarkable Past,* historian Pierre Berton tells the story of Mary's caretaker, Sam Grunall, who went searching for the treasure after the widow returned to North Carolina. On Valdes Island Grunall found a sunken concrete vault beneath an outbuilding. In the vault was a roll of tarpaper with a message written on it in Brother Twelve's handwriting: "For fools and traitors, nothing!" Was this, as Mr. Berton described it, "a defiant shout from another decade"? Or was someone having one last laugh at the expense of suckers?

THE MYSTERY OF THE MAD TRAPPER

Murder in the Arctic

The police and trackers who pursued him across an Arctic wilderness called him Albert Johnson, though his true identity has never been conclusively determined. To the press of his time, to the Canadians and Americans who sat glued to their radios to hear the latest bulletin on his one-man war with the Royal Canadian Mounted Police, and to legend, he was and remains "The Mad Trapper of Rat River." It is not known if he was even Canadian. But his bloody drama, played out in the wild Yukon, has made him one of Canada's most infamous murderers and placed him among the nation's most enduring mysteries.

The story began December 31, 1931, in the sunless depths of the long Arctic winter. Constables Alfred King and R.G. McDowell and special constables Joe Bernard and Lazarus Sittichinli of the RCMP approached a remote cabin on the banks of the Rat River in the Northwest Territories, not far from the Yukon border. The name of the man inside was rumoured to be Albert Johnson. No one really knew for sure, because the man was a loner who spoke to almost nobody. Local Indians had complained to the police that this stranger had been springing their traps and encroaching upon their legitimate livelihoods. The man evidently wanted all the furs in the district for himself.

The policemen had spent a day and a half walking and mushing by dogsled in cold that was far below zero on the Fahrenheit scale to reach this out-of-the-way cabin. They were cold and hungry and wanted to take care of what should have been a routine call quickly. They hoped to get to Fort McPherson in time for a New Year's party.

Nonetheless, the officer in charge, Constable King, urged caution. He knew that Johnson, or whatever his name might be, was something of an oddball. In a hard land where people relied on each other for survival, Johnson shunned human company. On his infrequent visits to settlements to buy supplies—for which he always paid cash—he was taciturn and sullen when spoken to. Those few who had met him up close said he had cold, blue eyes and spoke with a hint of a Scandinavian accent. Even when police asked him who he was and where he'd some from, as was their duty in this frontier territory, he'd been evasive. Some of his answers were contradictory, even outright lies. But he hadn't broken any laws that they were aware of, so they had no cause to question him further. A pair of Indians once mistook him for a man they knew named Albert Johnson, and that name, for lack of any other, stuck.

It was evident from the way the man lived alone in an eight-by-ten-foot cabin in the howling wilderness, and by the way he handled the frigid Arctic trails, that he was a woodsman of considerable experience. As long as he behaved himself, the Mounties had no reason to bother him.

Then the complaints from the Indians had started to come in. Johnson was pulling up their traps and hanging them in trees. There was no record that he had even acquired a trapper's license for himself. The first police party to go to Johnson's cabin had encountered a closed door. He looked at them through the window, but would not respond to their requests to open up. Very unusual in a country where everybody's door was always open to visitors, including the police. With no warrant to enter the cabin, and with the temperature almost freezing the blood in their veins as they stood at Johnson's door, the police had no choice but to go back to Aklavik, eighty miles away.

Now Constable King had a warrant. He knew that Johnson was inside the cabin because smoke billowed from the chimney and a pair of snowshoes leaned against the wall by the door. While his fellow officers waited by the river, King approached the silent cabin. He called out, identifying himself as a police officer. He said that he had a warrant, and that if he had to, he would force the door open. Still there was only silence from the cabin.

"Are you there, Mr. Johnson?" King shouted. Johnson did not answer. The Mountie knocked on the door. Instantly the silent, frosty air was shattered as a gun roared inside the cabin. A bullet smashed through the wooden door and buried itself in King's chest, sending him sprawling in the snow.

While the wounded Mountie crawled to cover, leaving a trail of blood in the snow, his companions opened fire on the cabin to keep Johnson down. The trapper replied with an occasional shot, just enough to discourage them from storming his cabin. None of the policemen had time to wonder why Johnson had shot a man. They had to get King to a hospital before his wound and the Arctic cold killed him. They lashed the fallen Mountie to their dogsled and whipped up the team. They made it to Aklavik in a remarkable twenty hours, stopping only to rub King's face and limbs to prevent frostbite. A doctor in the tiny Aklavik hospital saved King's life.

Now the Mounties pieced together what little they knew of "Albert Johnson" and wondered why he had tried to kill a policeman. Surely, not over a minor trapping offence? Could he be a fugitive who was wanted by the law elsewhere? Was he just plain crazy? He wouldn't be the first lone wolf to crack up under cabin fever. Only two things did they know for certain. The man was dangerous, and they would get no answers until he was arrested and brought in for questioning. What the Mounties did not know, was that the man they called Albert Johnson was no ordinary trapper. He would prove to be one of the most desperate, resourceful and elusive criminals they had ever encountered.

On January 9 a nine-man posse of police, civilian volunteers and an Indian guide moved in on the trapper's cabin. They were led by Inspector A.N. Eames and Constable Edgar Millen. Eames wanted to get this business over with quickly. The temperature was plummeting and his group was already running low on food for the men and the dogs. He called on Johnson to surrender. He said that King was alive, so there would be no murder charge. Johnson didn't say a word. He did his talking with his guns, and the police answered with theirs.

The police could not have known that Johnson was prepared for them. He had turned his cabin into a tiny fortress from which one man could hold off a small army. He had dug a rifle-pit in the floor, giving himself maximum protection and a good shooting position. He had knocked loopholes in all four walls so he could see in every direction and shoot from all sides. The thick log walls of his cabin were stout protection from bullets. He had warmth and he had food.

His foes, on the other hand, were out in the bitter cold and had men and a lot of dogs to feed. They had to expose themselves to his gunfire to attack the cabin. For now, he had the advantage. The police could not besiege him for more than a day or so. Not in the –50° F cold!

Several times the police attacked, only to be driven back by the Trapper's bullets. Once, a pair of Mounties got to the door and managed to jar it slightly open before a hail of lead from a shotgun and a rifle forced them to retreat. The police tried to blind the supposedly trapped gunman with flares, but that didn't work.

Finally, after a day of brutal cold and useless gunfire (fortunately with no casualties), Eames decided to try dynamite. He had given Johnson his chance. Now it was time to show him that the Mounted Police weren't playing games.

Even dynamite froze in that fierce cold, and thawing out the sticks over an open fire was delicate work to say the least. But soon the men of the posse were hurling the explosives at the cabin, hoping to blow open the door or cave in a wall. Johnson's solid little building held up to the blasts.

A civilian volunteer named Knut Lang dashed up close enough to the cabin to land a stick of dynamite on the roof. It blasted open a hole and knocked down part of the chimney. But a moment later Lang was scurrying for cover with the Trapper's bullets shrieking through the air around him.

The Arctic cold was crushing now, and even with campfires roaring, Eames knew that he would soon have to get his men back to the shelter of a settlement. He decided to try one all-or-nothing last shot. He made a four-pound dynamite bomb by lashing the last few sticks of explosive together, lit the fuse, and hurled it at the Trapper's lair. The explosion lifted the roof off the cabin and partially caved in the walls.

The possemen were sure that if Johnson hadn't been killed by the blast, he must surely have been injured or at least stunned. They rushed forward. A man named Karl Gardlund had a flashlight, so they'd be able to find whatever was left of Albert Johnson.

Johnson wasn't dead. Nor was he injured. If he had been stunned by the blast, the effect was only momentary. To Gardlund's astonishment, the flashlight was shot out of his hand. Once again the posse retreated, and this time they withdrew all the way to Aklavik. When Constable Edgar Millen and Karl Gardlund returned to the scene of the battle four days later, Albert Johnson was gone. They still did not know why he had shot King, and now they wondered why he hadn't run immediately after shooting a Mountie. What had the senseless stand at the cabin been all about?

By this time the outside world had heard of the shooting of King and the gunfights. The press quickly dubbed the outlaw "The Mad Trapper of Rat River." It was a sensational name that sold newspapers and drew people to their radio sets. It was a thrilling tale of one man against an entire police force in the far-off and exotic Canadian North—and never mind that he had fired the first shot. It was the Dirty Thirties, when people were losing their jobs and their farms, and people saw the police as the protectors of bankers and the rich. Even though Inspector Eames told the press that the so-called "demented trapper" was "shrewd and resolute" and "a tough and desperate character," there were many who sympathized with Johnson as an underdog, and hoped he would get away.

The chase that was to boggle the Mounties and astound the public began on January 16, 1932. A force of RCMP officers, white and Native trackers, and volunteers from the Royal Canadian Corps of Signals at Aklavik set out. They had homemade bombs and a portable radio. Once again Eames was in charge, with Millen as his second-in-command.

The search went badly from the start. The wrecked cabin turned up no clue as to Johnson's real identity. A heavy snowfall had buried his trail. Then a blizzard came howling down on the manhunters. For days they searched the Rat River countryside and found not a single clue. On January 21, faced once again with a shortage of supplies, Eames had to retreat with most of the men. He left Constable Millen with Sergeant R.F. Riddell of the Corps of Signals, Karl Gardlund, and a fourth man to continue the search.

For a week Millen's party tramped through the snowy timberland of the Rat River country. Once, they came upon a food cache and watched it for hours, hoping it was Johnson's and that he would return to it. But the Trapper never appeared. By January 28 they were almost out of supplies and were ready to turn back. Then Sergeant Riddell found the faint, two-day-old marks of Johnson's trail.

Certain that the outlaw was within their grasp, the posse continued the hunt. They lost the trail, then found it again. The searchers realized that their quarry was an exceptionally skilled woodsman who possessed incredible stamina. He walked a zigzag pattern so that he could spy on his pursuers from the side or from behind. That meant that he had to cover twice the distance—on snowshoes and with a heavy backpack—that they covered by dogsled. In temperatures that froze men to the marrow, he could build only small campfires under the shelter of snowbanks. Since he could not risk using his rifle to shoot large game, he had to snare small animals for food. He trekked his way across country that veteran trackers had thought impenetrable, and left a thoroughly confusing trail while doing it.

The posse was on the banks of the Rat River, wondering in which direction to go next, when an Indian came into camp and told them he had heard a gunshot in the Bear River area. Millen decided it was worth investigating. Perhaps Johnson had thought that he had left the police far enough behind to risk shooting a large animal.

The men picked up a trail near the Bear River, and followed it back to the Rat. They came across the remains of a caribou, and finally, on January 30, they spotted the Mad Trapper's camp. Millen couldn't believe their good luck. The wily Johnson seemed to have grown careless. He had made camp with a cliff at his back, cutting off his escape. And he was cheerfully whistling a tune, evidently unaware that his pursuers were near. They had him this time!

Then one of the men slipped, making a noise. Instantly Johnson grabbed his .30-.30 Savage rifle and opened fire. As the police shot back, Johnson leapt across his campfire and dove behind a fallen tree. He appeared to collapse, and Millen thought he might have been hit. The Mountie called out to Johnson, and got no reply.

Nobody dared leave his cover. For two hours they waited, not sure if Johnson was dead, wounded, or planning a new trick.

Surely, they thought, he couldn't just lie there in the bitter cold. They could feel their own sweat freezing inside their clothing.

With night approaching, Millen decided to close in. The men had advanced only a few steps when Johnson sprang up and opened fire. Sergeant Riddell ducked for cover as a bullet whistled over his head. Millen dropped to one knee and fired two shots. Suddenly he stood up, spun around, dropped his rifle and collapsed. He was dead, with a bullet through his heart. While the other two men kept Johnson pinned down with rifle fire, Gardlund dragged Millen's body to cover.

The surviving possemen retreated to a base camp where they found Sergeant Earl Hersey of the Corps of Signals. He had brought in a sled-load of supplies. The next day they returned to the scene of the gun battle and found that Johnson had escaped by scaling the sheer cliff behind his camp. The Mad Trapper had won another round. With Millen's frozen corpse lashed to a sled, they started back to headquarters.

In Aklavik Inspector Eames had to admit that the police were dealing with a most extraordinary man, and would have to take extraordinary measures. Not only was there a killer on the loose, but also the reputation of the RCMP was at stake. The whole world was watching their failure to outshoot a lone gunman who had been on the run for a month in the middle of the Arctic winter. He sent out a call for more volunteers and requested the use of a search plane. It would be the first time in the history of the RCMP that a search would be conducted from the air. The plane could also be used to ferry supplies.

On February 7, while Eames led a search party through the rugged country between the Rat and Barrier rivers, a Bellanca monoplane lifted a load of supplies to the men in the field. Flying it was W.R. "Wop" May, one of Canada's great pioneer bush pilots. He was the pilot who had been the target of the Red Baron in a 1918 dogfight, when the German ace was shot down by another Canadian, Roy Brown. May would be invaluable to the police, shuttling supplies and spotting the blind trails the clever Johnson left to confuse the police trackers.

For several days following the death of Millen, search parties roamed across the Arctic wilderness. The Mad Trapper seemed to have vanished. He'd been on the run for more than a month, living on scanty rations and tramping through hostile country in blizzards that kept the toughest men indoors. As one trapper put it, "'Tis rough enough just staying alive under those conditions, let alone having to be on the run."

Not until February 12 did the Mounties get a lead, and what they heard was unbelievable. Snowshoe tracks believed to be Johnson's had been seen near La Pierre House on the *Yukon side* of the Richardson Mountains! The outlaw had done what even the Indians considered impossible: crossed, all alone, the high passes through bare, windswept rock in the dead of winter! Was the fugitive even human?

On February 13 Wop May flew some officers to La Pierre House, while others prepared to cross the range through Rat Pass by dogteam. May soon spotted Johnson's trail from the air, but lost it again in the tracks of a herd of caribou. The outlaw was still using every trick in the book.

The next day, after a series of sweeps across the country, May found Johnson's trail again near the Eagle River. It appeared that the Trapper was heading for another pass that would take him to the border with Alaska. For the next two days Wop May was grounded by bad weather, but men on the ground stuck to Johnson's trail. On February 17 May was able to take his plane aloft again. He followed the trail of the searchers, and so had a bird's-eye view of the final confrontation between the Mad Trapper and the RCMP and Corps of Signals.

Johnson had been moving up the Eagle River, and had back-tracked, probably hoping to come in behind the manhunters, as he had done before. This time he misjudged and came face to face with Eames' party on a sharp bend in the Eagle. Sergeant Hershey, who was in the lead, swung his rifle up and began firing. Two other officers also began shooting.

Johnson ran a few yards, then turned and fired a shot. The bullet struck Hershey in the elbow, deflected down and hit his knee, then deflected up and smashed into his chest. Hershey was not dead, but he was badly wounded and out of the fight.

As the police outflanked him, Johnson threw himself into the snow on the frozen river, pulled off his backpack, and thrust it in front of himself for cover. He was determined to shoot it out with a dozen policemen and soldiers.

Three times Inspector Eames called on Johnson to surrender, and each time the Trapper answered with gunfire. But now his luck had run out. The police had him in a three-way crossfire. Six bullets struck him, one exploding some ammunition in his pocket and blowing off a chunk of his thigh. Still he continued to shoot. Then another bullet smashed through his spine, and the Mad Trapper was dead. Wop May zoomed low over the prone figure on the ice, then signalled to the police that the fight was over. But why had it all happened? Who was the dead man? Since the trouble began back at the cabin on the Rat River, he had not uttered a single word.

There was absolutely nothing on the body to identify the man. The fingerprints were sent to Ottawa and Washington D.C., but they matched nothing in the files of the RCMP or the FBI. Months later a magazine published a photograph of Johnson as he lay dead in an Arctic police post. A number of people thought that the emaciated face, leering in a death-grin, resembled that of a man they had known as Arthur Nelson. There is considerable, though not conclusive, evidence that Nelson and Johnson were the same man.

Nelson (that name might also have been an alias) seemed to be of Scandinavian background. He had suddenly appeared in northern British Columbia during the 1924 gold rush. He was a strange, withdrawn man who usually avoided people. He was an excellent woodsman and a crack shot. Nelson had wandered across the north, trapping and prospecting. Indians who met him thought there was something suspicious about him and called him "The Bushman," a type of bogeyman from Native folklore. Nelson was last seen in May 1931 heading in the direction of Fort McPherson. Weeks later the man called Johnson had appeared in the Rat River country.

Even if Nelson and Johnson were one and the same, that does not explain why he killed one man, wounded two more, and led the Mounties on the biggest manhunt the North had ever witnessed. It has been suggested that he was truly a madman, with a psychotic hatred for police. But there is another theory.

In some of the places Nelson had visited, men had disappeared without explanation. One man had been killed in a struggle before his cabin burned down. At a place on the Nahanni River, several headless bodies had been found. This has led to conjecture that Nelson/Johnson was a thief and murderer of long standing. Nelson was known to travel long distances to sell furs, passing a nearby trading post to go to one farther away. This suggests that his furs were stolen, and he did not want a local trader to recognize another man's marks on the pelts.

Among Johnson's possessions when he was killed were $2,410 Canadian and twenty dollars American. That was a lot of money for that time. He also had five pearls worth about fifteen dollars, a jar containing some alluvial gold, and five pieces of gold dental work. The gold fillings did not come from his own teeth, so where did he get them? From the headless bodies found by the Nahanni River?

To date, the identity of the Mad Trapper of Rat River, and the reasons for his forty-eight-day duel with the RCMP, remain among Canada's most perplexing mysteries.

Bibliography

Atkin, Ronald, *Maintain the Right,* Macmillan, Toronto, 1973

Anderson, Frank W., *Hanging in Canada,* Frontier Books, Surrey, BC, 1973

Berton, Pierre, *My Country,* McClelland & Stewart, Toronto, 1976

——*The Arctic Grail,* McClelland & Stewart, Toronto, 1988

Butts, Ed & Horwood, Harold, *Pirates & Outlaws of Canada,* Doubleday Canada, Toronto, 1984

Bandits & Privateers: Canada in the Age of Gunpowder, Doubleday Canada, Toronto, 1987

Campbell, Marjorie Freeman, *A Mountain & a City: The Story of Hamilton,* McClelland & Stewart, Toronto, 1966

Charlesworth, Hector, *Candid Chronicles,* Macmillan of Canada, Toronto, 1925

——*More Candid Chronicles,* Macmillan of Canada, Toronto, 1928

Colombo, John Robert, *Mysterious Canada,* Doubleday Canada, Toronto, 1988

Hall, Charles Francis, *Life With the Esquimaux,* Hurtig, Edmonton, 1970 (reprint)

Hicks, Brian, *Ghost Ship: The Mysterious True Story of the* Mary Celeste *and Her Missing Crew,* Ballantine Books, New York, 2004

Hunt, Jim (Contributing Author), *Outlaws & Lawmen of Western Canada, Vol. 3,* Heritage House Publishing, Surrey, BC, 1987

Jones, Richard Glyn (Ed.), *Poison: The World's Greatest True Murder Stories,* Lyle Stewart Inc., New Jersey, 1987

Kelly, Nora & William, *The Royal Canadian Mounted Police: A Century of History,* Hurtig, Edmonton, 1973

Leasor, James, *Who Killed Sir Harry Oakes?,* Houghton Mifflin, Boston, 1983

McGahan, Peter, *Killers, Thieves, Tramps & Sinners,* Goose Lane Editions, Fredericton, NB, 1989

Miller, Orlo, *Twenty Mortal Murders,* Macmillan of Canada, Toronto, 1978

Monet, Jean, *The Cassock and the Crown,* McGill-Queen's University, Montreal, 1996

Neatby, Hilda, *Quebec: The Revolutionary Age, 1760–1791,* McClelland & Stewart, Toronto, 1966

Parker, John, *King of Fools,* St. Martin's Press, New York, 1988

Patterson, Raymond M., *The Dangerous River,* Gray's Publishing, Sidney, BC, 1966

Robin, Martin, *The Bad and the Lonely,* James Lorimer & Co., Toronto, 1976

Wallace, W. Stewart, *Murders & Mysteries,* Macmillan of Canada, Toronto, 1931

The Dictionary of Canadian Biography

The *Toronto Star*

The *Globe & Mail*

The Canadian Historical Review, Vol. XX, "The Mystery of Walker's Ear", A.L. Burt

Theosophical History, Vol. IV, no. 6–7, Oliphant, John, "The Teachings of Brother XII"